RUNNING

Also by Ronnie O'Sullivan

Ronnie

RUNNING

THE AUTOBIOGRAPHY

Ronnie O'Sullivan
with Simon Hattenstone

© Ronnie O'Sullivan 2013

The right of Ronnie O'Sullivan to be identified as the author of
this work has been asserted in accordance with the
Copyright, Designs and Patents Act 1988.

First published in Great Britain in 2013 by Orion Books
An imprint of the Orion Publishing Group Ltd
Orion House, 5 Upper St Martin's Lane,
London, WC2H 9EA
An Hachette Livre Company

1 3 5 7 9 10 8 6 4 2

A CIP catalogue record for this book
is available from the British Library.

ISBN HB 978 075289 880 3
TPB 978 1 409149 56 9

Typeset by Input Data Services Ltd, Bridgwater, Somerset

Printed and bound by CPI Group (UK) Ltd, Croydon, CR0 4YY

The Orion Publishing Group's policy is to use papers that
are natural, renewable and recyclable products and made from
wood grown in sustainable forests. The logging and
manufacturing processes are expected to conform to the
environmental regulations of the country of origin.

www.orionbooks.co.uk

To Lily and little Ronnie, with all my love

ACKNOWLEDGEMENTS

Thanks to the following: Mum, Dad and Danielle, Lily and little Ronnie, Laila for their love and support; Damien Hirst, Antony Genn, Sylvia, Irish Chris, Scouse John and Little T for being in my corner; Jimmy White and Stephen Hendry for showing me the way; Django and Sonny for their management skills; the farm and the pigs for keeping me busy and sane; Tracey Alexandrou, Chris Davies, Terry Davies, Barry Elwell, Amanda, Mark, Terry McCarthy, David Webb, Alan, Sian, Claire, Jason Ward for being the best of mates: the brilliant Dr Steve Peters for teaching me how to cope; agent extraordinaire Jonny Geller, Alan Samson and Lucinda McNeile for their editing skills; and Simon Hattenstone for his friendship, ability to get into my head and for being as bonkers as me (it takes one to know one).

CONTENTS

PROLOGUE

I wasn't sure what to call this book. It was a choice between 'My Year Out', 'The Comeback Kid' and 'Running'. The first two are pretty self-explanatory – I took a year out for reasons I've not gone into until now after I won the World Championship in May 2012 and returned in May 2013 to win it again. It was the first time I've won successive Worlds in my career, and I was the first player to do so since Stephen Hendry, whom I regard as the greatest ever, did so in 1997. Happy days.

But in the end I opted for *Running* because this book is about what has sustained me through the second half of my career. In the first half, it was more drink, drugs and Prozac that kept me on the straight and narrow – crazy though that sounds. This time round, with the not so odd exception, it's been the running that's kept my head straight. Or at least as straight as a head like mine will ever be. It can't have done me too much harm, if I'm being objective about it. When I wrote my first book 12 years ago I was 25 and I'd just won my first World Championship. Nobody expected me to take that long to win it – with the possible exception of me. Until then I'd become known as the greatest snooker player never to have won the World Championship. And, believe me, that was a big old albatross to hang round my neck.

I was relieved when I finally won it, but there was always the worry that, despite the other big tournaments I'd won, when it came to the Worlds I'd be a one-hit wonder. Now I've won five, and only Steve Davis and Ray Reardon with six and Hendry with seven have won more. Despite all my talk of retiring (and whatever people think, it's not just talk – if I tell people I'm getting out, I believe it when I say it) I still reckon I could overtake their records. This year at Sheffield I overtook Hendry for the number of centuries made at the Crucible in the final against Barry Hawkins (131), and that was a great feeling. I also scored six centuries in that final, another record. So slowly but surely I am writing my way into snooker's history books.

Without running, I reckon I would have given up on the game a long time ago. Running is my religion, my belief system, my way of keeping calm. Running is painful and horribly physical, but it's also probably the nearest I get to a spiritual high. I want to share my running buzz with everyone – those of you who are already on the buzz will hopefully recognise what I'm writing about; there might even be the odd bit of decent advice here. And it might encourage others to get out in the fresh air, put your foot down and get a serotonin boost.

It made sense to me to write a book about running – not only is it my hobby/obsession, but it's been a recurrent theme in my life. As the sports psychiatrist Dr Steve Peters will tell you, I've spent loads of my life running away from shit, and running to shit – be it drink, drugs, bad people, good people, Alcoholics Anonymous, Narcotics Anonymous, running clubs, family, food, TV cameras, the snooker authorities, my own demons, you name it.

But, of course, this book is also about snooker – my game. The sport that I sometimes detest so much I can't bear to look at a cue; the sport that has been the love of my life. More than anything, the book documents the year between May 2012 and 2013 – even by my standards the craziest 12 months of my life. In 2012, I won the World Championship for the fourth time. It was the greatest feeling ever at the end – my son, little Ronnie, came to join me on the stage at the Crucible and I threw him in the air, the roars were going up and it was just pure bliss. Straight after I announced I was quitting the game, and I did – for 11 months. Then I agreed to come back for the World Championship to defend my crown. I don't really know what I thought I was going to achieve – after all, nobody had successfully defended the title since Hendry in the 1990s. I'd played one competitive match the whole season, my ranking had slipped down to 29th in the world, and even though they still made me one of the favourites I thought that was just crazy. Until I went into practice six weeks before the tournament started, I'd barely hit a ball all year.

Throughout Sheffield 2013 people asked me why I'd quit, why I was back, and though dribs and drabs emerged I knew I couldn't tell the story properly in a few sound bites. Some of them sounded daft or unconvincing in an 'Ah, that's just Ronnie' way – when I said I'd come back to pay the kids' school bills everybody laughed and said, how could you not have money for that? They thought I was joking. But I wasn't. So this book is to set the record straight.

What I want to do is to give an insight into a sportsman's life, and show how difficult it can be to balance family and professional life. Don't get me wrong, I ain't asking for your sympathy – I know just how lucky I am to be gifted, to have a huge following and to be able to make money and travel the world playing the game that I love (when I'm not hating it that is). And, yes, in one way it is a very glamorous life. But sometimes, if things don't work out as you'd hoped in your private life, it becomes impossible to keep a happy balance between family and work, and sometimes you're forced into choosing one ahead of the other.

1

GETTING THE BUZZ

'Wednesday, four miles, 30 minutes, six x 400m, off 30-second recovery, times of reps was 72 secs, 71 secs, 70, 72, 73, 71.'

'Oi, Ron, get up!'

'Ah, Dad, give us a break, I'm knackered.'

'Come on, son, time for a lovely little run. You know you want it.'

Jesus. I was about 12 when I started running. Dad made me run, and it was like the Chinese water torture. I hated it. I was always talking about leaving school early to play snooker. And Dad said, you've got to be disciplined about it – you've got to go to bed early, do your three-mile run every day, keep fit. Healthy body, healthy mind. He said if I was physically fit I'd be able to focus better when I went down the snooker club. Dad realised I was already capable of winning little tournaments if I could have the edge of being fit. Back then snooker players didn't bother with fitness. The opposite, in fact. Hurricane Higgins would always have a fag on the go, and a pint of Guinness at his side. The Canadian Big Bill Werbeniuk even got a sick note from the doctor saying that he had to drink beer when he was playing to control the tremor in his arm. That was his excuse anyway. As for all the up-and-coming kids, most of them spent their time playing fruit machines and gambling rather than keeping fit.

Sometimes when I ran, Dad followed me round in the car. It was horrible. I was always a bit scared of him – certainly too scared to say no to him. But there was sense in what he was saying. I wasn't fast, but I was okay – I was a bit porky, but I could get round three miles easily enough, and keep going.

In the end I stayed on at school till I was 16, when I turned professional. I also kept up with the daily three-milers. Not that I had any choice. But it all changed when Dad got banged up for murder. As soon as he was charged I stopped running and training. I stopped doing everything really. I wasn't in the right frame of mind. My mind was elsewhere. I couldn't believe what was happening to my world, or that my dad could be charged with murder – let alone be guilty. I was in pieces. Then he came out on bail, and he insisted I went back to the old routine.

'Just because I've been away is no excuse for you to stop the running, is it, Ron?'

No excuse? What, he's been in nick for months, I'm in pieces for what the police say he's done to some poor fella, and he's having a go at me for not having a jog. Bloody cheek.

'No, Dad,' I muttered.

'Right, let's go, son.'

So I got my running shoes on, he got the car out and stalked me for three miles.

Bloody hell. I thought I was going to die. All it takes is a few months off the pace, and it's like you've never run in your life. My heart was going like crazy, my legs didn't belong to me and my feet were already blistering.

'See, not that bad, was it, Ron,' Dad said with a huge grin.

'No, not bad,' I puffed. Not bad, my arse.

But Dad was right about body and mind. When I ran my snooker was better, and I did better in pro-ams, where both amateurs and professionals compete. Pro-ams are a long day; you'd get picked up at eight in the morning, get home at midnight if you got through to the final, and you had to keep focused throughout. Somehow, when I wasn't running, my mind wandered all over the shop.

Also, weirdly, running helped me with my sweating problem. I've always been a hairy fella, and I'd find myself sweating under my arms, through jumpers and shirts. It was horrible; embarrassing. I found that when I wasn't running my armpits were squirting like the Trevi Fountain. If I wasn't running, I'd forever be in the toilets, drying my pits under the heater. As soon as I started again the problem would disappear. I sweated while running but afterwards I was fine. It's like a detox – it just flushes the shit out of you. There were other advantages to running, too. My legs wouldn't rub together and cause me chafing hell because they were slimming down.

Dad was in custody for nine months, and then he came out on bail, and the first thing he said was, you've got to start with your running again. I'd put on a bit of weight, but not changed drastically – except in my attitude. I'd become a procrastinator: 'I can't be bothered, I'll do it tomorrow.' So I started running again while he was out, and then when he was finally convicted for murder that was it. Boom! The end. I fucked it off for about six years. I swapped running for bingeing – on drink and drugs.

I knew I was losing it but I didn't realise I was turning into a right porker. By the time I was 20, I'd got myself up to 15½ stone, a 37½-inch waist, and I could have fitted two 15-year-old Ronnies in my playing pants. I'd become huge – a rhinoceros of a fella – and I wasn't even aware of it. I just naturally grew into it, and nobody said anything to me about it.

I was out one night at a club with a mate, and someone said to this girl: 'That fella's Ronnie O'Sullivan.'

She looked at us and said, 'Is he the fat one or the skinny one?'

I was like, well, I know I'm not the skinny one because this geeza I was with was skinny. And I just thought, fuck, I must be fat. I'd never thought of myself as fat at all. It hadn't even crossed my mind. But that really hit home. If I could see the woman now I'd thank her and shake her hand and say, you've done me a massive favour. The next day I started training. I felt heavy, slobbish, gross, and I knew I had to sort it out.

So I started running regularly and got my weight down to a decent level. I lost three stone, and felt so much better for it. I'd had a big wobbly belly and now I'd started showing muscles. Wow! That was a mad feeling because it seemed to happen overnight. Until then, I couldn't see any results. Then one day, after about three months, I looked in the mirror and thought, fuckin' hell, I don't recognise that bloke. It was 1997, I was 22, and now I'd gone from 15½ to 12½ stone. Result!

I kept the running up for six to seven years. There were times when my head was in pieces – too many times to remember, to be honest – but I always think it would have been that much worse if I'd been doing no exercise. I'd go down the gym, run, get a swim in, play football occasionally. But nothing extreme. It was just a way of keeping myself in decent nick.

Then, in 2004 I started serious running. Competitive running. A mate of mine, Alan, who I ran with at the gym, said, come up to the running club, see if you like it. I was, like, alright, even though I didn't know anybody, and I'm shy by nature. I got to know a few of the lads there – they were a friendly bunch and said, d'you want to meet up on Sunday, we'll do a long run.

I was world champion at the time, but not in the best of spirits. I'd been in the Priory, come out, been clean for nine months, which was wonderful. I went to meetings every day – drug addiction, alcohol addiction – and I was feeling fantastic. I was reborn. I couldn't believe it. I was getting up in the morning, running, eating healthy food.

My life was good. I felt fit, fresh, alert. And that was all because of going to Narcotics Anonymous and getting structure to my days. Good structure. And because I was enjoying my snooker more my game was getting better and better, more like it was when I was a youngster.

I went to the meetings every night, and I was reminded where my addictions could take me. I kept away from all the nutters who were likely to tempt me, and got my head down on the pillow early every night so there was less chance of me weakening. I used Narcotics Anonymous as a drop-in centre, to stay around people who weren't using. And by 10.30 p.m. I'd be ready for bed anyway. It was that tricky time between 6.30 and 10.30 p.m. that was most tempting. I'd think, I'm bored, I've played snooker, done what I've had to do, I've got this three-hour gap to fill, what now? And that's when the meetings were so brilliant. They were perfect – I'd go to them, have a cup of tea, sit there, listen to what everyone had to say, say my little bit, have a cup of tea after, go for coffee. It was the company more than anything that helped.

I knew I didn't have the strength to say no to drink and drugs for ever. I was always tempted, and after nine months I gave in to that temptation. After that, every so often I'd go on a bender. I kept dipping into it now and again. Going on a bender here and there – a lot of puff, and I could get through

15 pints of Guinness a night. It sounds a lot, but it isn't really when you're on the other stuff. You could drink all night if you were taking drugs, then you'd take more drugs because you were drinking. I loved a joint. The only problem with a joint is that one spliff follows another, and another, and then you get the munchies and you eat everything in the fridge, and put on loads of weight.

At the end of the night I'd go to someone's house, start smoking, and, boom! I felt good. Great! I knew I didn't want to get back on the constant drinking and drugging benders, but also I knew I didn't have the strength just to say no, never again. Then every now and then you'd have a night where you got a bit out of hand and you'd go, fuckin' hell what's happened now, and you'd think about all the stuff you learnt in the Priory about addiction, and you'd feel ashamed of yourself.

After my first bender, I got clean again for three to four months, and then went on another bender. It became a pattern. I thought, lovely: so long as I was going to my meetings, and was just dipping in and out, I'd be fine – it was just a bit of a re-lease I was after. And, after all, the damage wasn't that bad – I'd justify it to myself, tell myself it was just the occasional drink or joint and so long as I wasn't doing it every day. But, of course, I was deluding myself because the reality was I was hooked on it.

At my worst I had to have a joint first thing in the morning just to function. Without it, I felt paranoid, uneasy in myself. So I thought, if I can keep the benders to once every two, three, four months and then have a blast. But loads of the time, the snooker got in the way of my benders rather than the other way round. It was as if I was in training for the benders. It was my Olympics. Every four months I'm going to get totally wasted. I'd tell myself that was a good reason to stay clean, you'll enjoy it more, you'll deserve it.

I'm not really sure how I managed to get through the drugs tests during this period. I remember getting to every World Championship and thinking, I can't wait till this tournament is over 'cos then there's no more drugs tests, there's nothing for three months, so I can go out and smash it. I'd got caught once early on in my career, but that's all. I'd get tested between events, and I was just trying to judge it perfectly so there'd be no drugs left in my system, but I was pushing my luck.

My mum said to me, 'You're going to get caught soon. You can't carry on like this.'

I said, 'No, I'll be alright. As long as I don't overdo it and stop a week before the tournament I'll be fine.'

In the end it took a new addiction to knock the drink and drugs on the head. Running. So Alan got me to go to the club. I still run with him now – he's 50 and killing me at the moment. He's probably running 10 kilometres in 36 minutes just now, but he's one of the best vets in Essex.

I'd had a bit of a bender and saw Alan at the gym. He took a look at me, and could tell I wasn't at my best.

'What's up with you, Ronnie?'

'Ah, you know, Alan, bit of a night last night.'

'Looks like more than a bit to me,' he said.

I didn't answer.

'You alright, Ron?'

'Yeah.'

'I thought you were doing your NA and all that.'

'Yeah, I am.'

'Well, I'm sure massive benders aren't part of your twelve steps, are they?' He'd sussed me. Anyone else, I'd think they were taking a liberty, but he said it so kindly. I knew he was just thinking of me.

11

I smiled at him – bit of a stupid smile, really, but I couldn't think of anything to say.

'Come on, Ronnie, come for a run with me. You don't need all this booze and stuff. Fresh air, get your heart pumping, serotonin, that's what you need.'

I did about five, six miles and it killed me. *Killed* me. Then he introduced me to the athletics club, Woodford Green in Essex, which is quite famous as it happens. Until then the only running I'd done was by myself or with a few fellas at the gym. And once I'd been to the running club for about two months I ran at the gym with normal members, and the other guys couldn't believe how fast I was.

The first time I went down the club I was a bit shy. I didn't say much, did my bit and sneaked off. But the runners were really friendly, and after two or three times they'd introduce themselves, and I'd go to the bar and have a glass of orange with them after we'd killed ourselves on the track. A few of them recognised me, but they didn't seem that interested in who I was. We never spoke about snooker; it was all running. Everyone left their job at the door. It was just about racing; who's running well. If you were into running, Tuesday night at the track was just the best thing.

There'd be 50 to 60 people on the track, running all kinds of distances, and javelin-throwers, shot-putters, long-jumpers, all sorts, and I just thought, blimey, there's so much going on here. Everyone had their own little group.

I've always tended to keep my head down when I've been out to places. People will recognise me, come up and talk to me. You get used to it. I don't mind people chatting to me, it's just when they start driving you mad and you think: 'Oh, mate, give it a rest!', and before long they do your head in. But this place was different. Just gentle chit-chat, encouraging you to run better. Eventually, once you got to know them, you'd get the odd one who might say: 'How are you doing with the snooker, Ron? I watch you', but generally they weren't interested. It was just times, races and who had decent form.

My first race was 3,000 metres, seven and a half laps on the track; 10.06 minutes was my time. I've only done it once, so it's my personal best. One of the coaches on the side was saying: 'Stay on his shoulder, stay on his shoulder', so I did. I was about 40 to 50 metres behind the next fella, and they meant use the one in front, to push yourself, then I'd come round for the next lap and he'd say: 'Push on now, Ron, push on to the next group', so I'd push on and I was thinking, I ain't got it in me, but I just found this speed. I thought, if the coach believes in me I must have it. So I went on and he'd be: 'Get on the next one, get on the next one now', so I'd push on to the next one, and by then I'd made up 40 to 50 metres, and on the final lap I was up with three of the faster boys and I remember just finding a sprint down the last 100 metres and I beat a couple of the runners who I would have never dreamt of getting in front of. So I surprised myself.

I'd been at the club around six months and was loving it. Then I started on the 10 kilometres. I don't know why 10 kilometres is such a perfect distance, but it is. I suppose it's a sprint, but still a long way. If you can run six miles you can run 10 miles, and if you can run 10 miles you can run 13. And the thing is, once I started running – really running – I wasn't interested in jogging, I wanted to give it my all. I'm not the first sportsman to get obsessed by the 10 kilometres – though maybe the others didn't to the same extent. The great England batsman Kevin Pietersen had the same thing. There was a time he was touring India, and all he seemed bothered about was getting his 10 kilometres down. He'd finish a day at a Test match, the team would all get in the coach and then he'd be, like, right I'm running six miles back to the hotel. At one point he said he had to decide whether to focus on getting a PB with his running or his cricket. I could understand it because that's just how I was.

I became a running bore. Just talked about it all the time. I knew I couldn't go to the snooker and bore them all with it because they weren't interested, but I could talk endlessly about it to the fellas at the club. In the end I stopped hanging round snooker venues or with players except when there was a match on. I used to get my mate to ring up the local running club if I was playing in, say, Telford, tell them I was coming down and that I'd like to join them for a run.

And if I wasn't out running I'd be having dinner with one of the runners I'd made friends with. The only way I could enjoy my snooker was if I could run while I was away, so snooker tournaments became like training camps – an opportunity to run with different runners and try different routes.

Running became so much more important to me than snooker. After a while I wasn't worried if I won the World Championship, so long as I could get my runs in and improve my PB. Everything else was secondary. I'd established ages ago that I had an addictive personality and that I tend to pursue things to the end. Now it was just about trying to make the addictions healthy ones. I knew if I was sitting in the pub or in a snooker hall I'd get bored and need a bit of excitement in my life – and that meant benders. So I thought, well, as long as I stay away from those places and hang around gyms and running clubs then I can channel that addiction for the good.

Running is such a different world from snooker. It's outdoors, it's physical and the very opposite of that claustrophobic snooker hall. Sometimes when I'm on TV I'm so aware of the camera picking up every tiny thing I'm doing – flicking my ear, picking my nose, twitching my eyes. It interrogates you. Horrible. But in some ways running and snooker aren't so different. You're still on your own – you get the disappointments, you get the glory, it's all for yourself. It's still a one-man-band sport. Whereas snooker is all about technique, running is much more blood, guts, determination and finding something within yourself to keep going. There are times when you think you can't keep going, but you do. And after a race you swear you're never going to put yourself through that again, as you cross the finishing line, but invariably you do. It's so painful, and you just wonder what made you do it. Nearly all runners feel the same – even those who make it look easy and win all the races. But when you see you had a good race, and you're getting somewhere, and getting rewards for it, it makes it all worthwhile.

When I did my first 10 kilometres at the club, it took me 39 minutes. Then I whittled it down by a couple of minutes – almost six-minute miling. The next goal was to get under six-minute miling. It was becoming an obsession. I thought if I could only run 5.50-minute miles I'd be happy. I did the Southend 10 kilometres and started off terribly. I felt really heavy legged because I'd been on a bender the night before; not a heavy bender, but I'd been smoking a few spliffs and that, and I remember getting out and feeling lethargic. The first three miles I thought, I'm going to have a nightmare here, then after that I started to get going. I picked a few off and ended up coming in my best time, which was 36.30 minutes. But I was still really pissed off because it meant I was just outside sub-six-minute miles.

Then I did the Essex cross-country, a tough 8½-mile race, and I came 27th. A decent result. I was cream-crackered by the end, no energy; I was just gone. I could have fallen asleep standing up. But everybody was saying to me, that was a really good race.

The biggest race I did was the Southern England cross-country. All the top boys who run in the European cross-countries and the World Championship were competing, and I finished 180th out of a field of 1,200. I came off saying that was horrible, and I never wanted to do it again. A friend said exactly the same, and he told me it was the hardest race I'll ever do – a three-mile loop over Parliament Hill that you have to go around three times. What a fantastic run, though – nine miles cross-country; it took me just over an hour up- and downhill. I didn't realise it at the time, but that was a good achievement.

The only time I'd miss my Tuesday nights at the club was when I found other runners to run with. For example, I found this Irish fella, Matt, and he could only run between 6 and 8 a.m., so I'd have to meet him in the morning. He was much faster than anybody else I'd run with on the track, and I was looking for somebody to push me on, so I'd run with him two or three times a week. They would be eight-mile runs and from the go it was fast. So I'd get to 3–4 miles and be knackered, but hanging on, and he wouldn't stop, he just kept going. Most of the time I didn't even know where I was, and I just had to keep him within my sight so I didn't get lost. Eventually that took my running on to another level.

I've often wondered if it's the same competitive instinct that makes me run and makes me play snooker. I'm pretty sure it is. It's not that I'm a bad loser but I don't like losing, and they are two different things. And with the running, it wasn't always about the winning, it was about how could I improve. Running taught me a lot about snooker as well. Even though the sports are so different, the tips I picked up running translated into the day job. In running, you could be a great trainer or a great racer, but you couldn't be both. What I mean is, you can't give your all to both. You either have to cut back on your training to be fresh for your races, or concentrate more on the training than the actual races. You'd get people flying round on a Tuesday night and you'd think they're unbeatable and they'd do the same on Thursday but come Saturday they've got dead legs. They'd still race, but they were well past their best by then. You had to leave a little bit in the tank in training: train your bollocks off Tuesday and Thursday but don't race Saturday; or train Tuesday, then go steady Wednesday, Thursday and Friday, and your legs are fresh Saturday and you'd have a good race.

Eventually I got 10 kilometres down to 34 minutes. I'd say anything under 36 minutes is decent club running, and this was 5.40 minutes a mile. I couldn't believe I was running that fast. Having said that, this is not great running: it's decent club running.

I learnt so much from the training regime and started applying it to snooker. If you run all the time you end up physically exhausted. I'd always thought you had to give your all to training in the build-up to a snooker tournament. Six hours a day for a month building up to, say, the World Championship. But the running taught me you can overdo it. Sometimes you can do half an hour, and that's just fine. The week before a tournament your practice should be done, and you should have started winding down.

I want to do it, I'm chomping at the bit, but the reality is it's not that good for you. Sometimes I wouldn't practise at all and just trust myself. Maybe a month before a tournament I'd put the hours in, but now the week before I just relax. A week before a marathon, runners will hardly run; they just do a mile or two or three to keep their legs ticking over. No more intensive stuff; that's already in the bank, and you've got to let your body recover. Then, boom! Whether you're playing well or not, now it's time to switch on and be ready mentally. As long as you've got a full tank to draw on, there's no point going to an event driving yourself mad and leaving your best form on the practice table.

The more I ran, the more obsessed I became. Now I had a new dream. I wanted to represent my county at cross-country. (To put this in context, my fastest at 10 kilometres put me in the top 1,500 in the UK, so I wasn't reckoning on an Olympic medal.) To do that you had to get into the top six in Essex, and I thought that was doable. I'd come 27th in my first year running, and I thought if I could just devote more time to it, give me two years, maybe three. But that was the problem. I couldn't devote more time to it. I was still a full-time snooker player and everyone in the game was telling me I was mad giving so much to the running.

I was doing a lot of road races – local ones within a 10- to 20-mile radius of where we lived. At one stage I was racing every other weekend, and running really had become the most important thing in my life. It was the only thing I talked about, yattering away on the phone every night.

'Alright, Alan?'

'Alright, Ron, how you doing?'

'Yeah, good. But not good enough. Got to get under six minutes. Getting there, I think. Fuckin' 'ell, I was done for by the end of my ten kilometres. Lovely out there, fresh, crisp, cold, but it killed me.' But I loved the fact that it took so much out of me.

I loved the routine. My mate would come over to me, we'd get there for 11.30, get dressed, ready for 12, ready to race at 12.30, timings done, shower, boom boom boom. In the pub for 3.30–4 p.m., just on the orange juice, focused, everyone talking about their time, the race, where they'd come.

It's funny that it became such a huge ambition to represent Essex. Let's face it, there was no money in it for me, and no status – you're not going to be remembered for having run for your county, are you? Certainly, I'd be better off concentrating on the snooker from a financial point of view. And yet still there was something pushing me on. I was desperate to do it. I began to think if I *did* represent Essex it would be the same as winning the World Championship. The running replaced AA and NA meetings in my life. There wasn't time for meetings, snooker and running. One had to give way, so it was the meetings. By now I looked totally different. I weighed 11½ stone and was down to a 31-inch waist. Everybody would go, you look really ill, and I'd think, great, that must mean I'm really fit. Then, when they said to me: 'You look really well', I'd think: 'Shit, I've put weight on.' I knew when I looked gaunt that I was in good shape and could run a good race. I'd be flush, I'd think, cor I'm flying.

In 2008 I was playing well and won the World Championship for the third time. I really was flying then. I'd beaten Ali Carter in the final, my daughter Lily was just over a year old, little Ronnie had just been born, I was world champion: life was good. About a week after the Crucible final I won my first race and I did it for charity. There were 150 to 200 people racing. When I was overweight and did it, I came about 100th. Middle of the pack.

This time round we got to the race in Epping Forest and my mate the mad Irishman's running. He was about 42, and he could run – about 33 minutes for 10 kilometres. He was a class act. I thought, there's no way I'm going to beat him so I just sat in behind him in about fourth or fifth. I thought, I'll stick on his shoulder and I did till mile two. After about two and a half miles I got in front of him and I thought, come on, you're in front, just push on. So I pushed on and pushed on and won it by 40 to 50 seconds. And I'd done five miles in 27 minutes. I couldn't believe it – the thrill of running through the tape, and winning £80 worth of vouchers. I was buzzing. Ecstatic. It was on the back page of the local Epping Forest paper. Me on the sports pages – and not for my snooker. I'd always wanted to make *Athletics Weekly* and I thought the only way I was going to do that was through running.

But that day in Epping Forest I peaked. I don't know why but it all went downhill from there. I'm still hoping it hasn't – that I'll get back and beat my PB. Maybe I just got a bit lazy. Maybe I didn't know where to go on to once I'd won a race. I suppose it was always going to be impossible balancing the running and snooker.

One of the problems was with Jo, my then partner and the mother of Lily and Ronnie. She always felt my running was selfish because she'd had two kids and was bringing them up and I was out playing snooker and running. She didn't like me going out racing, then she didn't like the mess I'd bring in – dirty running gear, dirty legs. Often I'd put my clothes on top of my clobber, run upstairs, get in the shower and wash all the mud off before she'd had time to complain about it. Running was probably one of the things that brought our relationship to an end.

2

WHEN LIFE KICKS YOU UP THE ARSE

'Monday, five miles, 47 minutes. Did not enjoy my run, calves felt tight, lost my love for it at the moment, it feels like an effort.'

Life has a knack of kicking you up the arse when things are going well just to remind you who's boss. It was 2008: I'd just won the UK and World Championships, I'd made three 147s that season, my running was going brilliantly, I had a beautiful baby and a two-year-old toddler. I was on top of the world. In theory. Unfortunately, my relationship with Jo was collapsing.

The role of dad has always been important to me – I knew what it was to have a good dad who would do everything for you, and I knew what it was like to lose one for the best part of 20 years. I'd always thought I would be a dad, but didn't really know what to expect.

I was only 20 when I became a father, but unfortunately I've never really been part of Taylor's life, so I had never properly experienced what it meant to be a dad. And then, when Lily was born, it suddenly hit me. Boom! It's hard to put into words what it's like. When friends of mine are having their first baby, I tell them this is going to be the best feeling you'll ever have.

That's what it was for me. It just gave a bit more meaning to life. Everything seemed to have more point.

I was there for the birth. Jo had an emergency Caesarean because the cord wrapped round Lily's neck, and they said, we're going to have to do a quick Caesarean and get her out. It wasn't planned, but it worked out well because it was short and sweet. I got a phone call, rushed down there, didn't know what to expect. It was 2–3 a.m. You get to the hospital and it's all quick, quick, quick. You're panicking, but for the nurses it's just an everyday thing. Then, within 10 to 15 minutes, it was done. The baby came out, it's a girl. Wow! Pure elation.

I was 28 and life suddenly made more sense. Until then I had just been playing tournament to tournament and one year rolled into the next; then Lily arrives and a sense of responsibility comes with it. It was a bit of pressure, I suppose, because I had to provide for this little baby. I'd provided for Taylor for eight years, but because I didn't have an active role in her growing up it didn't feel like it. You stop thinking so much about yourself as a self-contained unit and more about yourself as a father – making sure the baby eats and sleeps and has a good home.

When you're just looking after yourself you kind of know you can get through to the other end, and in the end it will be alright. The feeling I had now was almost primitive – I was the hunter-gatherer, the provider. Family has always been important to me, and we have always been a close unit, even when both Mum and Dad were banged up in jail. Mum, Dad, me and my younger sister, Danielle – the O'Sullivans. We'd always supported each other throughout, and this is what I hoped for with my new family. We were close in every way. Last year I bought a house in Loughton, a couple of miles away from the rest of the family in Chigwell, and I couldn't cope. I thought, what have I done? It was like another world to me, and I seemed to spend all the time driving from Loughton to Chigwell so I knew it wasn't right for me. Mum, my snooker table at Mum's, Dad, Danielle, my running routes, my local haunts, like the bagel bar, are all around Chigwell. Sometimes you don't realise how rooted you are in your community; it took me moving a few miles down the road to realise it!

So when Lily was born it was important to be around Chigwell. For the first few months Jo and I were getting on fine. We'd started going out in 2001 and had been together for around five years. Jo and I met at Narcotics Anonymous, where we were both being treated for addiction. We had a bond from the start, and in the early days we got on great. We'd always had our little tiffs, like everyone does, but soon after Lily was born things started to become difficult. Before, I'd always had my own routine. Ask any sportsman or sportswoman and they'll tell you the same. Without routine you're lost; you're not going to achieve anything. I would go for my runs, work out in the gym, play my snooker. But when Jo was pregnant there was more pressure on my time. She wanted me to go to all the meetings about childbirth and getting ready to have a baby, but I wasn't into all that. Perhaps I could have been more supportive, but I saw that as her role. I was there for her to tell me about it when I came home, but I couldn't break up my day for hospital appointments and meetings about birthing pools or how to pack your bag for the maternity ward.

I didn't feel it was something I had to contribute to until the baby came along, and I always felt we'd know what to do when it happened. I've never been one for preparing for things; I've always been much more, let it happen and see how it goes. I think men are just constructed differently from women biologically. There is something in women that makes them want to prepare for babies, and they feel it much earlier than men do – 'course they do, they're carrying the baby. Whereas for fellas, we're not really involved and don't understand what our contribution is supposed to be till the baby arrives.

I'm not saying I'm right, but this is the life of most successful sportsmen. We need our routine; we need to be focused; we are selfish; we do have to put ourselves first. Jo wanted more of my time, but I didn't know how to change and wasn't sure if I could change.

Sportsmen also tend to be superstitious, and I thought any slight change to what I was doing would detract from where I wanted to go. Also, practice is bloody important. As Matthew Syed says in his great book *Bounce*, it's not natural-born genius that tends to distinguish high-achievers from less successful sports people, it's practice – he reckons that you're never going to get anywhere in a sport unless you've put in 10,000 hours' practice, and he's got a point. Then, when you've put in your 10,000 hours you can't just stop. You've got to keep practising, reinforcing your good habits. So the idea that you could give all your practice a miss, then just turn up for tournaments, was always going to be a nonsense to me.

It might seem old-fashioned, but the way my life is it was always going to be my partner's main role to bring up the kids. I don't mean that in a sexist way. I'd be happy to do it if I wasn't playing. And I am happy to do it when I'm away from the game. But the reality of life for any sportsman is that you're on the road loads of the time, travelling from hotel to hotel, earning your crust. Obviously, I'd be there once I finished my practice and come home and bath them and feed them, do whatever, but it never quite worked out that way.

I spoke to other snooker players who had become dads to see how they felt, and how they worked out their fatherhood

responsibilities. So I chatted to Stephen Hendry and Jo Perry –
I chose them because Stephen's the best the game has known,
and Jo hadn't achieved as much but had still dedicated his life
to sport. In terms of application, there was probably no difference between the two, but one was seven-time world champion
and the other was a good player who hadn't won the same kind
of silverware. I wanted two different perspectives. Jo Perry told
me: 'I get up in the morning, go to do my snooker, go to the
gym, and when I come back from the gym my missus says, do
you want to help feed, put the baby down, and it's all great.'
Stephen Hendry said: 'My life didn't change at all, my missus
knew what I was like, I was down the snooker club five hours a
day, I'd be in the gym in the morning for an hour, my missus
was happy for me to do anything I had to. If anything she was,
get the fuck out of the house because you're getting in my way.'

For any sportsman a successful relationship is always tricky
to negotiate, particularly where kids are involved. Talk to any
golfer or tennis player, anyone who spends most of the year on
the road. Yes, they might well want to be home most of the
time, and share all the domestic responsibilities, but that's not
ever going to be the reality while they take their sport seriously.
It's impossible. The simple truth is that for those years you're
playing sport at the highest level, you can't maintain a true balance between family and job, and something has to give. In the
relationships that work, wives and girlfriends accept that they
are going to be left to shoulder the burden of bringing up kids
unless they hand over to childminders. It ain't ideal, but life's
not ideal. Of course, lots of women don't want that deal – they
want their own career, their fella at home most evenings, shared
responsibilities. My advice to them? Don't get involved with a
sportsman – and certainly don't have their kids. (One of the few
exceptions is football where it is much easier to be around a lot

of the time because you're only playing once or twice a week for 90 minutes, and after training you have so much spare time – but even then you're going to have loads of time when you're simply not around for your partner.)

Again, I want to stress I was never going to be the easiest person to live with. But that was obvious from day one. I've always been obsessive about practising. There's nothing unusual about that – Steve Davis once said he overpractised when he was at his peak, but if he didn't he felt guilty. If you didn't practise you felt guilty, and if you felt guilty you didn't play well. Daft, I know, but that's how it works. It's difficult enough to make any relationship work, but so much more so when you are on the road for so much of your life. I couldn't blame Jo for getting frustrated, but nor could I change my lifestyle unless I gave up snooker.

At the time, running was a huge help. It would clear my head. I was running well then, and keeping records of my progress. I was flying back then. And the running was holding me together. I learnt how to manage family, conflict and snooker as best as I could. I decided the best thing to do was move out of home three days before a tournament started, so by the time I got to the tournament I was clear-headed for the first round.

I was running away. I knew that was the only way to manage my career, and that I had to keep playing snooker. I wanted to be there as much as I could with the children and as a family man, but in my mind the most important thing was that I went to work and did as well as I could just to support my family.

My relationship with Jo broke down and I began to feel useless as a dad. There came a time when even running couldn't sort out my mind. I felt defeated. I wanted to be at home with my family, I wanted to be able to go to work; I was in a fortunate position and I should have been enjoying all those things, but it just wasn't happening.

Ever since I was a kid it had been instilled in me that you have to give your everything to your job, and my job was snooker. So the idea that I could only enjoy the family side of life if I gave up on the professional side was always going to be something I struggled with.

I was putting off the inevitable, which was that we would split up. I just thought if I stuck around, saw through the bad times, things would turn around. With Taylor I felt I'd done the wrong thing. I wished I'd been part of her life, and there was guilt there. I didn't want to break a family up. I always remember when I was younger and Mum and Dad would have an argument and he'd go away for four or five days and then he'd pick me up on Saturday to go to football. I'd always be crying, knowing that I wasn't going to see him for a week or so. I didn't want to put my family through that, too. In my heart I just wanted to be there and not separate the family.

Anytime I wasn't playing snooker I wanted to do something with Lily. Sometimes I'd take her over to the cross-country races. I'd wrap her up, keep her nice and warm, put her in the pram and off we'd go. I expected that would be how it panned out – when I was playing Jo would look after the kids; when I wasn't I assumed I'd come in and take over. Even though in lots of ways the life of a sportsman is uncompromising and in-flexible, in other ways there are huge pluses. If you're working a regular nine to five you're not going to be able to call for the kids from school, but in my job there was plenty of opportunity for stuff like that.

The first two months after Lily was born were great. We were both ecstatic about having a baby, but it wasn't long before it went sour again and we were living separate lives. Then Jo told me she was pregnant again, and I was delighted. I thought another kid would help us and I'd always wanted two anyway.

Eighteen months after Lily was born little Ronnie came along. His was a natural birth, and it seemed to go on for ever and ever. He was born at Harlow hospital. When I was there for Lily's birth, the feeling was unbelievable; ecstatic, shared, beautiful. I'd not been there for the birth of Taylor, so this was the first time I'd seen it. By the time little Ronnie was born, I was more prepared for it; I'd been through the emotions, so it didn't have quite the same impact. But it was great to have two kids. I'd always felt that when Lily was born we have to have another – it was only fair for her to have a brother or sister. I didn't want her to be an only child.

When Lily was born she was so aware; she looked as if she knew everything that was going on. Little Ronnie was quieter, a bit more away with the fairies. They were very different children, and still are. Ronnie is much more laid back, Lily is more talkative and outgoing. Yet Lily is shyer than Ronnie when she first meets people. He just stays the same whoever he's with. Little Ronnie is probably more like me.

It was such a buzz taking the babies to see Dad for the first time. He was at Long Lartin when Lily was born. Dad was excited for me – and for himself. Then, when Jo was pregnant for the second time, I told Dad she was expecting a boy.

'You've got to call him Ronnie,' he said.

'Yeah, I suppose so,' I said.

The name was pretty much decided. Three generations of Ronnie: Ronnie Senior, Ronnie Junior and little Ronnie. Mum has a brilliant way of distinguishing the three Ronnies. You can always tell who she's talking to. 'Ro-*nnnnie*', gentle and loving and going up at the end – that would be for little Ronnie. 'Ronnnnie', still fairly gentle and loving but more grown up

– that would be for me. And then the bark: 'Ron!' That's for my dad.

We went to see this marriage guidance counsellor called Jerry, who suggested that I was too close to my mum, and it might help our relationship if there was more distance between us. It crossed my mind that things might improve if we moved away from Chigwell, where I'd always lived, and where Mum, Dad and Danielle all lived within a mile of me.

We were having the house done up in Manor Road in Chigwell, and Jo said, let's move out. So I said, great, go and look for somewhere for us to live, and she came back and said, I've found a place in Ongar, which is 15 to 20 miles away in the sticks. I didn't fancy it, to be honest, but I thought, let's give it a go. It was probably the worst thing we could have done. It alienated us both – she was stuck out there, I'd travel back to Chigwell to play my snooker and then, when I got back home, there was nowhere to go.

I ended up getting on well with Jerry, the counsellor. He was into this Indian guru called Osho and always went on about the path to inner peace, and I said: 'You know what? I get that every time I go to play snooker. I know exactly what you're talking about. I get lost in what I'm doing, and it's a fantastic feeling.' Jerry was trying to attain this spiritual enlightenment through the Osho buzz, and I explained to him that snooker wasn't just a game or a job to me, it was more than that. I told him that was all I'd done since the age of seven, that I was a perfectionist and I wanted to be the best player I could possibly be. And we had a fair bit of common ground.

I think Jerry was fascinated by how passionate I was about my sport. He was almost a guru in his own right. I enjoyed my sessions with him. He wasn't there just for the money – sometimes he didn't even charge me. I went to see him five or six times, and I enjoyed my one-to-ones with him because I knew he wasn't spinning me bullshit.

I've tried a number of religions and gurus in my time, including Buddhism, but ultimately they didn't do as much for my peace of mind as snooker. There were moments when these faiths or spiritual paths held me together, but it was always only ever briefly. I discovered ways of switching from a bad place to a good place, and gaining peace, but they were only temporary solutions. Every time I tried something new, my gut instinct told me I was running out of ideas; that I was desperate.

After the kids were born I was thinking of giving up the game so that I could be a better family man. In the end, though, I decided I was too young to, and that it would destroy me; that however much pain it caused me, not playing it would cause me more. I accepted that I wasn't easy to live with. Sometimes I go into myself and shut down. I come home and don't talk, and I would imagine that must be hard for most women. Often I feel my mind is not here, present; it's on other things – ridiculous stuff like why can't I pot a ball, why am I struggling with this shot – and I shut out everything else. Everything else becomes unimportant, but that doesn't mean I don't care. I don't think I'm a nasty person. I get angry with myself, I get frustrated with myself and with the game. Even now, as I'm working on the book, part of me is replaying shots, asking why my arm isn't connected to my body, and fidgeting about. I wish I could forget about it, just get on with what I'm doing, but I can't. That's me. And I reckon that's probably the most difficult thing for people around me to handle – my inability to switch off.

But in other ways you could do worse than me as a partner. I was happy to settle down and be a dad. I wasn't out trying to get other girls – I was too interested in my snooker and my running to do that, so I was faithful. But in the end Jo and I ran out of patience and options. We were simply incompatible. It was desperately sad that we couldn't make it work, but for me it's much sadder when you see couples stay together when it's obvious that they no longer have a relationship. And I believe that can be awful for the kids, too – the last thing you want as a parent is for your children to see you rowing all the time.

In the end I moved out after we'd had a big row. I got my bags and lived out of the boot of a car for about a month – sleeping on people's settees. I had my mate in Ongar, Chrisy Flight, and I'd go round to his house at night, and he had all these old snooker books that I hadn't read. One night I picked up this Joe Davis book; he was never beaten at the old-style World Championship and won it a record 15 times between 1927 and 1946 and scored the first ever maximum. I'd never read anything about him – to be honest, I'd never even read a coaching book. And I thought, blimey this is good.

It took me back to basics because I've often struggled with my game, and I thought I'd see what he had to say, and my game improved. Joe stressed the importance of being still on the shot, get my cue nice and parallel because I was always jacking up at the back, get my bridge hand a bit lower, get my cue going nice and straight along my chest, get my feet nice and solid, get my body bolted down, and basically I was away. The game came easy again. I ended up hitting the ball really well, I couldn't miss – that season 2007–8 I won the UK and World Championships. It was one of my best years and it was all because I was reading the Joe Davis book. I was as fit as a fiddle, too, running an unbelievable amount – I weighed 11½ and was doing 10 kilometres in 34 minutes. I was too skinny really, but I felt great.

I'd come about 25th in the Essex cross-country championship, and that's when I decided I was prepared to give everything up if I could just get into the Essex running team. As I've said, you had to get into the top six to make the team and I thought I could do it. I looked at the fellas ahead of me and thought, they're fit and fast, but with my obsession and dedication if I put my mind to it I could achieve it. In hindsight, there was no way I was going to do it because I would have had to give up so much family-wise for the running, and I wasn't prepared to do that.

Having said that, apart from the kids running was then the most important thing in my life. I was putting off snooker tournaments if there was a race I could have competed in instead. The running gave me an outlet that made me feel good. I enjoyed the social side of the running, looked forward to the cross-countries at the weekend, I loved it all.

And perhaps, most importantly, it was helping my head. The first five or ten minutes are hard, but once you've got a sweat on it's impossible not to feel better than you did beforehand. Running really is pure serotonin. I hate to think what state I'd be in if I'd not found running. I might be four or five stone overweight because I do like my food, and I am prone to laziness. Running gave me a sense of professionalism and purpose. It made me want to get out of bed in the morning; it made me want to take care of my appearance; it made me have a bit of respect for myself and that all helped my snooker.

At the time I could easily have gone the other way. In fact, there were times when I did. I went through a period when, once a week, I did have a little release. Well, not so little, actually. I'd go out on the booze with my mates and not get in till seven or eight in the morning. It was always a Thursday; we'd play backgammon, have a few drinks, have a few joints. I'd get home for early morning, go to bed till early afternoon, then go out for a six- or seven-mile run when I woke up. I'd feel like shit when I got back and just sit on the settee, but by Friday I felt okay, so I'd do another seven- to eight-mile run, then, come Saturday afternoon, I was flying. The benders lasted about six months – drink, drugs, and backgammon. We'd start about 9 or 10 p.m. and just go on through the night. Vodka was my drink. It's the one drink I know I don't feel bad on. Beer gasses me up and bloats me out. Vodka is just smooth.

I'd fall asleep on the fella's settee, wake up then get a cab home; or sometimes I'd just run home. I was that fit. I'd have my big leather boots on, my top, big cardigan, and jeans. One day I was stuck in a jam in a cab, and I had to be home for Lily's birthday. So I told the cabby I was going to get out and run because it was quicker, and he said, but it's three miles, and I said, look I can do three miles in 16 minutes, and I'll get there quicker than in the cab. So with all my clobber on I just ran home, which turned out to be a pretty good way of coming off my bender. I was so fit that three miles was nothing.

I eventually gave up on the Thursday nights. I knew I was an addict, and I couldn't keep on doing it. So I said to myself, get to the other end and once you've stopped keep away from those people and places, and get your head down. I learnt that about myself when I went in the Priory. I knew that however much I wanted to continue caning it, I couldn't. It was the one road I couldn't go down. It was difficult because I needed escapism at the time, I needed some fun in my life. But after six months I just said that's it; end of.

Even though I had been smashing it once a week I had my best year on the snooker table, so how does that add up? Joe Davis's advice was stronger than the drink, the drugs and the backgammon. It got me through. Running and Joe Davis will conquer any drug! (Well, any drug in moderation.) Everybody was saying to me, when you stop drinking and taking drugs your life gets better and it does in some ways, but that brilliant year professionally was when I was having my weekly benders and my private life was in bits.

3

I FOUGHT THE LAW

'Wednesday: Went steady on the first lap, same on second, then picked it up on the last. Felt tired in the legs, hamstrings felt tired, lactic acid in the quads.'

In some ways it was a relief when Jo and I finally split up, but that's when the shit really hit the fan in terms of the kids. We couldn't agree on me seeing them so I got a solicitor. It was the last thing I wanted to do, but I couldn't go without seeing them.

I was feeling sorry for myself, but this wasn't straight depression. My life had been turned upside down; I'd not seen the kids much in 10 to 12 weeks. Altogether I'd seen them for probably 20 hours in three months and it was killing me. Initially I was granted five hours on a Saturday and two hours on a Wednesday. The courts said you can never mix access and money, but in a way that's just what they seemed to be doing. It felt like a simple equation to me – you pay more maintenance, you see more of your kids. This went on for 18 months, then two years, and all this time the meter was running, so every couple of months I'd get a monster bill through the post. I couldn't understand why we ended up going down this route.

I always wanted to give Jo money for herself and the kids, and I wanted to see Lily and little Ronnie – and it shouldn't have taken lawyers to sort that.

I started representing myself, which was disastrous. I didn't have a clue what I was doing in there. I was shocking in court – the worst thing I've ever done in my life. Laughable. They ran rings round me and I was paying for the privilege. After a while, the judge said: 'I recommend you get a barrister, Mr O'Sullivan, because this is going to cost you.' He had a point. I wasn't doing myself any favours. So I got myself another solicitor, and said, do what you have to do. I said I wanted it resolved quickly if possible. But of course these things are never quick.

Money and lawyers brought such ugliness into my life. In the end I thought there was one simple, if drastic, solution. Stop playing snooker. If I stopped playing then I wouldn't have any problem being with the kids on my Saturdays and Wednesdays, I'd get to see them grow up and I'd be more relaxed. Simple.

But, of course, there was a problem. It would also mean that there was no money coming in. When we finally settled on maintenance, the figure was based on 2008, an incredibly successful year. If I wasn't winning major tournaments it would be impossible for me to keep up such a high level of maintenance, and if I wasn't playing at all there would be nothing coming in. This didn't just mean no money for me, it also meant I wouldn't have money to pay for the kids' maintenance or their school fees because they were both at private school. It also meant I'd struggle to pay the lawyers' bill which had now topped £200,000.

I did feel angry. I'd spent all these years working hard earning money for the family and it was now being pissed away on lawyers' fees. Anybody who's been through this – and there are plenty of us out there – will know how it feels. And it didn't make any sense to me. I hated the fact that because of the legal system my relationship with my kids had been turned into a cash-for-access deal. Perhaps the thing that upset me most was when I was playing, to earn for the family, it would inevitably mean sometimes not being available on Saturdays and that might prejudice my chances of seeing the kids more frequently. I even felt angry about the fact that I was angry. Because this ain't me – I'm not an angry man by nature. I might be screwy in some ways, but I like to think the best of people.

I wasn't simply a virgin in the family courts, I was a headless chicken virgin. I was getting advice from family and friends and didn't know who I could trust. I didn't have a clue if people were telling me sensible stuff or whether I was being taken for a mug. When you receive huge invoices from solicitors, you question why you're now spending all your money on this. But once you're on that wheel, you can't get off. My mind runs a hundred miles an hour at the best of times – I think the same way I pot balls: bang, bang, bang. And I had all these thoughts going through my head at the same time, and it was driving me crackers.

All the legal stuff began to get to me after I moved out and I was playing in the Regal Welsh. I thought, I don't even want to be here. I got to the semis and thought, you know what, I've had enough, I just want to go home. I felt lost, lonely in myself, and I just gave up in matches. I never threw matches, and would never dream of throwing matches, but I did give up. There's a big difference – one is planned, illegal and something I would never contemplate. The other is unplanned, and unconscious. It's often only afterwards that you look back and think, blimey, what was I doing there?

I did it in the Regal Welsh in 2010 and in the China Open, which was straight after, then I did it against Mark Selby in the World Championship quarter-finals. I felt ready to win the Worlds that year, I was playing well enough, but then I just reached a stage where I couldn't bear to be there any more. It was mad, really – there's nothing that means more to me than winning the Worlds, and there I was desperate to get the hell out. I just gave up mentally and started going for shots I shouldn't have gone for.

When we were due to go to China I said to my manager, Django: 'I don't feel up for it, mate. I really don't feel I can get on that plane and travel across the world. I ain't got it in me.'

He said: 'Well, there's twenty-five grand for you, there's a sponsor there, you've just got to turn up, shake a few hands, meet a few people.'

So we got out to China and the people were amazing, and you've never seen anything like the hotel. It was the best hotel I've been in my life. They gave us the top-floor suite, and I just sat there every night crying my eyes out. I felt so lost, so fucking sad, and that's when it hit me. I thought, I should be buzzing, I've got a little girl and little boy, I'm staying in a fantastic hotel, top of my game, and yet I'm out here, feeling like death.

I was playing this fella, just after I'd been crying my eyes out in this hotel. And I said to Django, I've got to get out of here. I was going to pull out of the event, and he said, if you pull out there will be murder. They'll fine you heavily. So I said, alright. But I knew I was in no fit state for anything, and just wanted to get back home. I thought, maybe when I get out there it will be better, and playing will do the trick. But when I did get out there I just felt worse.

The geeza could barely pot a ball, but somehow it got to 3-3, then he went 4-3. I knew I couldn't play another day. I was desperate, frightened about what I might do to myself. In the next frame I was clearing up, and I had the black on the spot and I missed. It was a shocking shot. Not only did I miss, but I left the ball over the pocket. Lily could have potted it. In the end the geeza beat me 5-3 and he was in shock, but I just thought, I'm out of here, I'm done. I got in the car, boom, went back to the hotel, got my flight back the next day.

People had always said about me that there were days when I looked as if I wasn't up for it; that I just couldn't be bothered. And there was some element of truth in it, but nothing like this.

I never once went out saying, today I'm going to get beat, but I began to realise something was up when I read in the papers that I hadn't won a first-round match for six months. I lost the first round in six consecutive major events. First round! Six tournaments on the bounce, and I wasn't conscious of it until six months later when people were talking about it and saying it was unheard of. It was only when I read it that I thought, bloody hell, what's happened to me?

I was so down – upset with myself and the family situation and my terrible form – that I decided to change my life completely, so I bought a boat and went to live on it. I was at Sheffield, 2010, and things were bad between me and Jo, and I'd just been in China crying my eyes out. There's a canal in Sheffield and I went on someone's barge, and I thought, this is nice, this is what I need. So I bought myself a boat, spent about 80 grand on it, and moved into it. It only lasted three months. Typical, really. I sold it for about £60,000 so I lost a bit on that. Again, typical.

I lived on a canal in Hertfordshire, and for a while it was great. Peaceful, looking at the water, feeding the ducks in the morning. A little family of ducks would come to my window at 6 a.m. every day for feeding. I thought, wow, I've lost one family but gained another! These ducks were like my children. I named them Lily and Ronnie.

There were around 15 residents living in my spot. The only problem was they all had jobs, so they were out working and I was left on the canal all day. I'd wait for them to come home at 6 p.m. and then I'd have company. It was miles away in Hertfordshire and I didn't really know anybody there. I suppose, as so often, I'd not really thought it through. In the days I'd go and run down the canal – I knew if I didn't run I'd fall apart, and that was one of the reasons I'd moved on to the canal in the first place. There was a gym round the corner so I'd do my run then go to the gym and another half-hour there. I was in good shape, but I needed to be, and I still lost my way a bit.

A good measure of how much I've been running away from stuff is the number of houses I've lived in over the past seven years – eight, and a boat! I should do *Homes Under the Hammer*! If that's not a reflection on how unstable my life has been, I don't know what is.

Meanwhile, I was in the courts so often that one time the judge told me I might as well rent a room round there. (That would have taken it to nine houses!) We'd gone through the early stages where you tend to spend about an hour in court each time, but when it gets to final hearings for the maintenance and access it takes for ever. What I went through was horrible, but I've heard it's pretty standard when a separation is acrimonious.

I ended up going to Families Need Fathers for help. I heard them on the radio, and thought they sounded sensible. I found out where the meeting was and went to hear what they had to say. When I spoke to the guy there, he said, what you're going through is standard – fathers have no rights, that's why there are organisations like ours. He was great – really helpful – and

I still go to him for advice. But ultimately I didn't feel Families Need Fathers was right for me, either – talking to the other dads tended to make me more angry, and what I really thought was, I need to start afresh rather than obsessing with the past.

I never told World Snooker what was happening in my private life, and I probably should have done. They might well have been more understanding. Instead, as far as they were concerned they had a prima donna on their hands – a liability who simply wasn't turning up for tournaments. I got loads of disciplinary letters and was fined. Not surprising really – they must have been well pissed off with me.

At first it didn't matter so much because the tournaments I wasn't turning up for were minor events. I was thinking, my main goal has got to be building up my contact with my children, and I could only do that by being there for them at weekends, and that meant missing tournaments. If I didn't do that every time I went to court I would worry it might count against me when I asked for more contact.

I stopped sleeping properly in 2010. The solicitors' bills and demands were mounting up, and every time I opened a letter it was something threatening; if I wasn't in court there'd be costs. And I just panicked. They gave me a form E to fill out, and it's like a 40-page document with dozens of questions on each page. There were 350 questions I needed to answer just on one section. It did my nut in. Then they wanted to know every bank account I'd had, every mortgage I'd had, how many things I owned that cost more than £500, what holidays I went on, what pensions I had, who I owed money to, who owed money to me. They wanted to know everything.

An investigative accountant was hired to look into everything, and would come back and say things like, 'What about this American Express card you've got?' And this was a card that I couldn't even remember having, and it turned out I'd made one transaction on it in two years. So they said, no, we need to see the full receipts on stuff you've purchased with it, and I'm like: 'Well, I bought a couple of tickets on it once and that was that.' Then they said: 'What about this company you've got in China? We need to see the accounts for that.' And I'm like, I don't even know what you're talking about. Then I remembered I'd set up a company with my manager Django for some potential work in China, but the company didn't do any trading. And they said, no, that isn't good enough, we need to see the accounts. The whole thing terrified me. I was going bonkers with it all.

I feel I lost three years of my life to a court battle, and got so distracted from my job that it allowed competitors to walk over me. I'd go to tournaments, and I was so brittle – lonely, sad, all the emotions you don't want to be feeling when you're going to do battle at the big events. And the worse I played, the more sponsors lost faith in me and pulled out of deals. It was a lose-lose situation.

But one huge plus is that I've now got maximum contact – every other weekend Friday through to Monday – and every Wednesday Lily and little Ronnie stay overnight and I take them to school on Thursday. As a result I've got a much better relationship with my children. I want to be part of their life, and they're great to be around. Little Ronnie and Lily make me laugh. Don't get me wrong: they're hard work, and parenting, especially single parenting, isn't easy.

Both Jo and I have come to realise that. There were a couple of times we got back together and she did say to me: 'Ah, it's a lot easier when there are two of us doing it.' And it was. But the fact is we aren't temperamentally suited to each other. That doesn't mean we can't still work as a team, bring them up together, even when we are not actually together as a couple. We just have to be sensible about it. I hope we won't resort to the courts again because it's crippling – financially and emotionally. Lawyers are not good for the soul.

In February 2013 I decided I'd return to snooker for the World Championship. As well as being bored and missing it, the money issue was crucial. I'd never really had to think about money before because I'd always lived within my means, and had always had more than I needed to get by. So it was all stacking up, waiting for a rainy day. But with maintenance for little Ronnie and Lily and their school fees and maintenance for my older daughter, Taylor, I couldn't afford not to play. I think I had a romantic idea that somehow if I didn't have money life would be simpler and everybody would start helping each other. But I accept now that was naive. Not forgetting one other little factor – however much I moan about it, however pissed off I get with the game, I do love my snooker.

4

THE BARRY HEARN
REVOLUTION

'Three minutes hard, three minutes recovery. Two
and a half minutes hard, two minutes recovery.
Then 90 seconds four times off a minute recovery.
Then six at a minute off a 30-second recovery. Last
600m I pushed it; right ankle felt sore.'

Snooker was really in the doldrums when Barry Hearn took
over in 2010. At first I didn't have a clue what he was doing
with my sport. I thought he was having a laugh, but over time
it's all begun to make sense.

Barry was at the heart of snooker during its glory days in the
1980s when he formed Matchroom with Steve Davis and Tony
Meo. But in the 2000s snooker started to go down the pan. It
lost its main sponsor, Embassy, and TV ratings fell (not surprisingly because there was so much competition in the shape of
new TV stations). It was getting to a stage where even the best
players couldn't make much of a living from the game, while
the good, solid pros didn't stand a chance. Then, in July 2010,
Barry, who was chairman of the World Professional Billiards
and Snooker Association, decided enough was enough and that
he was going to sort snooker out once and for all. After a vote

in June 2010, he took a controlling interest in the organisation's commercial arm, World Snooker Ltd, and so began the Barry Hearn snooker revolution.

Barry and I go way back. I first met him when I was a 12-year-old lad standing on a box to play my snooker. He was already a snooker legend then – the former accountant who ran the snooker club in Romford and managed so many of the world's best snooker players, including Steve Davis. He phoned up one day out of the blue.

'It's for you,' Dad said. 'It's Barry Hearn.'

I thought he was winding me up. I got on the phone, and, sure enough, it was Barry. He wished me good luck for the Amateur Championship on Saturday, then said there was one other thing.

'I want to manage you,' he said.

Bloody hell! Barry Hearn, manage me! At 12 years old! Amazing. Dad had decided he'd taken me as far as he could, and now it was time to let the professionals take over. Barry and I have been close ever since. We've had our fallings-out, but he's family really.

I know I drive him crazy at times, but I also know he cares about me. Last year Sports Life Stories made a documentary about me, and he was one of the main people they interviewed. 'I've managed Ronnie O'Sullivan twice,' he said. 'Some of the greatest days of my life have been with Ronnie O'Sullivan. Ronnie O'Sullivan has also driven me round the bend; driven me nuts. There are times when I could hug him and there are times when I could kick him. I prefer the hugging.' I prefer the hugging, too!

As well as being a great businessman, Barry understands me. 'Sometimes he doesn't have that confidence,' he said. 'Sometimes he needs an arm round him, sometimes he probably needs a clip round the ear. His biggest strength is what God gave him; he's a natural player. He's born to play. His biggest weakness is Ronnie O'Sullivan himself.' I watched that interview and thought, this geeza could be a shrink.

Actually, Barry was lovely about me in the documentary – as well as perceptive. 'He is a player who has fallen in and out of love with the game, the authorities. Sometimes he thinks he's got the world on his shoulders, and yet he can be the nicest person that you'll ever meet. He's an enigma, and geniuses are enigmas.'

If I'd been a single fella or in a happy relationship, and the family was all sweet, I would have said from the off that it was the most fantastic thing Barry had done for snooker. I'd say happy days. More tournaments, more playing opportunities, more time away from home. Fantastic. But being in my position, it was actually the worst thing that could have happened for me. I would have wished it had gone back to eight tournaments a year, as it had been before Barry took over, because I could have played them and then I would have been at home a lot more, wouldn't have had to do all the travelling, and I would have been able to fit in my time seeing the kids without the lawyers using my schedule against me in the custody battle. But when Barry went from eight to 27 tournaments within six months that screwed me.

It was an incredible change, and in many ways one that was needed. Snooker had been going through a terrible time. People always talk about how snooker lost its popularity, but I'm not sure it's that simple. What happened is that it never prepared itself for when tobacco companies were banned from sponsoring events in 2005.

World Snooker was an association run by ex-professional players and many of them didn't have the necessary entrepreneurial skills. I think that if Bernie Ecclestone had been in charge of snooker, the moment he knew tobacco sponsorship was going he would have done something about it. Everybody was given five years to prepare for it, and World Snooker should have started securing new sponsors from that time on. But they didn't. They were arrogant. Their attitude was, once tobacco goes everybody will be wanting to sponsor snooker, so we'll deal with that when the time comes. And what happened is that all the other sports prepared and moved on, they got backing from telecommunications or banks or whatever, but snooker had no sponsor.

I'd won the Embassy World Title in 2004, and that was the last year of tobacco sponsorship. And World Snooker never had anything in place. They didn't put it out to tender early enough, and were left with no bargaining power. All they were left with was unsponsored tournaments. It was catastrophic for snooker. If Barry, never mind Bernie Ecclestone, had been in charge at that point he would never have let it get to such a state. There wasn't enough money to put into the events, and so they couldn't even put them on. They were left with their BBC events, a couple of Sky, a couple in China, one in Ireland and that was it. Pathetic. A true humiliation for snooker. It was basic maths.

Stephen Hendry's manager, Ian Doyle, who ran 110 Sport, was trying to set up a rival tour and get the players to come over to his side. If that had happened World Snooker would have collapsed. Not surprisingly, World Snooker got bottly and offered the top eight players big pay incentives to stay with them. They said, right, we're in trouble and our way out of it is to promote the sport. So the people running World Snooker went, how do we keep our top players? Because if we keep them we'll keep the BBC on side, but if we lose them the BBC will lose interest.

So World Snooker panicked and started offering the top players big salaries to promote the game. It was a salary to play, but we also had to do things like magazine shoots to promote the game. I felt that money was basically for my vote, but it was all a shot in the dark; just a desperate attempt to stop 110 getting hold of the game. World Snooker succeeded, but it wasn't good for snooker. You needed people to come in and look at the game like a business.

But did the game ever lose its popularity? I'm not so sure. After all that time when Steve Davis played Dennis Taylor in the final, and they got 18.5 million viewers on the BBC, there were only four channels on the telly. Once Sky came in and shook everything up, it was inevitable that snooker would never be able to enjoy such a huge share of the viewing figures. The world was changing, and snooker wasn't going to be the exception to the rule. Where snooker failed was that it never thought ahead – actually, it didn't even think in the present. Who knows? If it had got its thinking cap on, and Barry Hearn had been involved all along, it might be as popular as golf is now. Even though snooker's adored in the Far East, it was never exploited – in the best sense. The people running the game had tunnel vision. They were, like, well, we've got our four BBC events, a few invitations, a couple in Thailand, we've got nothing to worry about. But once tobacco sponsorship ended, there was nothing to fall back on.

Even though it suited me when there were hardly any events on, for most players it was a nightmare. They'd be practising for a month or six weeks between events, with no cash coming in. If your form went there was a lot of pressure on you to do well in the next event. Whereas the attitude now is, I'm playing in 30-odd events, I'm bound to do well in three of them.

The journeymen players, those who were on the circuit but would never win events, did actually find a way of coping. But that was more a reflection of how uneconomical snooker had become as a sport than anything else. With fewer tournaments they cut down on their expenses because, for example, you didn't have to be paying for hotels all the time. In a way it was more economical to play the professional game when there were fewer events because so many players actually lost money by turning up for events – hotels, petrol, eating, you name it, it all adds up.

Now, with so many events, some would argue that it's harder for the journeymen to make ends meet because, unless you're winning, the money is not much better and the expenses are still the same – the Hilton's still £100 a night, it still costs £100 to fill your tank up to get up to Preston (I know not everybody's going to stay in the Hilton or eat up as much fuel as me!). So if they're away for, say, 28 tournaments a year, they might be paying almost five times as much in expenses as they were doing pre-Barry Hearn. A lot of players are finding it tougher now because before they could get a bit of part-time work in a club. But the bottom line is the sport itself is in a much healthier state.

And the longer Barry's been in charge the more he's ironed out the problems. He saw the ranking system wasn't fair, so he changed it. We went from six to around 20 ranking events, and although the winner might only win £10,000 in lots of them, the events carried important points. What it basically meant was that winning four tiny PTC events was the equivalent of winning the World Championship, so a lesser player could easily find himself heading up the world rankings. Now the points reflect the prize money, so say you got £10,000 for a PTC event and £250,000 for winning the World Championship, you'd have to win 25 PTC events to get the same points for winning the World Championship.

That seems fairer to me because only the very best players are going to win the World – and you ask any player what they'd prefer, 25 PTCs or one world title, and I guarantee every single one will go for the latter. What the system meant as it stood was that all the top players had to enter the small PTC events just to nick a few points and avoid dropping down the rankings, so you were effectively blackmailed into playing in them.

We ended up with players ranked number one who'd never won a senior ranking event. It was like when tennis player Caroline Wozniacki was world number one, even though she'd never won a major and found it difficult to get past the quarter-finals. So when Barry started you could never really say there was a genuine number one, but what he did do was generate more playing opportunities which benefited the players who only had their snooker to worry about. For me, though, it turned into a headache. I was caught between playing for important points in these unimportant events or seeing my children.

I actually enjoyed these smaller events when I played in them. They were good for sharpening your game up, and it was nice to get away from home and play a bit of snooker and see where your game was at. In 2012, I played in most of the PTC events and I noticed a difference in my game. When you're playing so many matches you don't have time to worry about whether you're cueing right; you just have to switch straight on. So you become much more in tune with your game. If you were struggling you just had to find a way of getting through it; playing your way out of it.

It hardened you up. It was like I was back at Blackpool all those years ago when I was 16 and was playing, and winning, match after match. One match would turn into another and it became like going to have a knock down your local club whereas before, when there were only six or eight events, every one had to count. Now it was like you win one, you lose one.

In many of these PTC events there'd only be a handful of people allowed to watch each match. It really was like Blackpool! The games were held in cubicles, and the most you could have were four seats one end and four seats the other end, a referee and two seats for the players, and that was it. No TV, no nothing.

I loved it. I once had nine people watching me – that was a proper crowd. Lots of people complained about travelling for these events, but once I got there I loved it. Just like being a kid again. Cubicles? They didn't bother me. I just loved to play snooker, and it was such a throwback.

I had my running trainers in my car boot, I'd get dressed in my suit in the car park, jeans off, dinner suit on, go and play for my half-dozen spectators, then off for a run when I was done. Don't get me wrong, it was hard. There were times when I felt like shit, and thought, what am I doing here? But on the whole I loved it. I won three out of nine of the PTC events in 2012. They ain't easy either. You've got to win seven matches over three days to win each one. Three matches on a Friday or Saturday then four matches on a Sunday, if you got through. And you pretty much knew if you'd played on the Saturday you wouldn't be winning on the Sunday because it took so much out of you. The best draw was Friday match, Saturday off, then Sunday you'd be fresh again to play.

It was great preparation for Sheffield because it got me used to stop-start, stop-start, the rhythm of playing, and so it became easier preparing for a big tournament. You were permanently match fit.

What Barry did was clever. He saturated the market by putting on so many tournaments. Then, once you'd filled the calendar up if you had someone come up and say, I want to put a snooker event on, he'd go: 'There isn't much room, when d'you want it?' and they'd say: 'Well, I'd like it there', and he'd go: 'Well, we'd have to get rid of that tournament to put your tournament in so it will cost you money.' Basic supply and demand. Good business. You create the demand, and that's what Barry did. So when, say, the Chinese came along and said, we'd like another tournament Barry would be in a position to say, it's going to cost you. And it's worked. Now we've got five tournaments in China, one in Australia, three majors over here, one in Ireland. So in the few years he's been back in snooker, he's definitely been going in the right direction.

Although we exchanged words about his new regime – and, as he says, I've driven him mad plenty of times – I've always basically got on with Barry. Even our disagreement over the new contract was a misunderstanding. If I'd sat down with him just after the World Championship in 2012 I'd probably have been playing through 2012–13. The way I understood the contract was different from how Barry later explained it to me. The way I read it I thought, well, if you're going to get a ban for missing four tournaments I'm bound to fall short and that isn't going to be good for me. But I hadn't understood that was four tournaments *a year*; I thought it was rolling on and on.

But Barry told me the slate was clean every year. That had been the main sticking point for me. There was also the point about restricting your trade; you had to sign a contract that said you weren't allowed to play in any other televised event without clearance from World Snooker. In a way it is a restriction of trade, but the bottom line is that Barry's not going to stop you playing in an event unless it clashes with his event. And he's right in a way to put that clause in because he's trying to build a tour and he doesn't want me going off with, say, Stephen Hendry and putting on a rival tournament when his is on. What he did say is, come and talk to me about it, and when there's a gap in the calendar of course you can go and play Stephen Hendry in a one-off match, or whatever you want to do.

Barry has taken the maxi prize away. That's a bit of a bummer. There used to be £167,000 at Sheffield for the maximum – £147,000 plus 20 grand for the biggest break. He got rid of that because he said they were too easy to get. I said, you're having a laugh, there's only me and Hendry who have made them with any regularity, so it ain't that easy. I've had 11, Stephen's had 11 and John Higgins has had seven. I've had three at the World Championship, Stephen's had two. The first maxi at the World Championship was made by Cliff Thorburn in 1983. Nobody could believe that such a level of perfection was possible when it happened. Mind you, it took Cliff about a week to make his!

All in all, Barry's done brilliantly for snooker. If I was coming into the sport now I'd be buzzing. If I was 18 or 19, I'd think I've got another 15 to 20 years in which to earn good money. And the cash is coming back into the game. Next year the winner of the World Championship gets £300,000, the winner of the UK gets £150,000. Sure, we're not talking Premier League football figures, but we never were.

Although it was terrible for the sport when we were down to eight tournaments a year, it did give me plenty of time to focus on the running. In a way it was a perfect mix – eight events a year (six ranking events and two invitation events – the Masters and the Premier League), and I had my sponsorship, and my running, so I was happily occupied.

I was running in cross-country races every weekend and they became more important to me than the snooker. Obviously it was great to get to semi-finals and finals, but there was a down-side – I'd have to miss the races. Unconsciously I was thinking, well it's not that bad if I get beaten at this stage, I've got a few points on the board, I ain't disgraced myself, and I'm going to be back home for the cross-country Saturday morning. Running was taking me over.

It had become an addiction, but it was my best addiction yet by far. It's a continual high – one of those you can just repeat and repeat. I'm not talking about jogging, I'm talking about *running*. Jogging is hard, but running is easy. Running is as easy as brushing your teeth. When you watch runners doing 10 kilometres in 27 minutes that isn't hard; it's harder for the fella doing it in 54 minutes because he's using every muscle. When you're jogging it's a slog; you're using your shoulders, your hips, you're struggling to get your knees in front. When you're running, everything just flows. You get in such a rhythm, it's like a dance. Your body's not moving, your head's not moving, your shoulders aren't rolling. Your hips are coming through, your feet are off the ground a lot longer. You go past a set of lamp-posts and you're thinking, I'm covering this ground really fast. You're just listening to your breath, your heart and your footsteps, and maybe a few birds twittering away. It's beautiful.

I never listen to music while I run because I want to hear myself and the world as I run.

These days it feels more of a struggle. I'm running, but not like I was five or six years ago. If I go out for a run now and do three and a half miles it's an effort because I'm still trying to go at the pace I used to go at but I can't sustain it, so I have to stop two or three times. But I always think I'd rather stop two or three times and be running than jog and never stop. I feel like I'm wasting my time when I jog. But for me to get that feeling of running at a nice pace I have to put in the work. You have to get out and do your eight- or nine-mile run on a Sunday; you need to be doing 35 to 40 miles a week. Hopefully, by the time you read this I'll have put in the hours and I'll be flying again.

5

COMEBACK KID

'Forest 50 mins, about seven miles with John. Speed sessions 10 x 30 seconds with 30-second recovery. Five minutes recovery. Then 12 x 30 seconds. Felt good. Proper fit.'

It was winter 2011, and I was getting more and more run down. Not sleeping, miserable with the family situation, depressed and exhausted. In December 2011, I beat Ding Junhui 7-1 in the final of the Premier League. I'd not had any success in the ranking events for a couple of years, but this was the tenth time I'd won the Premier League, the seventh in eight years, and I felt in pretty good nick. I got home Sunday night and on Tuesday drove to Sheffield for a PTC event starting on the Wednesday.

I got beaten 4-2 in the first round. The fella played well, no excuses. I didn't play badly but I just felt I didn't have any energy. I went back to the hotel and there was me, Gay Robbie (who's not gay but is very camp) and my friend from Scotland, Charlie, and Patsy Fagin, who won the UK Championship in 1979. I'd asked Patsy to come down to help me with my game.

We'd spent a day on the practice table, and the next day I went downstairs for breakfast and I felt terrible – achy, drained, no energy. I phoned up Mum and Dad and said, I need to come home. I was going to stay in Sheffield for a few days then go straight to the UK Championship, which was in York, but I thought, I can't do this; I don't feel right. I couldn't eat, my stomach felt terrible. But I didn't think I could drive back. It was a three-hour journey, and if I got caught in traffic I'd be done for.

So I decided to leave my car in Sheffield and get the train home, and Dad went, well, you can't leave your car there, and I said, well, I can't get home, I won't make it, I don't fancy my chances. But as I walked out of the hotel, I saw the car there and thought, sod it, put the bag in the boot and drove home. I got to Peterborough, about an hour and 20 minutes from home, and I was done. I was driving down the hard shoulder, and I knew that I was about to fall asleep or have an accident, so I put a bit of speed on and just went for it.

I drove straight to Mum's house in Chigwell, lay on her settee and didn't eat anything for three or four days except clear soup. Then I spent a few days at my own house and felt a bit better, and I went to the UK Championship. I beat Steve Davis in the first round, and Judd Trump beat me in the second, but I was playing pretty well. I hadn't yet had a quarter-final in a major event for a couple of years, but I thought, you know what, you're playing well enough for a breakthrough.

I was so knackered, though. Wherever I was I'd just fall asleep. I'd go down the club to practise and just fall asleep on the settee. I had no energy. I thought, when I've got the energy I'll play, but I hardly ever did have. I'd get to my feet, play for 20 minutes, half an hour, an hour, whatever I could do, and that became my preparation for the World Championship – just lying on the settee and practising whenever I had the strength.

I'd come straight home from matches and sleep. It was mad.

I was ill from December 2011 to May 2012. Eventually I went to see the doctor and the tests came back saying I had glandular fever.

'What do I do?' I asked the doctor.

'There's nothing you can do, Ron,' he said.

There were times I felt I couldn't get to the top of the stairs, and all I could do was rest. So I thought, that's what I'll do – rest and play, rest and play. It wasn't a bad thing; I quite enjoyed it – loads of sleep, loads of chilling out. It could be plenty worse. It forced me to slow down. It meant I couldn't keep running, going to China, going up and down motorways. Glandular fever became a blessing in that it forced me to slow down and reappraise the way I was living. Trying to keep my family life in order and playing in all the tournaments took too much out of me. So I missed a couple of tournaments and started to take it easy, and that's when things got better for me.

In February 2012, I played in the German Masters. That kick-started my season. I felt I had been playing well till then, but I wasn't getting results. Two years without a victory in a ranking event was a first for me.

I had no problem with the Premier League. That was a tournament made for me. There's a stopclock, and you have to play a shot every 25 seconds. But because that so obviously benefited my natural game I never counted it as a real victory. The Premier League was almost a given, my banker – and my mortgage paid for the year.

I was so close to an inglorious exit in the first round of the German Masters. I was 4-0 down to Andrew Higginson and thought, I'm done for here; start the car. I've lost it. I obviously haven't got it in me to win these important tournaments any more. The German is a ranking event, which means it's classed as a major, whereas the Premier League is an invitation event so they often invite people like Jimmy White and Steve Davis just to put bums on seats. No disrespect to them (they are two of my heroes, after all) but they are past their best. It was seen as Barry Hearn's favourites who were invited to that, whereas a ranking event is open to all the top players in the world. Everybody wants ranking titles on their CV, the World and the UK being the most prestigious. But I'd just lost the ability to win them. Or so I thought.

So I was 4-0 down, first to five. And I thought, either the standard's getting really high or I've lost it. Or a combination of both. I'd been working with the sports psychiatrist Dr Steve Peters so I didn't panic. I thought I was cueing well. I'd had a couple of chances, but not made the most of them. Rather than panic or get the hump, I thought, no, I'm here, I'm playing okay, a crowd of 2,500, just try to enjoy the experience. If you get beaten 5-0, you get beaten 5-0, but just give it your best, and that was the stuff I was working on with Steve Peters. Stay patient, and if I get a chance to put some pressure on the fella, you never know what's going to happen.

I won one frame to go 4-1, then I won another. And I won them in one visit, and quickly, which is always good for morale. So at 4-2 I thought, if he's going to twitch he's going to twitch now. It got to 4-3, and then he had a chance – he was on a 60-odd break, and there was a red over the hole, and I thought, well, I'm done now. Fuck, I've got beaten in another ranking event early doors. Then he kissed the green and four-ball snookered himself on the red over a hole. Unbelievable. You would have got odds of 1,000 to one on him doing that. I've got a bit of a chance here, I said to myself. But I was still 60 down, 4-3 down, and there was 67 on the table. So if he gets on the red he's 61 ahead, 59 on the table and I'm out.

But he didn't pot that red. I then got a good long one, cleared up, 4-4, and I thought, bloody hell! Then I won the last comfortably. So I got through a match I was dead and buried in. He was gutted. I shook his hand, and he was gone. Andrew's a good player ranked in the 20s. All these players coming through these days can beat the best at any time. Andrew looked like he was going to fall over. He was in a daze, and I was so pumped up. He was deflated, and I was elated. I thought, wow, that was a touch! Four-nil down, one ball from going out: you couldn't have written it.

When I got through to the quarters in Germany I thought that was a result because for two years all I'd been doing was last 16 at best. And then I got to the semi, and I thought, fuck I'm near a final. It was a shitty match against Stephen Lee; one of the only matches that season I felt: 'I want out of here, I've had enough, count me out, I'd rather get home and watch it on the telly.' Somehow I got through that match. I was there for the taking, but Stephen sat on the fence and once it got close I reckoned if he's not been able to beat me yet and I've got this far then there's a good chance I'm going to win.

I got through to the final against Stephen Maguire and I thought, if I'm going to play in the final like I did in the semis, it's going to be a long day. At the interval I was 3-1 down – Maguire had had three century breaks, basically hadn't missed a ball, and I managed to nick a frame. And I thought, I've done well, I was 3-1 down, but I'd had a result. Was it always going to be like this against modern players? Every time you go out there you're going to get your head punched about. Unless you make three centuries you've not got a chance.

Then I thought, no, just enjoy it, give it your best. That's all you can do. And I managed to come out of the session 5-3 down, which was also a result. It could easily have been 8-0 or 7-1, so I'd avoided a whitewash and there was still a game on for the evening session. I'd avoided the embarrassment of getting absolutely hammered and having to come out 7-1 down; I'd done alright. I'd given everything, and there was no more meat on the bone.

Stephen played so brilliantly he probably felt disappointed going in only 5-3 up. He'd not made as much of it as he could have done, so maybe he was the one in the dressing room beating himself up. I came out in the evening and got to 6-6. It wasn't the best snooker in the world, but I came in and asked myself, how did I get to 6-6? I'd been outplayed all over the place. Then we came out for the last session and he started missing a few, and I was thinking, game on, it's the best of five now, I fancy this. I started to feel I was in charge. That's the thing about snooker, any sport really: so much is psychology – and the psychology swings one way then the other by the second. So I'd taken a battering all day long and then my rewards came later in the match, when you want it to come good for you.

I was 8-6 up, on the verge of winning, then I played a bad positional shot. I was convinced I'd just thrown it away. I'm on a 40-odd break, in my mind I've won the match, I'm doing the winner's speech and, boom, he clears up. And I was thinking: 'Oh no, I've done it again, got carried away in the moment.' I wasn't used to winning, and I tensed a bit. So it went 8-7. Eventually I potted the blue to win it 9-7, and I was twitching like mad. My backhand was shaking like a leaf, my arse was pooping all over the gaffe, 2,500 people in the house, and I was, like, get me out of here; this isn't the place to crumble and fall apart.

I'd not been so nervous since a semi-final in the World Championship against Stephen Hendry in 2002. The German Masters is a tournament that loads of snooker fans aren't even aware of, but this was huge for me. Huge. When the blue went in, I couldn't believe it. I was shaking so much I thought I'd miss it by a foot. At first I thought, don't worry about potting, just get the white safe. Then I told myself, don't think like that, that's not how a champion thinks. A champion thinks: 'That's going in the hole, pot the blue and get on to the pink; that's the shot.' Embrace the moment, I told myself. This is what top sport is about, this is how you separate yourself from the pack. You grab these opportunities, and commit.

I went back to my chair and I was gone. Exhausted. I thought, I've won a tournament, a proper ranking event. After coming out of the Priory and winning the Champions Cup, it was the greatest turning point for me since I'd started playing professionally. That was so massive in 2001 because I'd been drinking and puffing my head off for seven years and I'd come out clean and won this tournament, and I thought, I'm enjoying this, I've got a chance. After winning the German last year I felt the same, and I never thought I'd recapture that feeling. I'd been down for more than two years, I'd been knocked by everyone in the game, and I'd proved I still had it in me. I won about €50,000 – not a massive amount, but that was irrelevant.

Not winning for two years had a big impact on me financially. Not just the prize money. When I started to lose all the time, the sponsor money disappeared or went down. Snooker was unrecognisable financially from when I started. Back in the days of Steve Davis and Dennis Taylor the standard was nowhere near as high, but anyone in the top 30 could make a decent living out of the game. After all, the tournaments were on telly, watched by millions, tens of millions even, and the tobacco sponsors queued up to put their name on trophies. But the game was hit by that double whammy: cigarette sponsorship was banned and the viewing figures fell away.

When I stopped winning I went from earning £750,000 a

year to £150,000. Listen: it's still decent money, but once you subtract the costs of travelling and hotels, managers and agents, believe me it's not impressive. Actually, it seemed to bother my accountant more than me – he'd go, hold on, what's going on here. He couldn't get his head around it.

But as far as my lifestyle went, it never affected me because I didn't live an extravagant life anyway. I had my odd mad moment, like when I bought a Ferrari on the spur of the moment, and flogged it just as quickly at a fair old loss when I realised Ferraris are not me. I had a nice house and car, but I didn't really go out – all I did was run and play snooker. My running trainers are the most important things I own. I feel lucky in that I've never had to earn a huge amount to maintain a lifestyle. I've never felt that pressure because I've never wanted that lifestyle.

So it was the winning rather than the money that was always going to be the big thing for me.

And I'd finally won another ranking event. It was massive because I thought it was over for me. Before Dad came out of prison in 2010 I had this fear that once he was out I'd never win another tournament. I don't know why. The mind does daft things. When I was a kid I'd always found it difficult to win when he came to watch me, and that was probably in the back of my mind. But there was something else, too. I wanted to spend time with him, and psychologically I'd resigned myself to becoming a bit-part player and losing my focus. I knew I had to make up for lost time. I didn't want to be away, living out of a suitcase and not seeing him.

I'd waited 18 years, and there's no point waiting that long then when he comes out not to enjoy having a fry-up, watching a bit of Sky and a bit of boxing, and being there for him. I'd been there for him all that time he was in prison, and now

I wanted to be part of his life. It was important that when he came out I was there to support him.

When I was in rehab in 2000 I had to read out my life story; one of the fellas in there was called Max – we never really got on, but he gave me one of the most important bits of feedback I got there. When you read your life story out, they share back what they think is going on, and Max, he just said to me: 'It looks as if you're counting down the days till your dad comes home.' And he was right. It's like when you put your mind to winning a tournament; I told myself I was doing it for him to keep him going. Every time he saw me on the telly he said it was like having a visit, and I thought, if that's the most exciting part of his life in prison I couldn't jack it in even though I wasn't always in love with the game. The most important reason to keep playing was to keep Dad going.

I always knew Dad wanted the best for me; that he'd do anything for me as a child to give me the better chance of success. So I always felt he was largely to thank for my success. He taught me everything I knew, kept my feet on the ground, gave me the best opportunity, the best cues, the best practice facilities and best practice partners, and that needed paying back. When Dad was in jail I felt we were in it together. I wasn't about to abandon him when I was out here. I always felt it was a team effort – me, Dad, Mum, and my sister Danielle.

In those two years I also thought that was the end of my time as a champion because it is the age when most champions stop winning. Stephen Hendry won his last major tournament when he was around 34, but you can forgive him because he crammed so much into such a short amount of time, just like tennis player Pete Sampras did. Maybe he burnt out a bit quicker than his talent deserved as a result. I've had gaps where I've still played but not with the same intensity as somebody like Hendry would, and that's probably why I've been able to continue going over a longer period of time.

But sport is a business as much as anything else, and you have to look at things practically – when will I find my days numbered? Can I keep going on till I'm 40? It's my job, it's my life, it's what I like to do, and you want a sense of when it's going to come to an end. In your own mind you're trying to prepare yourself for it, and you can only go by the people who went before you. That's all there is – history. But in my heart I didn't feel I was coming to the end. I still felt confident in my own game.

At other times I felt I was past my sell-by. This was a new era of players, and I was deluding myself. I questioned the type of game I was playing and whether it was equipped to deal with the new generation. I told myself that even though I thought I was playing an aggressive game, the new players were looking at me thinking, who is this old codger? Perhaps it was like me playing Terry Griffiths 20 years ago; he'd so rarely take a risk. And maybe they were looking at me in the same light, going: 'This Ronnie O'Sullivan, he's a bit too negative for me. He don't fancy the job.' I was getting paranoid.

I did have to reinvent myself as a player because I felt I was on the back foot against a lot of these players; that they were more aggressive to me, playing a different game. When I started out, the likes of Steve Davis were more careful. They wouldn't just break the balls open. They were more percentage players whereas now, even though they don't miss much, they're still percentage players; they just go for harder shots and get them. Whereas years ago you would have thought a ball is safe, today's players now think, well, that's my chance. Against the likes of Steve Davis you knew you might get beat but you wouldn't get blown away. So you could start slowly and work your way into a match. With these guys, there's none of that. As I said, I was 4-0 down to Higginson, and I'd not done a lot wrong. Twenty years ago he would have won a lot of tournaments.

All the new generation are aggressive – perhaps 30 of them who, on their day, could beat anybody. When I started out there were seven or eight who could kill you off, but you'd never meet them till the quarter-finals; now you're getting them first round and you're thinking: 'Cor blimey, I don't fancy this geeza!'

It's funny how the standard has gone up so much while the incentive to play the game has fallen so much. Twenty years ago you could get close on 20 million people watching the World Championship final in the UK, but nowadays you'd be lucky to get five million. There was the tobacco advertising, and money in the game, and the financial rewards were massive. But this new generation were probably the ones watching it back then. It was a big sport, a glamorous sport. Perhaps I'm reaping what I sowed. People tell me my game encouraged others to come into the game and play aggressively and fast.

So I changed a few things in my game, developed a few new shots. My two lean years were partly down to me not playing well and partly down to problems off the table. In the 2011 World Championship I was ready to give up, then I was introduced to Steve Peters and he turned my thinking around. I rediscovered my passion for the game, and my attitude was a thousand times better than it had ever been before.

After working with Dr Steve for a while, I didn't feel I ever gave up in matches. If I lost, it was just because the other guy had played better on the day and that was a lot easier to live with. It wasn't easy because you then thought, well, I gave it my best and still lost, but it was easier. There was a transition period where I changed my game. I'm quite a good student of the sport, and I watched other players and thought that to move on to another level and last another few years I needed to improve certain areas of my game. The new players pot with such ease. Before, players made it look like hard work. The new bunch made it look like every ball was over the hole: I needed to start thinking like that. I changed my grip and technique and started committing to the shot – if I was going to miss I was going to miss positively. I wasn't going to twitch them in any more.

John Higgins was my yardstick. You looked at him and thought, he's doing a lot of things right; then Judd Trump came along, and he does a lot of things right as well. Neil Robertson was another big factor, and Ding Junhui. If you look at their technique, all four have similarities: they play the same sort of shots and the balls break the same.

There's a science to it. A lot of it is just how they release the cue; their timing, their grip, their balance. They are power players; they pot a red, get the right angle and go into that pack and the white will just accelerate through the balls. With one shot the balls are at their mercy. Years ago they were accurate, but they didn't have that one shot that could win them the game. With a lot of players you can see technical weaknesses, and you know they will break down, but with this four you look at them and think there's not a lot that could go wrong with them. Over 17 days or a season of course they'll lose matches, but they'll be 85–90 per cent most of the year round and I thought that for me to compete with those players I had to learn off them. I had to learn how to play as if I could win matches with one shot. To play the aggressive game you might give away a few chances, and it might be the wrong shot to go for, but my logic was that the game I was going to play would be more risky but it would also give much more of a message to the opponent: if you miss, I probably won't.

In a way it's counter-intuitive. As you get older the tendency is to become more conservative and take fewer risks. I was aware of what happened to Steve Davis and Stephen Hendry. I think Davis would have been better if he'd tried to match Hendry at his own game; he had the ability to do that, but he was so stuck in his ways. If he's convinced of something he ain't going to change, which is probably why he won so often. But I also believe you've got to look at the competition and think, if I'm going to move on I need to adapt and realise that there'll always be someone coming up behind me who will take the game to the next level. And the only way to stay in the game was to go with them and not get stuck behind.

When I was losing all the time, people's behaviour changed towards me. They were nicer to me, and I hated that. They were talking to me. Once you're not a threat, people want to be your friend. There are certain players on the circuit who are not like that – Matthew Stevens, Neil Robertson, Ding Junhui, Stephen Hendry, Steve Davis. They're always the same whether you're winning or not. But some players, and their managers and friends, change.

They'd be chatting away like they were your friend, then all of a sudden, when I started to win, you could smell their change of attitude. You'd sense you were on your own again. But if I had the choice I'd much rather be on my own and be a winner than be a loser and have: 'Hello, lads, where you going for dinner tonight? Yeah, yeah, great, and what day you going to China? When you get there we'll meet up.' All that bollocks. That's the loser's mentality. They're good in a group, they like to banter with each other. But Hendry never bantered with people, Steve Davis never bantered with people, John Higgins doesn't banter with people, and I'd never bantered with people. I was there to do a job, and yet I felt I'd become one of the banterers; one of the mob that would sit there and talk bollocks for three or four hours because that's where the level of my game had gone to.

I wasn't winning tournaments, and I felt I was just one of those players there to make up the numbers. I was not a threat to the real contenders. Hendry was an assassin. Davis was an assassin. At my best, I'm an assassin. We're not there to be mates with anybody. There's nothing worse than travelling 13 hours to China when you feel you're just making up the numbers.

When I won the tournament in Germany, the other players knew how important it was to me. I'm not sure I realised how important it was till I played in the next tournament, the Welsh Open. I went there, thinking, I'm still not cueing that well, but I've got a chance. In the first round I beat Marco Fu 4-2, and Marco has always been a bogeyman for me. Every time he sees me, he rubs his hands together and goes: 'Ah, lovely, I've got Ronnie in the first round, I'm bound to play well.' But now I thought I'd won in Germany and the pressure was off me. Beating Fu is like beating a Higgins or a Hendry because he always plays out of his nut against me. Then I beat Mark Williams 4-1, again not playing great but competing. No matter how badly someone like him plays, he always has that inner belief, that steel, that he can win. He was playing well then, so that was a result.

At this stage it was touch and go whether I'd qualify for the World Championship. I'd sunk to around 20th in the world rankings because I'd won so few world-ranking points for a couple of years, and every tournament I found myself slipping down the world rankings. When Barry Hearn came in he changed the world-ranking system. Before that you basically had your spot and pretty much stayed there the whole season. Then, when Barry came in, the rankings changed every two or three tournaments. He introduced loads of new events and every point mattered.

In the Welsh, I beat Judd Trump in the quarter-finals, and that was another turning point. He was one of the leading players coming through the ranks, got to the World Championship final and was playing with huge confidence. I thought, I'm not going to play cagey snooker, I'm going out to give it a go. And that's how it went. I went bang! Long red. Eighty. He went, bang! Long red. Eighty. I went bang! Long red. One hundred. He went bang! Seventy. And I thought, 2-2, we're having a row here, this is good! I'm enjoying this. Then, at the interval it goes 3-2 to me in another single visit, then 3-3 with another 70 odd. And I'm thinking, wow, he's hit me and I've hit him with everything. There came a point when he changed his game. He started playing shots he wouldn't normally. He started to not go for his shots, waiting for me to make mistakes. And I thought, whether I win or lose this match there's a chink in the armour and I've found it. Psychologically, he's no longer the machine everybody thought he was going to be. I know John Higgins beat him in the 2011 World Championship final, but that's how he had felt to me till then. From then on he didn't feel like a Higgins or Hendry to me – with those two I felt there was no chink. You might beat them, but there was never a chink.

You always measure yourself against the top four or five players, and to get to an important stage of a tournament and feel that you've got the edge on someone like Judd felt good. I thought, if you're not going to go for your shots I will, and I went bang bang bang bang, thank you very much, 5-3. And I got through a match that I thought I wouldn't be able to – I was 36, he was 22, and I didn't think I'd be able to keep up with him. If that was the standard, I didn't know whether I had the stamina or consistency. But the same thing happened that had against Maguire. When it got to 6-6 he started playing cautiously. It's alright playing the big shots in practice, and in the early stages of the match, but when it really matters is in the final stages of a big tournament.

Graham Dott or Mark Selby at 3-3 would have been a tougher match than Judd Trump at 3-3. Although Judd plays a lot more aggressive, attractive snooker, at 3-3 you don't want to be playing Selby or Dott; you'd rather be playing Trump. Sure, he can blow you away, but if you stick to him you've got a chance. And nobody can blow everybody away. I don't care if you're Barcelona; Manchester United can hold on to you, and if you get to 80 minutes, you're still 0-0 and you twitch, they'll nick a goal because they're used to it and they believe in themselves. Boom, miskick, boom, through the goalie's legs, Barcelona beaten. And snooker, or any sport for that matter, is no different. So Trump was someone to measure myself against. And I thought, okay, I might not be able to be as aggressive but I'm trying to play that game – or play the game I can play to feel I can compete with them – and when it came to it I fancied the job. Sure, I was nervous against Maguire and Trump, but the more I got into it the more I thought the odds were in my favour.

I got to the semis and played Selby. We nickname him the Torturer. Just as when you play Trump and you play a nice, open game, you enjoy it, and you know you're either going to get smashed off the table or have a good game, but you're going to play the shots you like to play at a nice tempo, so it was the very opposite with Selby. I didn't know my arse from my elbow, I couldn't cue, I didn't feel like a snooker player because he plays a game in which, unless you match him in certain areas and score, he's going to beat you.

I was matching him in the safety, but when I got in the balls I wasn't scoring, and I lost 6-2. But I came off and thought, well, at least he didn't aggravate me like he did in the past. With a lot of people, if you respect their game you don't mind losing to them, but there are certain players you don't appreciate. They're still very good and get the job done, so you have to respect them for that, but it is painful. Selby is the Torturer, just like Peter Ebdon (I love Psycho – that's what Dad nicknamed Ebdon – but he'll be the first to admit he likes to slowly strangle his opponents). Tactically, there is probably no one better than Selby in the game. He's prepared to play a lot of long frames – he's happy to take five hours to play five frames. But that's no good to me. Every punter's paid their money, and I feel like I've robbed them. They've come to see me play, and if I've given them ten 50-minute frames I feel shit, and want to go home and kill myself.

Selby and I have different mentalities. His way is not wrong, my way is not right; we just have different philosophies. A lot of people don't like playing him. He tortured Graham Dott, he tortured Neil Robertson in the Masters, he tortured Sean Murphy. They probably wouldn't admit it, but, watching, it was evident they were finding it hard going. And in some way I got satisfaction out of that because in the past I'd played him in the Masters and in the Welsh, and people went: 'See, Ronnie doesn't like this kind of player', but I still managed to get a couple of wins over him. I beat him 9-8 in the UK, and had a maxi. We've had tough matches, and I've got a certain amount of respect for the way he goes around getting a result. John Parrott's got the best name for him: Stickability Selby. He'll stick to you no matter how well you play. Selby does have issues with his cue action, though; his belief in his game. He has anxiety within himself. I don't think he's enjoying his game even though he's getting the results. I don't think he's entirely happy with the way he hits the ball. He's had about 20 different cue actions in the past 10 years, but, again, I take my hat off to someone who's prepared to change their game to become a better player. It shows that he loves the sport he's playing.

There was one match I played him where I just counted the dots on the spoon repeatedly. There were 108 dots on the spoon, and every time I lost count I went back to the beginning because it was difficult to watch; difficult to get any rhythm against him. That was the 2008 UK Championships and I was in good form then. But I found myself counting the dots because you're not allowed to go out there and read a magazine or put a towel over your head, or do this and that, so I thought, fuck it, I'll count the dots. I'd have found something in that arena to distract me. Everybody went, he's lost the plot: 'Ronnie's counting the dots.' But they didn't have to get in there and play him. Now they are playing him and crumbling, so maybe they should look back to those earlier matches and say: 'Well, Ronnie did well, and you can understand why he counted those dots.'

I pulled out of Ireland. I had a bad back and shouldn't really have got on the plane in the first place. To make matters worse, I was travelling on Ryanair – never a pleasant experience. You know they're out to catch you whenever they can – it's one of those airlines that just wants to make something from your misfortune. I was the last one on the plane with my mate Gay Robbie. We got on the plane and there were six spare seats together, and I thought, happy days, we'll sit there. As we got on the Ryanair fella is going: 'Anybody who would like the extra seats that are free it will be an extra ten euros.' And I'm going: 'Ten euros! That's Arthur Daley flogging you a seat for an extra ten euros.' Anyway, I went, I'll have 'em, and the geeza then goes: 'No, you can't have them.'

So I just went: 'Right, we're getting off, I've had enough of this, I don't want to travel.' I said: 'Thank you very much, we're getting off the plane, you've done me a favour. I'm in no state to travel, my back's in spasm, I'm off. I haven't got the hump, happy days, I'm going home, see you later.' So I got off the plane, rang my manager and told him I was going home.

The next tournament was China. I'd not played a tournament for a month and I felt a bit rusty. I went 4-2 down to Marcus Campbell, and ended up winning the match 5-4. Don't know how, but I did. Then I beat Mark Williams 5-1 in the next round, didn't play great, but was pretty match-sharp because I'd won the German and got to the semis of the Welsh. Then I played Maguire in the quarters and he beat me 5-4. Again, he outplayed me in the beginning, but I held on and it went 4-4, and I felt I was beginning to find my game at the right time. I had a fairly simple shot to stun in to win, but I decided to come off a cushion, then missed a red, we had to respot the black and he potted it. I lost the match, but came out thinking I could have had that, and again I felt I'd done well. You can't win every event and sometimes you have to save your wins for the right time. So win, semi, quarter, and I was thinking, I'm back. I felt I'd earned my right to play again.

I was playing in a lot of the small PTC events that Barry Hearn had introduced. This is how Barry was putting on more games – not televised, but it meant players were getting more match practice. If you got to the quarters you got a grand, if you got to the semis you got £2,500, 10 grand for the winner, so there wasn't much money in it, but there were ranking points. If I hadn't gone to those PTC events I would have had to qualify for Sheffield, and I really didn't fancy that. Barry had us by the bollocks – as I've said, we had to turn up for the minor events to qualify for the bigger ones.

I came in at number 16 and just qualified for the World Championship, so I didn't have to play qualifiers. That had been my goal – to keep my top 16 ranking – and I'd just about made it. I'd won a few of the PTC events, even ended up number one on those rankings, so my form was decent. It's just that I hadn't done it in the major events till Germany. But by then I thought, whatever happens at Sheffield, I'm back, I've had a great season. I'd proved to myself that I deserved to be on the circuit, that I was still a top 16 player.

6

ME AND MY CHIMP

'Worked well, felt OK then pushed up at the last. Good session. Wednesday, forest, easy run, 50 minutes, seven-minute miling, then did a steady push and finished off with seven-minute miling.'

Dr Steve Peters is a bit of a genius when it comes to the mind. A sports psychiatrist, he has worked for years with Britain's top cyclists, people like Bradley Wiggins, Chris Hoy and Victoria Pendleton, to help them get the best out of themselves.

It was my manager, Django Fung, who first suggested I go to see Steve. He was convinced he'd be able to fix my head and he also told me that he was on the running buzz, which of course appealed to me. To say he's got the buzz is to do Steve a bit of an injustice. He ran as a kid at school, then didn't run again till he was 40. Then he became world champion in the Masters category at 100 metres, 200 metres and 400 metres (you have to be over 35). He ran 100 metres in 10.9 seconds, and 200 metres at 22.21 seconds when he was 44 years old. The fella's a freak, a flying machine. He came third in the East of England all ages when he was 44, and he got a call-up from the Olympics training squad – they thought he was an up and coming youngster.

Django drove me mad about seeing Dr Steve. In the end I agreed, but at first he said he was too busy to see me. He had so much on, working with the British cycling team, who were preparing for the Olympics, and Team Sky. Then he did a bit of research on me, and went to Django: 'Right, get him in now! This fella's in trouble, I can help him.'

He said to me, 'I knew you needed help, and I knew I could help you.' And he has done. If my private life hadn't been in pieces, I don't think I would have seen Steve, and if I hadn't seen Steve I don't think I would have come back to win two successive world championships. He knocked the complacency out of me, and made me want to win again. As so often happens, something good has come out of something bad.

Steve used to be a forensic psychiatrist at Rampton High Security Hospital, and since then has worked with just about everyone in British sport. For most of the time he's based in Manchester with the Sky cycling team. Victoria Pendleton called him 'the most important person in my career', and before the London Olympics Chris Hoy said: 'Without Steve, I don't think I could have brought home triple gold from Beijing.' After Bradley Wiggins became the first British man to win the Tour de France in 2012 he thanked Dr Steve for 'opening my eyes on how to approach my worries and fears and for simply being the world expert on common sense'. He's helped loads of sportsmen famous for having a short fuse, not least footballer Craig Bellamy, and now he's working with Luis Suárez at Liverpool.

Steve is just as good with the brain as he is with his legs. It didn't take me long to realise he was a bit special. I chatted away to him, told him how I felt about this and that, what was happening in my life. He's very quiet and unassuming, but incredibly wise.

'Sometimes I just don't want to be there, Dr Steve,' I'd say to him.

And he'd just listen away, hardly saying a thing.

'Sometimes I want to pick up my cue and just run out of the room and head off home. And then when I get home I just want to pick up my cue and run away to somewhere else. Probably back to the venue. It's mad.'

'What you're talking about is common, Ronnie,' he said. 'Lots of sportsmen and women experience this. And lots of people do in everyday life. I call it freeze mode,' he said. The way he described it, you just stop doing what you're doing in the middle of it.

'You've just disengaged and said, "No, I can't do this, so I'm going to stop."'

'Then there was a match I played in when I actually walked out even though I was a long way from losing.' I told him I was 4-1 down to Hendry, and I just went to shake his hand, and everyone thought I was bonkers.

'Well, what was going on in your head at that particular moment, Ronnie?' he asked.

'I dunno,' I said. 'I was panicking, paranoid. I just wanted out. Couldn't stand being there, couldn't stand people looking at me. Wanted to be by myself.'

'That's flight mode,' he said. 'Now it's much rarer to see sportsmen in flight mode. Flight mode is an extreme form of freezing. Often they'll freeze less dramatically – and that can take lots of different forms; pulling out of matches or races saying they're not fit when they probably are, giving up in the middle, bottling it. But it's much more unusual to actually get up, shake the opponent's hand and admit you've had enough.' He explained it all in very simple terms, telling me that freezing or taking flight was disengaging from battle, which made perfect sense.

'What you're doing, Ronnie, is an act of sabotage. You're sabotaging your chances, and most sports people do that at one time or another, and in various different forms. What I'm here for is to try to help you stop sabotaging yourself.'

He told me about how the head worked, and said that he divided it up into two different bits; the chimp and the human.

'The chimp is the emotional bit. You know every time you feel like putting down your cue or taking the first train home or not even turning up for tournaments that's your chimp having its say. Having too much say.'

He told me the chimp was vital – without it I wouldn't be the person and player I am. But when the chimp took over all hell could break loose. Bloody hell, it made perfect sense to me. I had a huge chimp on my back, shouting in my lugholes, giving me all sorts of advice I could do without.

Then he told me about the human, the opposite of the chimp. The human is all reason and logic, and if you start listening too much to the human you think too much and tend to become over-deliberate or too cautious. That made sense, too. I thought of the time Ray Reardon coached me – it was fantastic the way he improved my safety game, but I gradually became more and more cautious, and more and more boring to watch. Dr Steve says the perfect balance, the computer, is when the human and chimp are working in harmony, and that's what he always aimed for.

'I'm on edge,' I told him. 'I'm always on the edge; I put myself through such anxiety.'

'Well, you don't need to be,' Steve said. 'You just have to work out what's important to you.'

'Snooker is pretty important to me.'

'It's just a game with sticks and balls, so try to get a perspective on it,' he said.

'Yes,' I said, 'but unless I'm playing really well I don't enjoy it.'

'So unless you're playing really well you're never going to enjoy it,' he said. 'The reality is you're not always going to play well. It shouldn't stop you enjoying yourself and just trying your best. It's a sport, there has to be a winner and a loser, and we can only do our best.'

Because he was also an elite sportsman Steve knew exactly what we were going through and could relate it to his own performances in the Masters sprinting world championships.

'My chimp can kick off if I go to a world final, and I'm lining up,' he told me. 'If you look at the brain, I've tried to say as a simplification that you've got one part of your brain that is highly emotional and it's very quick to think impulsively but it can be very inaccurate. Another part of the brain is logical, rational and calm. And they form teams across the brain. One team is what I call the human, and one team is the chimp and then you've got a computer system that is sprinkled around the brain and both of them rely on that for reference and for automatic behaviour. So if your blood supply goes to the chimp you think in a very emotional way, and if the blood supply goes to the human you'll think in a very rational, logical way. When I go to compete my chimp starts kicking off, and gives me the usual thoughts. It's all about me managing what my chimp throws at me, like "I can't lose this", "I mustn't look stupid", "I'm not fit enough at this point", it's the classic stuff I get when I work with elite athletes. So I can relate to that and the intensity of the feelings.'

If the human takes over you become too rational and analytical and you lose your spontaneity, he said. If the computer's working nicely and suddenly the human wakes up you can choke.

This fella really knew what he was talking about.

I worked with Dr Steve for the whole year building up to Sheffield in 2012, and he was great. For the first time I was really getting my emotions under control. I never felt I was going to lose the plot, and if there was any danger of getting overemotional I was much more aware of it than I had been before. I thought that however bad I felt during the match, I could put those emotions on hold till it was all over. He was there for me throughout the finals in 2012. Whenever I had a bad moment, he'd come into the dressing room in the break and talk me through it. He was incredibly calming and sensible. Steve is probably more responsible than anybody for my comeback.

But I didn't want to become reliant on him. I didn't want to feel I had to have him around me 24/7. That would have been unhealthy, and he couldn't always be there for me anyway. He had so many other successful sports people to be dealing with. He wanted to give me the model for what I needed to work on, so I could then go and do my homework, practise, and become good at it on my own. Then, when I'd go to see him it would be like servicing a car. I wanted to be a good pupil, I had a lot of respect and love for Steve and I didn't want to pull the wool over his eyes, so there was no point in not practising what he'd taught me.

He'd come down and watch me play at Sheffield, but I'm not sure if he likes snooker. It's funny; we don't really talk about it. He likes his dogs and his animals and his running. He's got two huge wolfhounds, rescue dogs, and he likes having people around him that he feels comfy with.

I've never wanted to become too reliant on any one thing. Even when I've got into my religions, I've thought, well I can work out things for myself. I've tried the lot in my time

– Buddhism, Islam, Christianity. I was reading the Koran and bits and pieces, and loads of my friends were Muslims. Because I was open-minded going to Narcotics Anonymous and stuff, I thought, let's go with Allah, the Muslim God, find out what he's all about. Allah wasn't too bad as it happens. Again, it was just a belief in something, but in the end I thought, I just want to be me. I want to be happy being me. Friday night at Regent's Park mosque in London, prime location, the big gaffe. I was with Prince Naseem and his brother Murad. He said he was going to the mosque and I said, well, I'll come with you because I didn't want to show a lack of respect. I thought, maybe I can just hang around outside, have a cup of tea. I didn't want to be rude.

So I ended up going, washing my hands this way and that way, kneeling there, on my knees, hundreds of people there. I'm doing all my bits and pieces, and I thought that was it – we'd sneak out, do a bit of grub, and then they suddenly dragged me down the front, and they were doing the business with me, whatever it is, and I'm getting kissed by all these other Muslims: 'Welcome, brother, welcome, brother ...' Bang! It's in the paper. 'Ronnie's converted to Islam.' Just after 9/11. I thought, I need that like a hole in the head. I phoned up Naz and begged him, and said: 'Naz you need to get me out of this, I'm terrified.' So that was another fine mess I got myself into. It was a one-off. I tried Christianity for about three months, but that didn't do the trick either. I'm destined never to be a member of the God squad. Everything with me is a one-off. I believe in people rather than gods.

And Steve Peters was a person I believed in because he taught me how I could conquer my chimp. Whenever I feel him coming to throttle me (the chimp, not Steve) I have to repeat the following steps to myself. Actually, even when the chimp's not on the prowl I need to repeat the steps to myself. Steve called it the five-point anchor:

1. Do my best; that's all I can do.
2. I want to be here playing and competing – period.
3. I'm an adult, not a chimp. I can deal with anything that happens, any consequences.
4. It's impossible to play well all the time.
5. What would I say to Lily and little Ronnie if they said their game was not right?

Steve said that, rather than pretending the chimp didn't exist, I had to accept him, and get to know him. 'If you have to put the chimp back in his box, one shot at a time, do so,' he said. 'Listen to the chimp without panicking, but always know it's the chimp and not you.'

Steve asked me to keep a diary of my relationship with the chimp. Here are a few typical entries from the build-up to the 2012 World Championship:

Wednesday 15th

Got up. Felt like the chimp was on me. Telling me I'm over playing, should be at home with the kids, should be training, running, obsessing about getting fat. Told him that I was not gonna discuss this now, I want to go and enjoy my breakfast. I then want to go and enjoy the snooker.

I went to snooker, and started off great. Not missing anything, my chimp was very quiet. I stayed in a great space. There were times when I played, or felt not quite comfortable on the shot, but I quickly put the chimp away, I gave it some logic and facts. Facts: that I have actually played lots of great shots. Not true that I'm no good. Logic told me that I should not beat myself up. Once I put that in place I really did shift and start to find momentum again.

Once I came home I did start to think about my shoulder, and my approach to the shot, and telling myself this good form can't continue. I did put the chimp away and felt better, but he kept coming out. But it was okay, not that bad. I kept putting him away.

BELIEF: That I can't play bad and win.
FACT: I have played bad and won three world titles.

BELIEF: Everyone is better than me.
FACT: M. Williams says I'm the best.

BELIEF: That I'm getting old and that my potting is not very good.
FACT: I have been potting long ones in certain games.

PERSPECTIVE: If I'm lying on my death bed what would I say to little Ronnie and Lily? ENJOY LIFE!!!

What would I prefer – to lose and enjoy or win and be unhappy? LOSE AND ENJOY!

Thursday 7th

Got up, felt like the chimp was at me. Telling me you're not consistent, that you're gonna start mistiming balls. I let him have his say, and then said, right, now I'm gonna give you some logic. I'm enjoying the game and I want to play, I have been feeling really good about my game recently. I'm thinking a lot clearer, I'm with Steve now, I understand the chimp, and you're telling me SHIT. I'm not going to panic, I'm one of the most successful players ever. No one thinks I'm bad because I play a bad shot or frame or match or even a bad year, so it's all nonsense. I'm going to do my best, that's what I'm telling myself. The chimp went quiet, my mind started to think very clearly.

Tuesday 24th

Woke up, chimp was there. Not as bad as morning before. He was saying, your right hand/arm will lose its accuracy.

Thursday 29th

Got up. Chimp was talking to me, saying my right arm is not going through the ball correctly, it's mistiming, not solid, cutting across the ball, your right arm is not in sync with your body. The chimp would not go away. I could not get out of bed at the thought of it. I felt him have his say, then tried to give him some answers … I ended up going for a run.

Chimp was telling me my stance and technique let me down, chimp was telling me after the game that if you play like that you won't win a tournament. Forget it!! Felt quite panicky in the evening when I got home.

Keeping the diary made me feel better. It is really useful to look back at, too – if painful. It's a reminder of just how possessed I can be by this self-destructive demon, and how pointless the quest for perfection is.

Sometimes there were no dates.

Got up chimp is on me. Again. I can't stop thinking what went wrong with my game, pains in my chest, shallow breathing. That's how it feels. (After beating Judd 3-2 in Prem League then losing 3-1 to Ding.)

There's a scrappy entry, accompanied by a happy face.

No snooker, three weeks off. Loved not playing.

Then there's an ecstatic entry in capital letters alongside a huge happy face.

17 DAYS SNOOKER
WON THE WORLD CHAMPS
UNBELIEVABLE
NICE REST REQUIRED
DON'T BURN OUT

That was in May 2012, just after I'd won my fourth World Championship. But, of course, by the beginning of the next season the chimp was back, tapping me on the shoulder or staring me in the face, telling me I was shite.

NEW SEASON

Started practice. That felt good for a few days, then the new gremlins/goblins/chimp started again. Long deep thoughts crept back in, which disconnect me from the real world. Can I handle this stuff? Do I want to handle this stuff?

Now I'm gonna list the gremlins/goblins!

Shoulder gets stiff and feels bunched when I'm not playing.

Think I'm gonna lose it, my game is not strong enough.

They're expecting me to win now. Waiting for me to fall again.

Should have gone out on a high.

Gotta fly to China 3 times etc.

I know it must read like madness to most people, but this is what goes through my head, and has been doing for the past 20 years. And I know it might seem like even more madness to write it down in diary form, but actually the diary advised by Dr Steve has done so much to keep me sane. The results speak for themselves.

7

TOP OF THE WORLD: SHEFFIELD 2012

'Sunday morning, Epping Forest, easy eight and a half miles. 62 minutes, seven and a half minute miling.'

Then came Sheffield. Bang! It was the best tournament I've played in my life. It smashed all the other world titles I've played into pieces. None compare. I felt every moment of that tournament because of the work I'd done with Dr Steve. Before going to Sheffield I was in his house near Sheffield saying, I don't fancy this; I don't think I can do this. There's a diary of all the work I've done with him, and I did work really hard.

When I first came to see him, he told me, you'll only get out of this what you put in. The more you practise, the better you get kind of thing. So I wanted to learn all the skills he could teach me, but sometimes I couldn't take it all in. I'd be writing stuff down as I was talking to him, then I read his book, *The Chimp Paradox*, which helped me make sense of his theory about how we sabotage ourselves and how to manage it. But despite all the work I'd done with him, I was still me. So of course I had major doubts. I was petrified, convinced I was going to get beaten first round. I had Peter Ebdon and thought, that's the worst draw I could get. As soon as I saw the draw I thought, oh no, he's going to torture me again. Psycho has always been a great competitor – and a lovely fella despite the scary appearance.

So Steve and I started preparing for Sheffield. I'd spend between an hour and three hours with him each session, depending on how much I could take in and how much time he had. The most important thing he taught me was the ability to put behind me what would normally have festered for a long time – i.e. that's a bad shot but I'm not going to let that carry on into the next shot. My natural thought process was, you hit a bad shot, you're shit, your cueing's crap, you can't hit the ball, you're going to get beat, boom! Then you'd be 8-1 down, and think, well, I'm out any way, so I'd start playing well the next session, and make a game of it and lose 13-9. But really the damage was done in the first session. He gave me the ability to play a bad shot but have enough knowledge of what I'd been working on to reinforce what I knew about myself – I was three-time world champion, four-time Masters champion, four-times UK champion. I had to reinforce all those elements because I was always frightened of the worst thing happening, and assumed it would do. I had to say, well, that can happen, you can lose, the other fella is capable of beating you, but you could also win this match. I had to look at the facts in my favour – my game very rarely deserted me, these players are good but I have a better record against them than they have against me.

I had to keep reinforcing these thoughts so I wasn't scared of going into these situations.

Once I got out there to play that was the easy part. It was the build-up I struggled with; coming away, having time to think about what had gone on and how I'd play in the next session.

I had to learn how to manage the time between matches and between sessions. And I think that's why ultimately I enjoyed 2012 at Sheffield more than any other because there were times when my game wasn't great but I stuck with it, and I came out of it thinking, I'm only 5-3 behind or 4-4, and the next session I found my game and would win six frames on the trot. So with the help of Steve I learnt the ability to feel present in every session and absorb every emotion. Every time I panicked I controlled it. I didn't rush or go for stupid shots because I was getting frustrated; I played every shot on its merit, then once I found my rhythm I started to dominate games. And when my game wasn't great I didn't let it affect me.

Steve showed me there was a more adult way of dealing with the emotional side of my brain.

He said: 'This part of your brain will never change. All you can do is manage it, and if you don't practise managing it every day your emotional side will take over again and you'll end up in the same place you were when you first came to see me. You've had twenty years of conditioning that mind, and you're not going to rebuild it overnight, so just accept it and deal with it.' He removed the idea that I was looking for this spiritual path to inner peace. This was much more about me being in control of my own mind; me deciding how I wanted to react to certain situations.

When I got to Sheffield in 2012 I didn't think there was any chance of winning. I didn't actually think I had any chance of winning the World Championship again. It has never been my kind of tournament because it goes on for ever, and it's over longer frames, and there's so often been a session where I've felt I've lost the match through getting the hump with myself. So I always thought to win the World Championship once was great, twice was unbelievable, three times even more so. But even though it's never been my thing, it's always the tournament your career is going to be judged by. It's the hardest one to win, and the most prestigious. It's the opposite of the Premier League, where you pitch up on a Thursday night, play your match, go home, happy days. Sheffield is tough. Epic. The tournament doesn't really begin till the semi-finals. A lot of people watch the earlier rounds and by the time it's the semis they think it's the end of the tournament, but it's not. Although you've already played 60-odd frames and had 10 or 11 days of intense pressure, it's only the beginning.

By the quarter-finals you can sense who's going to be there till the end. You'll have a quarter-final line-up and some of the players look dishevelled; they look as if they want out. And you spot it instinctively. You think, he didn't look like that six days ago; he looked fresh, but now the pressure is building up and you can see that certain players will only go so far. They might win another match, but they're not going to go all the way. Winning the World Championship is not just about talent, it's about resolve. That's why both Graham Dott and Peter Ebdon have won it – both of them really know how to dig in.

Although I didn't think I'd win it again, in the end it was probably my easiest victory. Ten-one in the first round, 13-5 in the second, 13-9 in the quarters, 17-10 in the semis, 18-11 in the final against Ali Carter. It didn't feel comfortable at the time, though. Often I went in thinking, I can't go through with it. It was scary, I didn't want to go out there and play. I didn't want to fail on the big stage and make myself look silly. But the great thing is that even though I had those thoughts, thanks to Dr Steve they were in the back of my mind, not the front.

For so long I was known as the greatest player never to have won the World Championship. It took me so long to win it that I thought I never would. I was 25 years old and had been playing professionally for eight years by the time I beat John Higgins 18-14 in the 2001 final. I got knocked out in the quarters and semis nearly every year. Even though I'm now a multiple winner of the world title I keep thinking back to the days when I just fell short. Peter Ebdon, John Parrott, Stephen Hendry, Darren Morgan, David Grey, they all beat me. I'd be playing well up to a point then my game just went. I'd collapse at crunch time. You have nine to ten good days at Sheffield, then one bad session and it's over. It's the equivalent of the Iron Man; it goes on longer than the Olympics, 17 days for one event. That's three weeks of intense pressure.

Last year there were spells in every match when I just couldn't play any better. I was seeing the ball so clearly. My potting, my safety, everything was on. I broke with my left hand, and that was massively important. My break had always held me back till then. I'd always leave something on, they'd pot it, boom! Frame over. But last year I got it more consistent than ever with my left hand. My left hand gives me a better throw, a better spin, a better pace, a better contact on the ball, the white finds the danger zone with more regularity, and I don't always leave the shot to nothing.

There's a science to breaking, and with my left hand I can get through the ball much more effortlessly. I've got more room, more time, and I'm able to hold the shot off like a golfer, or when you kick a ball you keep your foot on the ball longer and you have more control over it. You're with the ball that bit longer, and that's how I feel with left-handed breaks. Right-handed is more hit-and-miss. Left-handed is more controlled and I can penetrate through the ball and not cut across it. With right-hand, sometimes I get a bit of sidespin on it, and it loses its momentum, comes up short or throws off line and you lose the pace. If you hit the ball solidly, nine times out of ten the reds stay solid. And if you get a good white you're in business. So for the break-off the left-handed shot was key for me at last year's World Championship.

I was worried about becoming over-reliant on my left hand. I felt so good with it, but I didn't want to end up playing left-handed shots when I didn't need to. For a while I was getting confused. I felt more relaxed with my left hand, but I'm a better player with the right. Did I want to feel like shit and win or feel good and lose? Sometimes I just wanted to feel good, even if it meant losing.

The funny thing is when I started playing with my left hand other players thought I was taking the piss. They don't now, but back then they got the right hump. Now a lot of players use their 'other' hand – about seven or eight of them on the tour and two or three could build a decent break with their wrong 'un. I was the first 'ambidextrous' player, but I wasn't trying to be clever; it just made sense to play certain shots with my other hand.

Last year, there were times I was hitting the ball so well that all the shackles came off and the demons disappeared. I'd been waiting 20 years to feel like this, and when it finally came it felt bloody good. It had all come together – I was potting at will, playing safety shots like you couldn't believe, getting out of trouble and not leaving them with chances, scoring nineties and hundreds. You can hear it when you're playing well. The balls make a lovely sound when you hit the back of the pocket – you're hitting them with authority. I felt like a champion; I felt like I was playing a different game – a game that nobody could go with. Then, when my game wasn't so good, they couldn't put me away either. They could win a session 5-3 or draw it 4-4 – that was the worst that happened to me – but the sessions when I was in the groove it was 7-1 or 8-0, and by then I'd done the damage.

It felt like when I was 16, and I went on an amazing run, winning 74 out of 76 matches and then winning my first 38 ranking matches as a professional. I always think back to that period when I was 14, 15, 16, and everything felt good. People think I'm bullshitting when I talk about that time; as if I've got an Elton John-sized pair of rose-tinted shades on. But anyone who played me at that time would know what I was talking about. Ask someone like Mark Williams, and he'll remember.

For all my success, I knew I hadn't been as good as I was when I was a kid, and someone like Mark would back that up because he was there to see those days. Mark knows that how I played last year at the World Championship was the norm when I was a kid. That's why I was so frustrated all those years because I was used to playing to that standard before I really made it. And for various reasons – loss of technique, loss of balance, loss of confidence, poor posture, whatever – I forgot how to play.

I know that sounds daft when I'd already won the World Championship three times and had won 23 majors, but it really is how I felt. That I wasn't producing the goods. Then last year it finally came together, and, boy, did it feel good. The supporters were definitely glad to see me back winning, but I'm not so sure the players would have been. Why would they be? If I was playing me, I wouldn't have thought, isn't it great to see Ronnie come good again. I would never have said: 'It's great that Stephen Hendry has come back, and is flying again.' Of course I wouldn't be happy about it. It's like asking a turkey to vote for Christmas.

The experts and former players were pleased for me. Dennis Taylor has always supported me. I love Dennis. John Virgo was genuine, and Steve Davis was chuffed. Even Stephen Hendry, since he stopped playing, has taken an interest in my game. He kept sending me little texts, saying: 'Come on, mate! Get back on that table.' Amazing. My hero asking me to get back to playing. It's lovely to know that all those people you looked up to when you were younger, idolised in the case of Hendry and Davis, want you to do well.

There was a point in the final frame. I had made 50 or 60 and I was on 20-odd, and as soon as I potted that ball I started thinking about little Ronnie. He was up in the box, and it just felt that it was only me and him in the venue. Lily wasn't there – she's not much of a snooker fan. And to be honest I didn't expect little Ronnie to be there either. I asked Jo, and she said, how is he going to get there. I said to Jo, I know you've got worries about little Ronnie coming down, but Damien Hirst's personal driver, Ross, will come down, put a film on for him, and he'll only talk to Ronnie if Ronnie talks to him. I said he'll be treated like a king for the day, so he'll be in safe hands. Jo gave the go-ahead, which was great, and he came down.

About twelve noon on the second day, Sylvia, Damien's PA, brought little Ronnie up to my room. We had a cuddle, which really set me up for the afternoon. I was so happy to see him and be able to share this day with him, and for him to see me on the biggest stage performing. My dream had always been for the kids to come and watch me play and share in the wins and losses. And I hadn't had that apart from when Lily danced on the table when I won the UK in 2008.

It calmed me down seeing little Ronnie because I was feeling the pressure. On the Sunday morning, the first day of the final, I'd been really sick – whether it was down to a meal or down to pressure I don't know, but I was spewing up and my face was coming out in blotches. I didn't eat all that day, and I burped my way through the afternoon session. But I managed to get through it, and I was much better the second day. I was winning 10-6. How I came out on top that day I don't know because I felt terrible and hadn't eaten all day.

As I was clearing up in the final I had a lump in my throat. I wanted to cry and I thought: 'No, you can't. You can't.' I held it back. That's all I was focusing on – holding back the tears. I knew it couldn't get any better for me. After all that had happened in the last two years with the kids and the custody battle, and when I was ready to quit and losing first rounds every tournament, I'd come from that to winning the World Championship. And to have little Ronnie there was the icing on the proverbial. To go from barely seeing the kids to having my little boy who thinks the world of me and who I love to pieces being there, sharing that moment with me, was just perfect. It couldn't get any better. He was only four, and I'm sure he didn't have a clue what it all meant to me.

At that point, I thought, I've done everything I want to do. It's all downhill from here – it's got to be. I felt it in a good way. I was the oldest winner since Ray Reardon, had come back from nowhere and I was on top of the world. Damien was with me, and Sylvia – they had been with me from day one and were a calming influence throughout. They are the only people I can remember at the end when I won – Damien, Sylvia, me and little Ronnie. Someone brought Ronnie down and put him in my arms, and I got hold of him and I just held him, and it was mental. Unbelievable. I wasn't interested in picking up the trophy. It was just me and him, our moment. Priceless. It didn't go too quick, it didn't go too slow. I enjoyed every second.

We went to the presentation dinner, and I only stayed about half an hour. Ronnie was asleep in Damien's car with Ross. I kept getting up to make sure he was alright. Then I got him back up to the room at the Hilton at 11.30 p.m. We had a McDonald's – me, Damien, Sylvia, Sergio Pizzorno, the guitarist with Kasabian who is a good mate of Damien's, just sat in the foyer of the hotel eating Big Macs and chips. I went upstairs to check on little Ronnie. He was asleep, and I had the world title trophy on the side, little Ronnie in bed. I went to bed, cuddled him, got up in the morning, and I just thought, this is the best thing I've ever had.

8

SELF-IMPOSED EXILE

'Steady on the first lap, same on second, then picked it up on the last. Felt tired in the legs, hamstrings felt tired, lactic acid in the quads.'

I announced I was going to take six months off straight after the World Championship. I couldn't balance work, family and the custody battle, and work had to give.

Sometimes I had to decide whether to go to a tournament or see my children because, if I didn't see the kids on the days the court said I could have them, the next time I went to court I would worry they might well say, well you couldn't make these visits, you couldn't do this and that, so they wouldn't give me any more than my two hours on a Wednesday and two hours on a Saturday. I didn't want them to just look at my life and say, well, he's away playing snooker on Saturdays, and for that to count against me. In the end I got so confused with it all that on one occasion I didn't even know there was a tournament. All I knew was that I had Ronnie from 10 a.m. on Saturday till 5 p.m. and then I had to take him home. Meanwhile, that weekend I was supposed to be in Belgium, and I hadn't turned up and hadn't told them I wouldn't be turning up. Not surprisingly, World Snooker and Barry got the hump. I just had so much going on in my head that I ended up missing 12 tournaments over a period of two years and that's when they brought the new rules in.

I pulled out of the German tournament and the Irish tournament in 2011 at the last minute, and then they brought up the other 10 events I hadn't turned up for. In my head, I thought, well, they're not that important because they're not on telly, but that's unfair on both World Snooker and the punters – when they're selling tickets on the fact that I'm going to be there and I don't turn up it doesn't look good and fans are disappointed. The other 10 were minor PTC events, and I had the choice of going or risking the court telling me I couldn't see my kids because I had missed the set days I was supposed to see them.

At one point I went seven weeks without seeing Lily and Ronnie. I was in bits. I had no motivation, I had no incentive to want to play well, I felt I was missing out on seeing my children grow up. I felt sorry for myself, I was so down I couldn't see the point in anything. The legal battle was so sapping and drawn out and pointless. One court dealt with access, the other dealt with money, and it felt as if the lawyers were just bleeding me dry. I got to the point where I said, I've had enough.

There were rumours about Barry Hearn's new contract. I thought that if I missed four tournaments, the first tournament was a £250 fine, the second £500, then a grand, then £5,000, then it was a ban from tournaments, and then it was a three-tournament ban. I was told there was a points system, like when you get points on your licence for speeding, and that the points stay there for ever. So in my mind I thought, there's no way I'm not going to get banned. Because of the inflexibility of my home situation, there was no way I could continue playing.

I'd had three shit years because of stuff going on off the

table; I had World Snooker on my back for not turning up to events; I'd had Jo on my back for not turning up on Saturdays. I thought, fuck it, I've had enough.

I've won the world title, shown everyone I'm still capable of doing what I'm doing: what better time to call it a day? World Snooker had put pressure on me to play in all these tournaments, and I couldn't cope. They knew that I was bums on seats. World Snooker was sending me disciplinary letters every few weeks, and in the end I'd open up emails or letters from them and get panic attacks. I had to write to them and say, please don't send me any more emails, send them to my manager because just seeing them does my head in. 'You're in breach of this, in breach of that, we need a letter from your doctor.' Meanwhile, until my World Championship victory in 2012 I'd gone three years not earning much because my form was so bad and I'd missed so many tournaments, and what I was earning was just going on legal bills.

Everything seemed so hopeless and vulgar. It was all about money and I'd had enough. Even though my decision came just after winning the world title, it was based on everything that had been happening in the years building up to it. I also knew I'd have to spend loads of time in court fighting for custody, and I wanted to be with the kids when I could, so there was really no time for snooker. I put myself into retirement, not because I wanted to, just because of the stress I was under.

It wasn't depression I had – depression's a dark hole when you can't go out of the front door and face the world. This was just pure stress. I had to go to court and listen to lawyers tell the judge that I wasn't a good father. The things they said about me killed me. I was choking in court. It knocked the stuffing out of me.

I'd go to bed and my mind would be racing. All I wanted was

an end, but there was none in sight. I'd go to bed at 11 p.m., wake up at 1 a.m. and then I'd be awake all night, and then I'd go and practise early morning. For two and a half years I didn't sleep properly. Even in 2012, when I did really well, I was still only getting two to three hours sleep a night. I'd wake up in the day and I'd be fucked. Sometimes I'd just have to sit down and rest all day between matches.

I agreed to pay Jo the maintenance her lawyers demanded to draw a line under it. But I still couldn't sleep because I'd got into a pattern and couldn't get my life back in order. Straight after my victory in the final against Ali Carter I said that I'd spend my six-month sabbatical with the kids. After five months off, I decided to pull out in October and not go to China. Then in November it was announced I was taking the season off. It was Django who issued a statement to the press. He said I was finding it difficult to balance family and work, that I'd been sick with glandular fever and I thought it was unfair on the sport to withdraw from tournaments at the last moment.

The press didn't know what to make of it. Some papers said I was just having a laugh, and would be back by the next tournament. Others said I was gone for good. Barry Hearn was supportive. He told the media that I needed to sort my head out and I'd made the right decision in taking time out.

I picked up the phone to Barry Hearn and said: 'I'm out. You can pull me out, withdraw my membership, whatever's easiest for you. I'm not interested in playing.'

He talked me out of resigning my membership.

'Just pull out of these tournaments, and see how you feel come February/March,' he said. He talked a lot of common sense.

'Do what you have to do,' he said, 'but don't resign your membership. If you resign that you've got to go to qualifying school and that's no good for you. You might change your mind in six months. You might sort yourself out.'

'Alright, whatever, but pull me out of the rest of the tournaments because all this "Am I going, am I not going?" is destroying me.'

If I'd talked to Barry Hearn earlier I would probably not have stopped playing at all. But I didn't. I just assumed there were things in the contract that didn't favour me. It wasn't until I sat down with Barry who explained it to me, and I realised it was just a different interpretation of the contract. Once I talked to Barry I thought, well, that contract's fair, I'm happy to sign it. He explained that I would only get banned if I missed four tournaments in one season. At least I knew then that I've got four strikes, and that next year it goes back to zero. I can deal with that. If I miss four tournaments in a season I deserve to be banned.

Part of me did think that a year away might turn into fully retiring from snooker. Soon enough I'd have to look for a career away from snooker and now was as good a time as any. And having just won the world title, at least I was marketable. I thought of doing some radio work, TV guest appearances, punditry.

When I first made the decision I felt relieved. For the first few months it was one of the best things I'd done – I saw loads of the kids and Dad, and de-stressed myself.

With my first child, Taylor, I never had any involvement in her life. Taylor is now 16, and I regret not having a relationship with her. About a year ago she got in touch with me, and hopefully we will develop a proper relationship over time. What happened between me and Taylor made me determined not to lose Lily and little Ronnie. I couldn't let it happen again.

Not playing made it easier to negotiate life on a day-to-day basis. It meant I didn't have to look at my calendar five months in advance and work out if I could make this weekend to see the kids; and would it clash with that tournament? It simplified my life.

My routine was transformed when I stopped playing. It became a non-routine. I got up when I wanted to get up, went for a run when I felt I had the time to do it; when I could be bothered. I went out for lunches, saw Dad, saw the kids. But even though it was great in a way, it did get boring pretty quick. I missed having something in my life; missed going to work. The media work wasn't happening quickly enough and before long I didn't know what to do with myself.

By December I thought I couldn't carry on like this. I was so bored, itching to do something. Snooker had dictated virtually all of my life for me. Up at 7.30 a.m., running gear on, glass of water, 8.30 out for a four- to five-mile run, a little bit in the gym, shower, breakfast (porridge, banana, raisins, boiled eggs, always tried to eat healthy) then I'd go down the club for 11 a.m., play for four to five hours. Come back, chill out, watch a bit of telly and just relax in the evening. That was my routine every day. By 10.30–11 every night I'd be in bed.

When I stopped playing, the routine became get up 10–10.30 a.m., breakfast, run 1 p.m., shower, then just visiting friends, finding things to do, going for coffees, going for lunches, sitting down the bagel bar, no pressure, no stress. It was nice in a way, but it did my nut in. I became much less disciplined. I thought, right, I can pursue my running now, set myself a target of running a marathon in two hours 45 minutes, run twice a day and when I've got the kids I could use that as my rest days. It never happened like that.

I got lazier and lazier – you've got all this time on your hands and you find yourself doing nothing with it. I became one of the world's great putter-offers. Everything became 'I'll do it later'. I began to realise that snooker simplified my life; it didn't give me time to veg. If I was to be as good and as successful as I wanted to be, I needed the discipline so that I could feel I deserved those victories. I had to feel I was doing all I could do to give myself the best possible chance of winning. The reality was that I would probably have been just as good, maybe better, with less practice, but that's not what my head thought. I'm not good with guilt. If I think I've not given it my best it becomes a self-fulfilling prophecy.

I lost my confidence when I wasn't working. I began to feel guilty about going out to dinner, about spending money, filling my car up. I was looking at bills for the first time in my life, and thinking, I've got nothing coming in but I'm still putting £100 of petrol in my car, I'm still spending £120 at Waitrose, still going out for a meal three or four times a week and that's £60–£70. I know I have other bits and pieces like property to enable me to do that, but I did feel guilty. I was still paying Jo her money, still paying the school fees, and in the back of my mind I thought, this is eventually going to run out. So I was beginning to panic that I wouldn't be able to support the children, or myself, like I wanted to, and it would get to the point where we'd all have to cut back.

Yet at the same time, this was where I wanted to be. Money caused so many problems – but not having money caused even more.

Before long, you realise the phone has stopped ringing, you've got no work coming in and reality kicks in – you've got two beautiful children you care about but you've had to go down to the school to explain you've got no money for the fees. All these things were happening and I thought, fuck, I've got to go to work, this isn't sustainable.

I felt my year off was forced on me by events. But it was also a test to see if I could cope without work, and to see what impact it would have on the family having nothing coming in. In the end, it was a test we failed. It was obvious that none of us would be happy unless I was working and supporting the family. More than ever, it made me realise that Jo and I needed to work through this together, support each other, make it work. We were never going to be a couple again, but that was no reason why we couldn't bring up our kids happily. We're lucky to have them, and we needed to realise that, before their childhood was gone, lost in pointless legal rumblings. If I didn't go back to work properly, I wouldn't have money, Jo and the kids wouldn't either, and none of us would be able to enjoy the lives we had.

I was also missing the snooker. It might not always seem like it, but I do actually enjoy travelling, getting away from home now and then, into the hotel, seeing a bit of the world, meeting up with local runners and getting a nice little run-in. Then, at the end of it, I'd enjoy coming home, see the family, get my bag unpacked, get everything cleaned and ready for the next event. Snooker was the discipline that gave me purpose.

In my year off I became more reliant on Chigwell than ever. Between tournaments I'd always turn back to Chigwell, come home, to prepare for the next event. But now that there were no tournaments I barely moved out of the place. I had everything I wanted there – my running routes, the bagel bar, the park I took the kids to. And I could go wherever I wanted without being hassled. Savills, the estate agent, are also important to me because I move house so often! There's also Macey's, the convenience store, and the health food shop. If ever you're ill she'll sort you out.

Essex has such a reputation. For decades people have been talking about Essex Girl and Essex Man. You know the clichés:

the girls are dolled-up slags, the men are flash, thick bastards in sports cars. And it's got even worse now with *The Only Way Is Essex* on TV. But when I watch that show I don't recognise Essex from it. I don't know people like that. You see some of the people in the show around locally, but they've always got their heads down or they're on the phone because they're celebrities now and have got fed up with people driving them mad. Typical story really – you crave celebrity and then, when you get it, it ain't all it's cracked up to be.

Chigwell's my manor, my life. I love this place, but even I can have too much of it. When I stopped playing and never set foot out of the place, it made me realise how much I miss getting away from home. Taking something away from you is a great way of showing you what you had. And it's amazing how quickly your self-esteem can ebb away. Not that there was that much to ebb away in the first place! I'd take a 10-0 beating at Sheffield rather than feeling I was doing nothing with my life, just allowing it to vegetate.

My self-imposed exile has also taught me something else too – that I'm lucky to be paid to do something I love. I hate calling snooker a job, but at the end of the day it is my job and I need to go to work. It's what I do.

The best thing I did in my year off was work on a farm, which was in the middle of Epping Forest, where I used to run. By December 2011, I realised all the things I'd planned on doing weren't happening. The radio show hadn't happened, nor had the punditry. Even the running had tailed off. I was getting out once or twice a week, which was rubbish. I thought the only way to get me out of bed was if I had some sort of a commitment, so I started doing voluntary work at the farm.

A girl who worked at the pizza place I took the kids to told me about this little farm, about 40–50 acres, in the heart of the forest in Hainault. I went to check it out. I told them I didn't want paid work, but I'd love to help out, put a shift in. Outside, fresh air, lovely. I thought if I could get myself out of bed, it would maybe start me off on the running again.

So I turned up and the girl in the office said, you've got to fill this form out. I filled the form out and they said, we'll be in contact with you in a couple of weeks. A couple of weeks went by and I got an email saying, can you come down Sunday morning, 9 a.m. So I turned up Sunday morning, old boy called Tony was there, lovely fella. He was a paid worker and he took me round, showed me all the little jobs that needed doing. He recognised me, but what I liked about him was he didn't make a fuss: 'We're here, we need help, thanks for coming.'

He didn't talk to me about snooker. Not once did anybody talk about snooker. Nor did they want to know why I was there. They were just pleased to have help. There were six or seven full-time staff, and about 25 volunteers. I told them, I'm not interested in going on courses, all I want to do is turn up and if you've got something for me to do I'm happy to do it. So I didn't have to commit to anything.

It got me into the fresh air, and I felt I was doing something with my time. I did two days a week, sometimes three. I'd never done anything like that in my life before. I used to like fetching the bales of hay to feed the animals because you had to walk up the hill, over the mud, fill it up, come back down, again and again. I was pretty fit so I'd get a lot done. Green wellies, pure manual work, love it. I cleaned out stables and pigsties, removed the rubbish, took down fences. Lovely.

I also enjoyed digging the mud out from the pool, and once it was on the side we had to shovel it into the wheelbarrow, run it up the ramp on to the back of the lorry. Because the brickwork was ancient, they had to dig it out and put a retainer wall in to make it safe. The farm didn't have much money to employ people, so it made sense for the volunteers to dig out the mud. So we did that from 11 a.m. to 4 p.m.; my back was killing me, my arms were killing me and I got home and I was absolutely cream-crackered, but I enjoyed it.

I did my run in the morning, went for a four- or five-mile run, did the work, then came home, and I think all the work and fresh air made me sleep again.

One woman there was a bit like me. She said: 'I don't work any more, I've got a few properties I take rental income from, nothing complicated. I used to work on the markets, but I've given that up now. So I just wanted something to do for a couple of days a week.' She was a lovely woman, and me and her were grafters. You got a lot of kids there who had been kicked out of school, and sent to special schools because they'd been naughty. Then they'd send them to the farm to work, and they were good as gold. It was an eye-opener for me.

One kid said: 'Are you a policeman?'

'No, I'm not a policeman.'

'What car d'you drive?' he asked.

'A BMW.'

'Yeah, you're a policeman!' he said. 'They all drive BMWs.'

He didn't have a clue what I did for a living. So I just got chatting to him. I liked him; he was buzzy and hyperactive, and had good energy about him.

'What are you doing here?' I asked.

'I come here once or twice a week,' he said.

'Why?'

'I've been kicked out of school, and they make me come here.'

He was 15, and it made me think, some people have had it

hard. Perhaps he's not had much discipline in his life, and had just been able to get away with things.

'What did you do at school?' I said.

'Oh, just fight with the teachers, they get on my nerves.'

'What do your mum and dad say about it?'

'Well, they don't care,' he said.

I thought, these kids have had nobody to support them. Their mums and dads just don't care about them. It made me think about Lily and Ronnie, and I thought it was so important to be there for them, to try to steer them in the right direction, to make them feel loved and wanted, and have respect for people. I wouldn't want my little boy or girl going to school and treating people the way that boy was, yet he was a nice kid; he just needed someone to tap into that and get the best out of him, make him feel good about himself and loved. It made me think about how lucky I was growing up, having a father and mother to support me like they did, and to discipline me, and tell me right from wrong.

I don't think I ever managed to convince the kid I wasn't a copper. Part of the fun of working there was being anonymous. The volunteers didn't have a clue who I was, or they didn't care. Normally wherever I go I'm not sure if people are just nice to me because I'm famous, and I get fed up of that. You get people wanting an autograph and picture and to talk to you about snooker, whereas these people were just talking to me as if I was a normal person, a proper civilian as Liz Hurley would say. The only other time I'd had that was when I went to New York on holiday; they don't watch snooker out there, so they were just treating me as a normal punter.

But this was great because it was only two to three miles from home and I was anonymous. For once I wasn't having to worry about why people were talking to me. It was like going back to basics, and seeing how you could interact with people who know nothing about you. You're all on a level playing field.

You could tell a lot about the people who were there. There was one kid who wouldn't move a muscle. For five or six hours he didn't pick a shovel up, didn't do a thing.

I said: 'Mate, what is the point of you being here? You are just a waste of space', and he looked at me and we got on really well. We had a laugh. He was 14 or 15. Another naughty kid.

'Come on,' I said, 'get involved, just get a shovel, you'll feel better, trust me.'

But he wouldn't. He was just flicking stones in the pool, winding people up. He was good to have a laugh with, but a genuine waste of space. Whatever I said to him made no difference. He had no intention of doing anything. He'd just sit back and tell me how to feed the animals.

'Well, don't do that,' he'd say. 'Put this over there, put that over there, do this, do that.'

I remember Tony coming in and saying: 'He'll drive you mad, he will. Good kid, but he'll drive you nuts.' And in the end he was telling me everything I should do, but he wasn't doing any of it himself. He was just making it up. Even if he wasn't sure what he was saying, he'd blag it. That's when I told him he didn't have a clue.

I fed the pigs and the goats. The pigs were good fun. You'd just lob their pellets in, and they'd eat anything that mob. Frightening. Unbelievable. I don't even eat ham now, seeing how they live. I'd loved a bit of ham till then, but seeing the shit the pigs eat I won't touch it now.

The goats were alright, but I was a bit frightened of them. As soon as you gave them their food they'd bang you about. We'd leave the barrels of hay for the cows right by the field and somebody else would go to feed them.

Working on the farm has made me like chicken more because chickens are not dirty animals. But I didn't get too involved with them because they'd come flying out and I've never been keen on live creatures flying around me.

I worked on the farm for around six weeks. They sent me an email early February saying they hadn't seen me for a few weeks and was I still interested in volunteering; if not, no problem. I emailed them back and said, I've just decided to go back to work, you probably won't see me for a while, but in the future I'd like to go back to do a bit again.

I liked the idea of the community spirit at the farm. They were a genuinely nice bunch of people just getting on with their lives. There was no rush to get things done whereas outside everything was pressure, pressure, pressure. On the farm I found myself in an environment where people appreciated your help but didn't demand anything of you. If I gave them half an hour of my time they were grateful; it was like, thanks so much, d'you want a brew? It was great being around people who didn't care what I did or what I drove. All they were interested in was, can you help us, can you feed a few chickens and ducks because if you can that allows us to get on with the more important stuff. It restored a lot of faith in life for me. I felt I'd been battered for three years, and it had made me ill and dispirited. Going to the farm was a way of grounding myself again.

As I've said, it made me sleep better, too. I think I've tried every sleeping aid in the world – Nightnurse, Piriton, Zolpidem, Stilnox, the lot – and none of them worked for me. I went to this doctor and he said, insomnia's a common problem.

'Take this pill,' he said, 'it's an anti-depressant, but it's the only thing that will give you eight hours' sleep guaranteed.'

Lovely, I thought, and that got me back sleeping. Not sleeping was killing me. Now I'm getting about four to five hours.

If I go to bed at 11 p.m., I'm up for 4 to 5 a.m. It's not great, but it's better than going to bed at midnight and being up at two, which I did for two and a half years. In the end my brain was gone.

Despite allowing me to see more of the kids and giving me time on the farm, part of me thought I shouldn't have stopped playing. I'm sure that whatever happened Jo wouldn't have banned me from seeing them just because I was playing snooker and had to miss a few of my scheduled times with them. After all, she's a good mum and has the children's interests at heart. I still don't know what the right thing to do is. I couldn't love my kids more, but snooker is my career. And not one that's going to last much longer. Over the past year I have seen lots of the kids and it's been wonderful but you'll never convince me that it was the only way I could have done it – to sacrifice my career for my children.

9

WE ARE FAMILY

'Ran hard, pace felt fast, slowed down at halfway
for a bit then worked hard up the hills.'

I'd run a bit at school. Everyone had to do the old cross-country, and a bit of sprinting for sports day. But I can't say I liked it. It was Dad who got me running regularly when I was 12, and then it became even more of a chore. This was way before we struck up our deal about leaving school early so long as I kept disciplined and did my daily three-milers. He was always a fit fella, with the football and going down the gym regularly, boxing and skipping, and maybe he looked at me, saw all the shit I was eating, and thought, if he doesn't watch it he's going to be a right lardy fucker. Whatever: from an early age he told me to get myself out for a regular jog. Dad wasn't the kind of person you argued with. He was dead right, of course – by the age of 10 I was already spending a lot of my waking life in snooker halls, and you needed a balance to that. Not only would I become a little chubster eating crisps and chocolate, but stuck in those the horrible, dark, smoky rooms I'd start to look like Dracula for lack of fresh air. Dad instilled in me the belief that exercise and fresh air meant feeling better, and feeling better meant playing better.

The first time I played snooker was on my cousin Glenn's table. His parents, Peter and Maureen, my aunt and uncle, had a little table at their house in Orpington, Kent. When I was over there I'd hit some balls on it, wasn't very good, but I enjoyed it, and Dad bought me a table for Christmas. I was seven years old, and it was my first table. Dad got it fitted a few days before Christmas, but I wasn't allowed to play till Christmas Day. He and his mates were playing on it, and I kept going to look at it. I just wanted to hit a few balls on it, but he was, like: 'No, just wait till Christmas, then it's yours!' It was a lovely table. Little Ronnie now plays on a similar one, and when I see him it reminds me of my young self – head just popping over the table. I've given Ron a few lessons, told him what's right and wrong. In a way I'd hate him to play snooker professionally because it's such a mentally tough sport. I'd much rather he played tennis or golf and was out in the fresh air. But if he decided snooker was what he wanted to do I'd back him all the way, and I do believe he's got a talent. I watch him play, his bridge hand, the little things he does, and I think he's got the natural hand-eye coordination. But I hope he doesn't take it up professionally.

Playing snooker's a horrible life in some ways. For one, you're told to keep your emotions in check so you don't talk a lot, there's no interaction and you can spend five hours without saying a word. You learn to become a recluse, an automaton. Look at a lot of snooker players: they shut down and walk around like zombies. You can spot a snooker player a mile away. You can see the character in most of the players, too – they're not big conversationalists, they're quiet, introverted. And I wouldn't want little Ronnie to be like that. I'd like him to be more outgoing, confident, playing in a band, anything like that, interacting with the world.

Snooker is a lonely sport, too. You have to work lots of things out for yourself. You'd rarely go to anybody and ask for help because that's seen as a sign of weakness. You never want to share what's going on in your mind with competitors – having said that, there are times when I overshare! – just in case they psychologically get one over you. Maybe it's the same in every sport.

When I was a little boy, Mum and Dad were away working most of the time, but we were still a tight unit of three, until my sister Danielle came along when I was seven – then we became a tight unit of four.

From an early age, Mum and Dad left me with other people as they put in the hours – au pairs, friends, neighbours. There was one au pair who terrified me. I can't remember why, but I was in total fear of her. That's the only bit of my childhood I look back on negatively. The rest was good. Part of the time I lived with another family who were just round the corner. They had two girls and a son, and that's where I stayed most of the time. Again, it was because Mum and Dad were working all hours. I'd sleep over at their house or, sometimes, the girl would take me back to my house and stay over with me. They were like older sisters – they had already left school while I was still in primary school. So even though I haven't got older brothers and sisters, it felt as if I did have.

Mum and Dad were young parents. When I was six, they were still only in their mid-twenties, just beginning to get on in life. Mum's family had quite a successful ice-cream business in Birmingham, a load of vans, and they tried living there. But Dad couldn't hack it, so he came back to London and got a flat, and as soon as he got a flat Mum came down with me. I was 18 months old, and my parents had no money at the time. Because she was Sicilian and she had married an Englishman, Mum's family decided she had dishonoured the family.

They thought Dad was lazy and didn't want to work, and Mum's family couldn't stand him back then. They would sit there and talk about him in Italian in front of him, saying: 'Look at him, he's useless, all he does is eat all the food, sits on the settee, won't drive the ice-cream vans, he's lazy.'

Dad was sitting there, eating his pasta, thinking he's having a wonderful time, and Mum would be sticking up for him in Italian and then she'd turn to him and say: 'Right, come on, Ron, we're going!'

And he'd go: 'Why? What's the matter? I'm having a great time here.'

He said it was only later on that he found out they didn't like him. But Mum's family did grow to love him as a son.

Mum's always been a grafter – old-school. And Dad's still lazy, despite building up a business. He's never been overly keen on a day's work, although he was forced to do one when I was young. Mum just said to him: 'Okay, you've got to go and earn some money now. All this playing football and that, I don't see no money coming in. Go and get a proper job and bring some money in!' So that's why they ended up working so hard.

First of all, he was cleaning cars with Mum – Mum was doing the ins and he was cleaning the outs. Then she started waitressing in the evening, and he got into the porn game. The porn business suited him down to the ground. Mum was the one who gave him the little shove he needed, and once he got a taste for it he thought he'd found the dream job – instead of sitting behind a desk, he was up the West End, having a laugh with the lads. He just landed a job working for someone in the first place. He was pretty good at selling, pretty good with figures, and they liked him.

The police were raiding a lot of the sex shops at the time, and the people running the shops got a bit bottly and worried

Me when I was little Ronnie and Dad ... Dad has been a powerful presence in my life ... and a powerful absence. When he went down for murder, I was in pieces.

Me and Mum ... When we went into business together, I said to Mum, whatever I earn and whatever you earn we'll pool together.

With Stephen Hendry back in 1996 when we both looked like kids … for me, Hendry is the greatest player ever. When we fell out it hurt, but it was my fault. (Louisa Buller/PA)

2004 … winning the World Championship and celebrating with a pair of Dracula teeth. Everyone thought it was a tribute to Ray 'Dracula' Reardon, but I'd promised my mate Scouse John I'd stick 'em in if I ever won the World again. (Rui Vieira/PA)

Me with six-time world champion Ray Reardon ... I love Ray, he's the funniest man I ever met and a great coach, but I started playing too cautiously. (Trevor Smith Photography)

The great snooker cover-up … 2005, UK Championship, I put the wet towel over my head because I couldn't bear watching Mark King play. (Eric Whitehead)

Giving Lil a kiss after winning the World Championship in 2008 – my third world title, and a lovely feeling. (Getty)

Me and the trophy in 2008. I was so gaunt everyone asked if I was ill, but I was just super fit. (Anna Gowthorpe/PA)

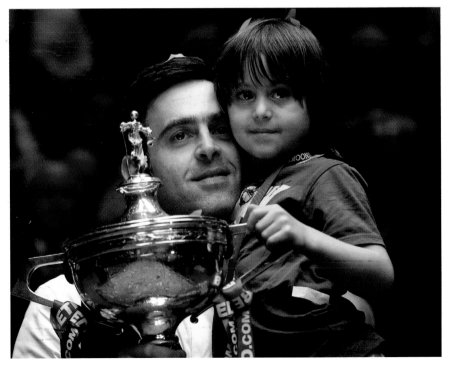

Me and little Ronnie in 2012. To go from barely seeing the kids to having my little boy sharing that moment with me was just perfect. It couldn't get any better. (Getty)

Me and little Ronnie 2013. What a way to cap off the craziest year in my snooker life. After my self-imposed exile, I came back and won the World Championship for the fifth time. (Rex)

Me, Sylvia, Damien and little Ron partying after I won the 2013 Worlds – Sylv is Damien's assistant and part of the gang.

Me and Damien Hirst, giving the world the finger. He makes me look almost civilised!

– they didn't want to go to prison, and they thought if they were nicked under the old obscenity laws they'd end up doing time. But Dad just thought, there's good money in this game and if I get six months or a year it's worth it. He never went down for running the sex shops – but he did end up doing a lot longer than that in the end.

He was selling pornographic magazines. He told me that a lot of people would put stars on the vaginas and the penises so when they went to court they'd go: 'Yes, it's obscene, but there's a star to cover it', but Dad left the vaginas and arses exposed, and began putting stars on elbows and armpits and feet and toes because he said he found them obscene! These were the days before sex shops were licensed. His brothers have still got a few shops left in London's West End called Harmony, but Mum and Dad are out of the game now. I think Mum got frightened when she got banged up. She did six or seven months, and she never wanted to go through that stress again. She thought she'd rather take less money and be out of the firing line. She's chilling out, going on holidays and having a good time these days.

I had a snooker room built for me at the end of the garden when I was 11. It was a huge room with the table, obviously, a settee, a telly, and I'd spend 10 to 11 hours a day in there just hitting balls. Now I'm not sure that's healthy for somebody starting out in life but then again to be successful it's necessary to go through that.

There's that old cliché that being good at snooker is a sign of a misspent youth. It's funny that people never say it about golf or football or cricket. But there is an element of truth in it. Why would you spend all those hours in the dark when you could be outside in the sun? I was such an early starter. By the age of 10 I was making centuries, at 12 I won my first pro-am tournament and when I was 15 I made my first maxi. In snooker terms, I was ridiculously precocious. I don't think Stephen Hendry began playing till he was 13 or 14 and Steve Davis was 14 when he started the game. Maybe it's not that they were late starters, it's just that I was a ridiculously early starter.

I soon discovered that snooker messes with your head more than any sport. There's no other sport where you just have to sit down till your opponent has finished their business. You're sitting there knowing there's nothing you can do. But in a way there *is* something you can do. If you play to your potential you definitely have an effect on what your opponent does. So although physically you can't do anything, if you dominate the game when you are at the table it does have an effect on your opponent. In some ways that is even more satisfying because you can see him making mistake after mistake, unravelling in front of you. Even though you are not getting punched in the face, or punching your opponent in the face, you are bullying your opponents in some respects.

Having said that, I think I'd rather be punched in the face than bullied on the snooker table. There are a couple of players who have bullied me on the table – sometimes I've come away from playing John Higgins and Stephen Hendry feeling I've been battered. There is nothing worse than sitting in the chair, at the Crucible or any big venue, for eight or nine frames taking the punishment, not potting a ball, watching your opponent clock up the scores. You feel embarrassed, you start questioning your ability. But in a sick way for many fans this is the joy of snooker – watching someone sit in his chair, shrivelling, falling apart. There's a sadistic pleasure people get out of it. It's total punishment.

When you go through matches like that you come off and feel devastated but you just have to pick yourself up and get on with it. But it's not easy – you collect a lot of mental scars during a career. When you're younger you are fearless and just go for your shots, but as you grow older and take a few beatings along the way, you begin to question your game. When I started people would say to me: 'Oh, it's alright for you, you've got no fear, just wait till you're a bit older and you miss a few and people start punishing you.' They were right.

When I won my first tournament against Stephen Hendry I remember feeling scared because I was playing my hero, and there was no chance I was going to win. I ended up beating him, and now, when I watch myself playing then, I see someone who looks as if he's playing with no fear. I think, wow! that kid there looked so confident, so assured.

When I was 10, I had fear but I never showed it. I'd go out and think, you can't show your fear. Beforehand I'd think, I can't go out there and play because I'm too nervous but then the performance I put in was really good. I didn't look nervous. Sometimes I look back at more recent matches, when I know I've been in pieces, and yet I look really calm out there. So what you're feeling and what you're projecting out there can be two entirely different things. I always wonder where that comes from. I know my confidence has been affected over the years by doubt and by trying to perfect my game, but on the outside it often doesn't show.

That frustrates me at times. I'd rather somebody came up to me and said: 'It looks as if you're struggling out there, Ron; you're doing this wrong and doing that wrong.' But nobody's ever felt able to say that to me. They just say, well, you look great, you're playing great, you look calm, it doesn't show. And I just think, are they lying to me? I would hate to see little Ronnie struggle like I have.

But I didn't always think like this, of course. By the time

I was 10 I already had it in my mind that snooker was what I wanted to do. I didn't have time for anything else. I loved playing. Competing. I used to get excited about the thought of going away at the weekend to play in junior events. I'd get a buzz out of just going down the club and playing. I just loved it; you couldn't keep me off the table. I'd be playing hour after hour, player after player. I never wanted to stop.

Winning was never important to me until I got a few victories under my belt. At 12, I was making 20 grand a year. Unbelievable, really. When I think about it I was earning more than most adults. I was a bit of a freak at that age. The other players didn't believe I was only 12 – I was already shaving, and they'd go, look at the size of him. By the time I was 14 I had a hairy chest.

The reason I was making so much money was because I was winning proper amateur events. A lot of these kids would win the odd junior event so they'd make £300–£400. But on the amateur circuit, where the prize money was £1,000 or £1,500 or even two and a half grand, I was regularly winning. I was mixing it with the top amateurs and that's why I was earning such good money.

A lot of the adults didn't like it. The dads would look at me and think: 'Ah no, my little boy's got to play him!' And it was often a mauling. It would be 3-0, they wouldn't pot a ball, it would be over and done with in about half an hour.

I was merciless. I never felt sorry for anybody. When I was a kid, the killer instinct was drummed into me by Dad, just like Ray Reardon did later on – you never let them off the hook, always nail them, when they want snookers, you get the snookers. When you shake hands you shake and you mean it; none of that floppy wet-fish rubbish; look into the man's eyes. That wasn't in me naturally, Dad instilled it into me. I remember shaking some old girl's hand and I just squeezed it accidentally, and she went aaaagh!

By nature I think I'm a gentle man. Dad moulded me into what he thought I needed to be. I probably would have been even more ruthless had he not gone away. But when he was inside I found myself, and became much closer to the person I naturally was. I haven't got the killer instinct to want to dominate the world. I enjoy the game, but I've not got that thing in me where I've got to win eight titles, break this record, or get revenge on the last player to beat me. It's not my way of thinking. Having said that, I think I'm still ruthless when I'm on the table because then it's just me and the game I'm trying to master.

Dad thinks we're very different people. He knows there's a lot of stuff I'm just not bothered about. He's driven to succeed; driven to want to be the best. He only loves winners. Messi's a god, everyone else is shit, that kind of thing. 'They call him great, he ain't great, he's fucking shit, look at him, cunt, shit. Shit. What are they all talking about, he's shiiiiiiiiit.' He's funny when he goes off on one – like Peter Cook in an old 'Derek and Clive' sketch. I listen to him and think, well, is he right or wrong, and by my reckoning the player he's going on about is playing for Arsenal or Tottenham and obviously isn't shit. He's a harsh critic. It was drummed into me from an early age to have that mentality, but it just wasn't me. Often I'm so quiet, so withdrawn, that I just turn my phone off for days to get away from everyone and everything. As soon as I switch it on, I see emails and texts and I don't know how to cope with it. It scares me. I don't want it, I just want to keep my life as simple as I can, which is hard. And I'm finding that now because everyone wants a piece of you.

When I played the adults some got annoyed losing to me,

and some loved it. I remember this Canadian fella, Marcel Gauvreau; he was about number 30 in the world and he turned up at the pro-am, and I was due to play him, and I thought, god, he's a legend. I'd been watching him on the telly. He'd got through to the quarter-finals of the Mercantile Credit Classic; he didn't win events but he was a regular quarters, last-16 man. And I played him in a quarter-final at Stevenage and this was a major pro-am – about 128 players, anyone who was anyone was there. Steve James, who was ranked number eight in the world, was playing, so we're talking quality.

I played Marcel in the quarter-finals and I had an 80, a 90 and 130, and I beat him 3-2. When I got a frame off him, I thought I'd done well. When I got two frames off him, I thought, fuck, if he beats me 3-2, I can go back to my local snooker club and say I took two frames off Marcel Gauvreau. That was how much of a scalp he was. And I ended up beating him 3-2.

I came off the table and he went: 'Hey, man, that kid's unbelievable! He's made a hundred and thirty and a ninety. Who is this motherfucker?'

And I was like, wow, because he became my fan. After he played me he wouldn't leave me alone. Every pro-am I turned up at he'd come up to me and go: 'This is the kid! *This is the kid!*' and I'd think, what's he on, this geeza, is he mad or what? I could never see what he thought was so special about me, but I was just glad to make a friend. I'd love to know where Marcel is now.

But a lot of the adults hated playing me, and hated getting beaten by me even more. Many players are driven to playing for the wrong reasons, and they'll do anything for a result. I know sport is about winning trophies and getting silverware, but I've always been more of a believer in playing for the spirit of the game. I really believe that if you took all money out of the game, it would be much fairer and more sporting. It would be a nicer sporting planet; having said that, though, I'd be a lot poorer.

There was a lot of jealousy from the older guys. On a couple of occasions I owed them money. I owed Nicky Lazarus a tenner, and his dad was Mark Lazarus, who played for QPR. They were quite a hard-nut family in Romford, and I owed Nicky the money because I was into fruit machines. I was shit scared of him. Every time I went to tournaments I avoided him. He was probably 20, 10 years older than me, always had a nice bird with him, so he was one of the dudes on the circuit. He was a good player.

Nicky caught me one day and said: 'Oi, you give me my fucking money back! You think you can get away with it, but my dad knows more villains than your dad.' I thought, shit! He's really coming after me. And it was all over a tenner. Maybe he was showing off his alpha-male qualities.

Without Dad I don't think I would have got anywhere in snooker. I think I would have got in a lot of trouble, probably been banned from tournaments. Dad was good at punishing me, getting me out of bother and sending messages to certain people at snooker tournaments not to lead me on because I was so easily led. He'd tell people to keep an eye on me because I needed to be watched. I was a little fucker, and Dad had told them: 'If he misbehaves make sure you tell me.' I know they all reported back to him because he found out everything I'd been up to.

I was gambling on the fruit machines and when I was eight or nine I was swearing a lot. When I missed a shot down the club, I'd be: 'Fucking cunt, fucking this, fucking that', and I'd be smashing my cues. I was terrible. I hated missing the ball and I'd just get the hump and become so angry with myself. I got banned from Pontins when I was 10, and of course Dad found out about that, too.

I threw a beer glass full of Coke across the ballroom when I was being chased – I wasn't throwing it at anybody, I just smashed it on the floor so the fella behind me would stop chasing me. Eddie Manning was a bit of a lary geeza from Leicester, always had a suntan. Fast Eddie they used to call him; he'd have all the birds and he was having a go at me. He'd started poking me and taking the piss, bullying me. I threw the glass in his direction. Splat! He went: 'You cunt', and started chasing me. I still had the glass in my hand so I threw it on the floor, obviously it smashed, and that wasn't right. But then they claimed I'd throw a glass at an old lady, which I wouldn't do in a million years, so I got banned for that.

Even though I got in trouble all the time, Dad was my safety net. He was a tough disciplinarian, and when I'd done wrong I knew I was for it. He'd humiliate me in front of my mum, his dad, his friends – verbally more than anything, intimidation. When I got banned from Pontins he called round the snooker player Mark King and his dad, Bill King. Dad had paid for the holiday, paid for all our spending money, and had said to Bill: 'Just look after him, make sure he doesn't misbehave and if he does just give me a call.' So we went there, and I got banned.

But when we went up to the disciplinary hearing, the report was written by the snooker referee John Williams and he said that on the Monday Bill King came up to him and said, you've got to get hold of Ronnie because he's messing around. So it turned out that the man who was looking after me now appeared to be grassing me up to the tournament official. Dad invited Mark and Bill round to our house to explain what had happened and Mark said: 'They were calling Ronnie Mighty

Mouth', and just shit stirring. I knew from Dad's face that I was going to be in shtuck when they left.

Dad gave me the slipper treatment. I couldn't sit down for a couple of days because my bum was so sore. Good old-fashioned put-you-in-your-place stuff; it probably didn't do me any harm. Not that I thought so at the time.

I was quite independent from an early age because of the snooker and also because of Mum and Dad working. I was left to go away by myself a lot. I was given petrol money, money for spends etc. from the age of 11. A lot of kids would travel with their parents, even when they were 17 or 18. I'd just turn up on my own. I loved it. I could play the fruit machines, mess about; if I got beat I could have a laugh with some of the older lads. I was buzzing. Those weekends were great.

Not surprisingly, I paid less and less attention to school work, and left school without taking exams. I had got on well with most of the teachers. I think they were all curious about me, and the snooker. When I was 10 or 11 my headmaster, Mr Challon, heard that I had got £450 for winning a competition, and he didn't believe it.

'Ronnie, is it true you've just won £450 in a snooker tournament?'

'Yeah,' I said.

'Can you bring in the trophy and cheque to show me?' He was particularly interested in seeing the cheque.

I got home and told Mum. 'Mum, is it okay if I take in my trophy and cheque to school tomorrow. The head wants to see it.'

She smiled. 'Course, you can.'

So I put them in my school bag, got called into his office, he had his mate there, and he went: 'Show me this trophy!' So I got it out, and he said: 'Well done! Very well done!' I liked Mr

Challon. The teachers were supportive of me. They knew my mind was fixed on being a snooker player and as long as I went to school they didn't push me about exams.

I was a bit of a loner. I didn't have a bigger brother or a bigger sister. A lot of my friends were in my year – George, my best mate, was like a brother to me. George is into computers and designs football websites. No one at school had a friendship like me and George – we were inseparable. He wasn't into snooker. Football was his game. George was a bit of a freak, like me. He had great big legs, and he'd get the ball and fly down the wing and he'd hit it and it would scream into the net, and everybody would go, there's no way he's only 12 years old. He was shaped like a man.

Dad wanted me to make a career out of snooker. From a very young age he instilled that dedication in me. He was always trying to steer me down the right path. I suppose back then he was moulding me into a successful sportsman. He's a bright man, and he knew the messages he was trying to put into my head. A lot of the kids I grew up with were mollycoddled: 'My boy this, my boy that.' My dad never gave me compliments. I never got any praise. He never said well done to me. Occasionally I felt I was doing quite well and I was still getting criticised. But in the end I didn't care, and it probably helped me get a good perspective on things – 'You've won a trophy, it's history, put it behind you, and now win the next one.' And that's actually a positive way for a sportsman to think. So that became my mentality. I was never allowed to think: 'Yes, I'm British junior champion', and rest on my laurels. That was knocked out of me at a very young age.

Perhaps he was moulding me into the sportsman he had wanted to be himself. Dad had ambitions to be a professional footballer. I don't know why he didn't make it because he was talented. Maybe he didn't have the mentor that he became for me. Also, because he'd been lazy when he was young, he was determined that I wouldn't fail for lack of effort. He understood that if I was going to be successful it had to start from a young age.

I was thinking a lot more clinically than some of the adult amateur players I was up against. Most of them were 18 to 20 and had been playing for 10 years down the club, but none of them thought like me. They were often lazy in their mind and approach, and it was obvious they were not going anywhere because their attitude was so wrong. If I'd had that attitude I wouldn't have made it. I needed to think as I did in order to become a top sportsman.

Mum didn't play much of a role in my development as a snooker player other than cooking and making sure the house was looked after. She had her own life. By the time Dad was around 30 he didn't really need to work any more. Amazing – especially since he's naturally lazy. He told me that he used to be asleep in bed when the wage packets came through the door around 1 a.m., and he said: 'I used to listen, and if it wasn't heavy enough when it hit the floor I used to ring them up and go, "Stop nicking so much; the packets are too light."' And that was his work. He'd check the takings, tell them they weren't doing well enough and had to up the takings, but really by 30 he was a man of leisure.

At 14, Dad started me off on my serious running routine. It was a deal – if I took my snooker and my fitness seriously, and learnt how to discipline myself, he said I could leave school at 16. But I had to prove my intent for a couple of years before that.

'Ronnie, if you want to leave school early you've got to do a three-mile run every morning, come back, shower and down the club for 10.30 a.m., back for 5.30 p.m., you have your dinner at 6.30–7 p.m., you're in bed at 9 p.m.' I didn't like the idea of it, but thought, I'll take it.

10

MUM & DAD: INSIDE STORY

'Finished 86th in the Met league out of 300. Room for improvement.'

When Dad went down I was devastated. I was 17, I'd just won 74 out of 76 matches, I was professional, I'd qualified for the World Championship, so all I felt I could do was get on with stuff. I was a young man, independent, so I tried to put everything to the back of my mind. But, of course, that was impossible. It was tough. I didn't have a clue anything was wrong before he was arrested. I was busy with my snooker, kept out of the way, was either in my room at the end of the garden or down the club so I wasn't witness to what was going on. I saw lots of people coming and going, there were always people in the house, and Mum and Dad were usually out clubbing, having a good time. But so much of that world is show. A lot of it is being out, drinking, having a good time, Page Three birds, boxers, sportsmen. There were always stories about George Michael or Gazza, mingling with celebrities. Your ego gets caught up with it, you get sucked in by it, and shit happens. It's easy to forget that you've got a family and kids, and all the important values.

I dabbled in that lifestyle, too. I looked at Dad, and thought, that's something to aspire to. It seemed like the good life – he didn't need to work, had a great time socially, lots of friends. So when he went away I thought I'd carry on where he left off. I thought this was what success brought you; that once you'd done your grafting it was time to enjoy yourself. Sod the snooker, I wanted to be out clubbing like Dad had been and I tried it for a couple of years and ended up in rehab. I went down that road because I thought that's what you did, that's what I had seen, but it never felt right for me, even when I was smashing it. I saw them going out late, coming in early morning, parties, barbecues, everything, but my dad was a different character from me. He enjoyed that lifestyle, but I didn't.

There'd be times when I'd look around at the people I was with and the places I was in, and think, what am I doing here? I'd go to the toilet and tell myself, you've got to get out of here, and I'd get a cab home and be full of self-loathing. I'd have been hanging round with the local knobheads from Chigwell, who'd smoke dope and talk bollocks and think they were small-time criminals. We'd go to Charlie Chans and Epping Forest Country Club, and now and again we'd go into the West End, but it was all rubbish. I never fitted into that world. I always told myself: 'Hold on, Ron, you'll begin to like it at some point because everybody else seems to be having a good time', but it didn't work out like that.

I didn't understand the discipline you needed to be a good sportsman, despite everything Dad had told me. In my mind I thought you could do all this stuff and still have a successful snooker career. I thought everyone did this with their lives. Eventually I realised they didn't; that it wasn't so normal. I was always happy doing my run, playing my snooker, going out for a nice little Chinese or kebab.

I was in a hotel in Thailand when I was told that Dad had been charged. Mum phoned me in the middle of the night so I knew it had to be serious. Just not this serious.

'Daddy's been arrested,' she said. 'He's in police custody. He's been involved in a fight and someone's been killed.'

I was in shock, and burst out crying. It turned out Dad had been arrested the previous week. At the time Mum thought it was all a big mistake, and to protect me they shipped me out to the World Amateur Championship in Thailand. Mum thought by the time I got home it would all be sweet and he'd be out. It must have been obvious that the press was about to pick up on it, so Barry Hearn said to Mum, you better tell him before the press does. When she told me, I just collapsed. I was gutted. Desperate.

Dad hadn't really been in trouble before, despite working in the porn industry. When he got bail I was convinced he wouldn't go down – why would they let him out if they thought he was guilty? I was told that if they thought he was guilty they'd be scared he'd do a runner so they wouldn't give him bail. So all the signs were that he was going to be alright; that it wasn't a murder, it was just something terrible that happened when two people were in the wrong place at the wrong time. All the signs were that he would get off, but he didn't.

Dad pleaded not guilty to the murder of Bruce Bryan, a driver for the East End gangster Charlie Kray. He didn't only plead not guilty to murder, he said he'd not even stabbed him. Now we obviously know he was there in that Chelsea nightclub and he did stab the fella and attack his brother. He should have just held his hands up, admitted to it, and I think he would have got a few years for manslaughter. What seems to have happened is that Dad and his mates were arguing about who was going to pay the bill (they all wanted to pay!). Bruce Bryan and his brother got the wrong end of the stick and thought they weren't going to pay at all, and it ended in a row. Dad went round to talk to them, said, let's sort it out, when one of the fellas lifted an ashtray and went to smash it on his head. Dad put up a hand to protect himself and two of his fingers were severed. That was when Dad picked up the knife on the other side of the bar, and that was that.

He told me the prosecution offered him manslaughter, and he said, no, he wasn't taking it. It was stupid, really; pigheaded. He went against the advice he was given. Once he gets something in his head he doesn't budge. He sticks to his guns. He's so stubborn. At the time I didn't realise how the law worked and the significance of his decision not to take a manslaughter plea. But eventually I realised there were people he went down with who'd done worse crimes and who were out within five years. I'd ask how come they got out earlier than him and I'd be told, well, they took a manslaughter, or they pleaded guilty. I thought, Jesus he's got to do 18 years because he said he wasn't there and didn't do it; he's mad.

In the end, he was given a longer sentence because the judge ruled it was a racist attack. But that was nonsense – Dad's always had loads of black friends. It just turned out that the fella he killed was black. Dad says time and again he can never forgive himself for taking a man's life and causing so much pain to another family.

At least I was doing well with my snooker. It gave him something to hang on to. In a way, it felt that we did the sentence together. Dad was on the phone a lot, still keeping me in check – what was I doing, who was I practising with, who was I hanging out with? So we still had our relationship when he was in prison. He couldn't boss me around as much as if he was out, of course – he couldn't knock on my door and go: 'Oi, what you up to?', but there was a respect for him that meant I didn't want to embarrass him or piss him off.

'Every time you're on telly, Ron,' he'd say to me, 'it's like I'm getting a visit.' And I thought, if my playing snooker is the most important thing in his life, I can't stop playing because that's all he's got to hang on to and all he's got to look forward to.

So it was always a big motivator for me. That's his currency, I thought; that's what's getting him through; me and my snooker. Even if he was down in the block, segregated for bad behaviour, he could go: 'Well, I know the UK Championship is on now, he'll be in Preston, he'll be doing this', and he felt that he was doing time with me; I was still there for him. And he would think that when he did finally get out at least he would have known what was going on in my life – there wouldn't be that much catching up to do. The snooker was Dad's motivation and mine. Perhaps if he hadn't been in prison I would have lost my enthusiasm, or sense of purpose.

Dad used to tell me about the good times in the nick. 'It's marvellous, three meals a day, lots of exercise, watching plenty of telly, reading my papers, fantastic,' he'd say. 'It's not all bad, this prison.' But he was putting on a front. He hated being away from the family – especially the first 10 years of his sentence when he often got himself in trouble for being mouthy. The other day he admitted it for the first time.

'The trouble with me, Ronnie, was that I couldn't do my bird. Couldn't accept it. I had verbal diarrhoea towards officers and towards authority in general because I had my life taken away from me. I lost my wife, my kids, my business, my liberty. The fact that I was so verbal wasn't a sign of my confidence, it was the opposite.' What he said next touched me. I'd never thought he really listened to what I said to him, but he told me that just wasn't true. 'When I had eight or nine years left you came to me and said, you've got to slow down a bit now, things are good. Then the penny dropped. I became institutionalised, didn't challenge everything, and I could do my prison a lot earlier.'

Dad says it took him a long time to learn how to talk to people and how to approach them, but once he worked it out it made doing his time so much easier. 'You can't make people feel uncomfortable, and if you want something done you've got to persuade them rather than tell them. If you're going to talk to somebody who's a bit of a bully on the wing you don't walk into a cell with a pair of trainers, a top and a hat on because you're looking for a fight. But if you walk in with your dressing gown and your flip-flops and sit down and chat, as soon as they spin round they see you're not dressed for a fight. So I learnt that over time. If you stick your chin out in jail, they'll whack it. And I had my chin whacked loads of times in there, but then I grew up. I read books and stuff. A lot of psychology books.'

Even now, he'll say: 'We had some great times in prison', and he'll tell me some of the stories and I'll think, come on, Dad, they don't sound that great to me. He'd talk about the times down the block when they're trying to pin a fag to a piece of string and throw it over the line, and there's this great excitement when one of them gets it. 'All this for a fag! And that's what got you through – after 10 days down the block nothing matters. Everything goes. You don't bother about your appearance, brushing your teeth, your telly's gone. Your papers have gone.' He sounded nostalgic when he talked about it. 'I ripped all my photos up. Even pictures of you,' he'd say. 'If I've not got photos up, nobody can rip them up, and they can't do you emotionally. You just go, fuck it and put it out of your mind. When you get through it and you've been moved on you come out feeling jubilant that you've got through.' It's a test of mental endurance down the block. I could understand the satisfaction he got from that, but I thought, I'd rather be out here having a bad day than in there having a good one.

For his first decade inside he was a rebel, never one for accepting rules or bowing to authority. It was always: 'No, this is what I'm doing, take it or leave it.' You've got to stand up for yourself in prison, fight your corner now and again, but I think he had more of a reputation for looking after people. He'd take the new boys aside, and advise them – 'Do this, don't do that, don't do that, do this, and you'll be alright.' And things tended to run pretty smoothly after that. He wasn't a piss-taker; people said they could rely on Dad inside.

His currency was phone cards. He'd see a fella wearing a T-shirt he liked. 'I want that T-shirt, here's twenty phone cards,' he'd say.

'Lovely, sweet!' they'd say. And it was a deal.

He bought phone cards, he sold phone cards and most of all he used phone cards to call home.

People would send him money in prison and he'd buy up all the phone cards with it. He'd buy the cards off people who didn't want them – lots of people didn't have anyone to ring, and they'd much rather have a bit of money sent off to their mum or sisters. He said: 'I'll have everyone's phone cards in here, and there's nothing nobody can do about it.'

Dad's always been sociable, a talker. Whenever he rang anybody it wasn't a quick hello or goodbye, you got the full 20 minutes. He phoned me when I was in Thailand and he had 40 phone cards on the floor. The screws saw him, and he was putting one in after the other, and they said, right we've got him, and sent him off down the block.

It was a little business really. He'd get people's phone cards, and say to the people working in his shops: 'Okay, take this address down, send a few quid here, send a few quid there', and that's what we did. The shops were still going so there was plenty of money about. 'Tony put that there, Darbo put that there', and they'd just do it.

At one of the prisons his nickname was Chairman Ron. It meant we didn't have to send anything in for him. He'd just see things he liked and buy them – tops, jeans, radios. It was a good way of doing business and saved us time. Whenever he saw anything he fancied, he'd just go: 'I like that. How many d'you want for it?' So he'd barter phone cards as well as stock them up for his own use.

Prisons fill me with dread. I became so used to them they were like a second home. But not a happy home. I always hated them – as soon as I went in on a visit, I felt trapped. It was like the end of the world; doom and gloom, end of freedom, no-where to go. Horrible.

I also did a few exhibitions in prisons. They would never let me do an exhibition where Dad was because it could be seen as favouritism, so now and again I'd do it for one or two of the other boys he knew. One time I was doing an exhibition at a young offenders' prison in Doncaster; they showed me round the wings and I was stunned by how quiet it was. They were having their breakfast and there wasn't a sound. Eerie. Other times on the wings it was so loud and echoey that it sounded like a madhouse.

I did one exhibition at Wormwood Scrubs with Jimmy White. We were there for one of Jimmy's mates. They all loved Jimmy of course, but I was new on the block back then. That was mental. It reminded me of the film *Scum*. Really intimidating. There were all these screws, but even more inmates and I thought, any minute now this lot could overthrow this jail.

There must have been about 100 prisoners watching me and Jimmy play. I kept thinking of that scene in *Scum* when Ray Winstone smacks another inmate in the face with the pool ball hidden in the sock. I was a bit scared, I have to admit. You just don't know what could happen in a situation like that. Charles Bronson might think: 'Hey, here's my next victim!' Don't think I'd fancy making the front pages for that reason.

But when I went in there, they were like: 'Go on, Ronnie!' I had great support from the prison world. I felt I wasn't just playing for Dad, I was playing for most of the fellas in the nick. 'When you won the world title that first time, Ron,' Dad said, 'every prisoner was banging on the doors.' When he told me that, it really hit me. Even though they were in their cells, they were rooting for Dad, and me. They felt like I was one of them; that Ronnie's done it for us. He said the wing was buzzing for weeks after my victory. Months even. It was the talking point for so long afterwards.

Jimmy was great in the Scrubs, but then he's great wherever he goes. They all love him – he's got that charm, everyone just wants a piece of Jimmy, he'll fit in everywhere. We played about an hour in the Scrubs and they were all buzzing. They were quite far away from the table – I wasn't sure if that was for safety reasons or it was just the way it had to be done. I looked round me and thought again, there are fewer screws than prisoners and they're taking a bit of a chance here. This lot could overrun the jail if they want to. I was just there to do a good deed for somebody, but a good deed could always turn into somebody else's opportunity. In the end, things were fine, and I was glad we'd gone in.

The more you go into prisons the more you realise that a lot of those in jail are not bad people, they just get caught on the other side of the law, often because of the way they've been brought up, lack of education, or just the world they live in. Don't get me wrong: some of them are lunatics who would be a menace out on the streets, but loads are just unlucky or made one stupid decision in life.

As for me, I'm terrified of breaking the law. Maybe it's something to do with what happened to Mum and Dad. I'm scared to breathe sometimes in case I get done for it. I just don't like trouble. In general, if I get a gas bill and don't pay it straightaway I start to panic and think I'm going to have the bailiffs around.

World Snooker threatened with me everything for not turning up to tournaments – you're in breach of this rule, in breach of that rule, we don't believe you've got glandular fever, we need another doctor's letter; no, that one isn't good enough, we've got our own independent doctor we want you to go and see. In the end, I got panic attacks every time I had to meet up with World Snooker. I felt they were out to get me, and in the end I thought, I don't want this in my life; it's causing me too much stress.

All the legal stuff in the custody battle terrified me as well. If I could avoid that, whatever the cost, I would. Again, I got to the point where I just wanted to get away from it all. And I did just that by staying at home for a year, running, cooking and becoming a hermit. One of my greatest pleasures in life is cooking – a nice spicy Indian or a Chinese. I've learnt so much about cooking from two friends in particular – Django and Damien Hirst. When I wasn't playing the lawyers seemed to lose interest in me, as well. Their attitude seemed to be, well he's not earning, he's got no money, he's no good to us.

The truth is I'm not built for conflict. I know I seem to have found plenty in my time, but I don't think I ever seek it out. It's not me. Having said that, I'm not built for being nailed down either. You nail me down, you kill me. You try to squeeze me, and I'll run away. Sometimes I feel as if I'm being suffocated – often by people who haven't got my best interests at heart (lawyers, hangers-on, certain agents) and sometimes by people who genuinely do love me. I feel like so much of my life is running – running from lawyers, agents, hangers-on, running from World Snooker, even running from the family at times. I'm running from everything.

There are times when I feel alone, and I think I need Mum. So I'll go there, and it's all good for a couple of weeks, then she gets on my nerves and I get on hers. She won't have hot water or the heating on 'cos she's always trying to save on bills. After a week of freezing at Mum's I start to think I need my own home. Then I'd go to stay with Dad and run away because he's always telling me what to do. In the end I'll be thinking, right, time for a break, I'm going to Sheffield where I'll do my runs, get left alone and do my snooker. Whenever I want to get away from stuff, I go up north because the people are so much friendlier and you're out of the rat race. 'Have a brew, duck!' As soon as I hear that I think, I'm in safe hands.

I suppose it's that classic thing – can't live with them, can't live without them. Yet as a family, we couldn't be closer. The fact that we can't bear to live more than a mile apart says it all. Mum, Dad, me and Danielle, all in different houses in Chigwell, down the road from each other.

I often think of me and Dad as a team. But perhaps me and Mum have been an even closer team because of circumstances. When Dad went down, she was in effect a single mum and Danielle was still a little girl. Then, a couple of years later, when I was 19 and Danielle was 12, disaster struck.

Weirdly, I was in Thailand again when I heard what had happened. My mate gave me a ring.

141

'Ron, I've got some bad news for you.'

'What is it?'

'Your mum's in nick. They've taken her away for tax dodging.'

'You're having a laugh, aren't you?'

'I'm not. Little Danielle's with us, and they're holding your mum at Lime Street police station.'

When I discovered Mum was going down I couldn't believe it. The investigation into Mum took place just after Dad went down. They watched our house for 18 months, and by the time they raided it they had everything they needed. I remember thinking, they really are out to get the family. It was like, right, we've got him, let's now destroy her.

When she went down it was mad. Everybody kept saying, they won't put her away because she's got two kids, and one of them's a young girl, and she's paid the VAT. Then, bang! She's gone down. We were in court and I still couldn't believe it when they found her guilty.

I felt so sorry for Mum. She was brave – she just looked at me. I was crying. She's a strong old girl, like a tiger. She didn't show any emotion.

Dad is tougher physically, but I think mentally Mum has become a much stronger person because of having to live in a man's world. She changed when he went away. She realised she had to be tougher, and I've seen a difference in Mum these past 10 years. She won't take any bollocks from anybody whereas before she'd be so sympathetic to people – too sympathetic. After Dad went down we were a powerful team. She had her business and I had mine.

Mum had always been willing to help people. Then I noticed the change. And I understand why, perfectly. She'd had enough of running around for me and Dad, and she thought, sod this, I'm getting on with my life – I'm running my business, going on holidays. If they need stuff they can look after themselves.

She made a conscious decision that a lot of the stuff I was asking her to do I could do for myself. And that was fair enough. She decided to become more selfish. She just got fed up with being a single mum always doing for others, and thought: 'I need a life of my own.' I agree with her. In recent years I've put my children ahead of my career, and when I look back I think that is probably not the advice I'd give other people. Don't be held back from what you want to do because you think it's the right thing to do. In hindsight, I should have just played my snooker and hopefully things would have just worked out over time. Just as I put my life on hold for three years, so did Mum – only for far longer. And she just got sick of it.

Before she went to prison, Dad had been calling her lots and they'd been having conversations about everything. Then when she went down she saw the big sign on the prison walls saying, all your conversations are being recorded, and she got the hump with Dad then because he'd been telling her all the time on the phone what to do with the money, and where to put it. And when the police came in the house they knew exactly where to look. I think she did blame him partly for the fact that she went down. He couldn't contain himself, he was so desperate to run his business even when he was in jail, and he ended up implicating Mum. She was angry, and when she was released she reconsidered her life.

When she came out we were like a couple. We were very close. She had the big house in Chigwell, and loads of people were waiting for her to fall and be forced to sell up. And I thought, no, we're alright, I'm playing snooker, she's got her business, we're doing alright. And that drove me on. I said to Mum, whatever I earn and whatever you earn we'll buy properties together and expand. Originally, of course, snooker was my business and sex shops was hers, but with the profits we thought we'd build up a little empire of properties and see where we'd go with it. I said, we'll invest our money cleverly and do it together. And that's what we did. We always put our money together. I said, what's yours is mine and what's mine is yours, and I was probably doing better than she was, but it didn't matter. She took care of business, managed the company, and I just pumped money into it. We're still business partners. Obviously, there's not as much money there now because property prices went up and snooker prize money went down, so my buying power was drastically reduced years ago. Properties were too expensive to buy for what I was earning. So I've not really bought anything over the past decade and recently, because of the custody battle, I've had to sell a few properties to find money for the lawyers.

I always know if I need anything Mum will bail me out tomorrow. I trust Mum with my life.

11

ME & DAD: OUTSIDE STORY

'In the gym with Terry. He worked me very hard. Was nearly sick.'

One of the first things Dad and I did when he was home on day release was go for a run. Well, not so much a run, more a jog. It reminded me of all those times he made me pound the streets when I was a kid. But back then he wasn't keeping me company on foot, he was chasing me with a car!

When he came out on day release he was overweight – had a belly on him and was a bit jowly. I'm not sure why. For so much of his time in prison he was fit as a fiddle, ripped, and didn't have a spare ounce on him. Maybe he allowed himself to go to pot in his final months inside.

The paparazzi managed to get shots of us having our little jog, and it got into the papers. The tabloids love any opportunity they get to tell Dad's story. In February 2009 the *Daily Mail* showed him in all his tubby glory with his blue Hackett's shirt on, blue gloves, shorts and woolly hat under the headline: 'Snooker champ Ronnie O'Sullivan's father celebrates freedom after 17 years ... by going jogging'.

They reported that Dad was now out on his rehab scheme and that he was due back in jail at the weekend. Dad didn't give them a quote, of course, but Mum issued a statement through World Snooker saying: 'We prefer to have our privacy at this time. We just want to be left alone.'

After day release came weekend release. Then, in 2010, he was finally given his full release on licence – this means that he's a free man, but if he commits any crime, or doesn't report to the police station when he's supposed to, he can be recalled to his life sentence at any time.

That was a fair old day when Dad was allowed to leave the prison premises for the first time. I didn't know what to expect. I turned up at Sudbury prison in the East Midlands, pulled up outside, walked over, got Dad and boom! We're off in the car. It was 2009.

I could probably play *Through the Keyhole* with Britain's prisons, I've visited so many of them. At least a dozen, probably more. Sudbury is my favourite – it was open, which meant they were on their way home. It was a lot more relaxed than other prisons. Sudbury was so different from the likes of Long Lartin and Belmarsh, high-security prisons that were prisons within prisons within prisons. As you walked through one set of barriers, you were met by another, then another. For 15 to 16 years I visited Dad in that kind of prison, and you'd feel you were never going to get out of there – even if you were just visiting!

At Sudbury, there were no gates, no nothing. You could walk out and you'd be on the road. So when I visited him there for the first time it made me realise, if he behaves himself he really is coming home. It was so much more relaxed than anything he'd been in before.

For me, the worst prison was Brixton – that was proper nasty. They wanted to strip-search me when I went in. I wasn't keen on that, to be honest. It put me off the place. It felt that they were humiliating me deliberately; just making a show of me.

Fast forward to Sudbury, and he gets in the car, and I can't believe it. We're together again, on the road. Or in the prison car park anyway.

'Well, where d'you wanna go?' I said.

'Well, I don't fuckin' know,' he said. 'It's my first time out in seventeen years!'

'I know a nice hotel where I've stayed before. We can go and get a bit of breakfast, read the papers.'

'Yeah, that'll do,' Dad said. 'Let's go!'

But we had all day to kill. A day's a long time, and we didn't know how to fill it. So we got there, and spent the whole day in the place. Both of us cried. Neither of us cries easily. I've only ever seen him shed a tear twice before. The first time was when I came back from Bangkok and he'd been charged with murder. I was crying, and he got choked up when saw that. The only other time I saw him cry was when he got bail, and we were driving up the motorway going to a tournament the day after he got bail. There was a song playing in his car by Deacon Blue, one of those that makes you well up, and I looked at him and he had a tear in his eye. The song was 'Real Gone Kid', and it must have felt so personal to him at that moment. It was all about old photos and records, memory and loss – and I suppose at that moment I was his real gone kid.

When we got to the hotel, and he was speaking to Mum for the first time on the phone, he was shaking. Then he let it all go. Mental. I was gutted for him. I thought, this is what prison has done for him – he's got his freedom, but he's shaking, crying, an emotional mess. But, then, how else would you be, banged up for the best part of 20 years and your first day out?

It was tough for me to see because he was my dad and my hero, and all I could think was, it's me driving the nice car now, it's me buying the breakfast, it's me supporting him. It was role reversal, and it didn't feel right. The last time we'd been together like this was at Blackpool when I was 16 and qualifying for the World Championship, and he was certainly in charge back then.

After breakfast Dad went and had his hair cut and got a manicure. Then we got a room, and spent the day there, watching the footy, chatting.

I was nervous because I didn't know what to expect, didn't know what to do. I was used to him telling me what to do, so it was weird for me to say, well, we're going here and we're going to do this and that.

Ever since he first went away I'd been looking forward to his release. It was what kept me going. Friends, journalists, everybody had spent 18 years asking me when Dad was coming out, and finally the day was drawing near. I suppose my vision of how things would work out was rose-tinted. I thought everything would return back to normal – Dad would be at home, Mum would be cooking for us all, everybody would feel secure, he'd be back running the business, we'd all go up the West End, it would be fun, the house would be busy again, he'd say the right words to me which would make me start playing better. But none of that ever happened.

The whole family had fantasies about life after prison. Not least Dad, of course. When he wasn't dreaming of a happy home life, his alternative vision was that he'd go off to Brazil when he came out. 'You can come to visit me,' he'd say, 'but I'm going to have a huge pair of binoculars here, and when you get off the plane if you've got any women with you I ain't seeing you. But if you come on your own, you're alright.'

'You're mad,' I said. For the final four or five years of his sentence that's all I heard – when I get out we'll do this and that.

None of it has materialised. Brazil? He's got a house round the corner in Chigwell.

Mum made it clear she's moved on. She changed so much when he was in prison – became an independent woman – that it was always going to be hard to try to resume life as if nothing had happened. Mum was happy with her life, in control of it, and she didn't want it being disrupted again. Dad had to accept that, and to be fair he did.

Now he's started telling me what to do again, and that can also cause problems because I'm used to being independent too, just like Mum. I've been self-sufficient for the past 20 years, and even though I make plenty of mistakes I don't necessarily want anybody to tell me where I'm going wrong. I don't feel I need to explain myself, yet I find myself doing just that because he's my dad. He does it all for the best reasons, but it doesn't always come out the best way.

Dad doesn't see the logic in the way I live my life. Maybe because there isn't that much.

'You'll always be all over the gaffe,' he says. 'You'll always be a mess. You'll always have money problems, you'll always have this ...' I suppose I could say, I'm a multiple world snooker champion, I can't have made that much of a mess of my life, but I don't bother. Dad likes to rattle cages. I don't say anything, just go quiet, get out of the door, turn my phone off and go on the missing list for three or four days, get back to my running, play some snooker and get my freedom and sanity back. I know Dad loves me, cares about me and understands me, but sometimes it just all gets a bit too intense.

Occasionally I think he tries to put me down. And that guts me because I think the world of him, only want the best for him, only try to support him. He knows he can have the shirt off my back. I've told him that whatever I've got he can have, but sometimes I feel I'm just caught in the middle of him and my mum, in the middle of him and one of my managers when he's got an issue with them, in the middle when he doesn't get on with my friends. Dad always makes his feelings known, and it can create tension. The bottom line is, these are my friends, these are the people I work with, this is my mum, and I don't want to be in the middle. My family mean the world to me, I love them to bits, but I've had it with being the middleman. If I can get on with my graft, make my own way, then I can begin to make sense of life. If I'm expected to step in for everyone else, fight their battles, I'll make a right pig's bollocks of it, or simply look for the exit door. Push me too far and I'll run. Or, as Dr Steve says, I'm prone to flight mode.

My sister Danielle gets on great with Dad. She and Dad are very similar, and it's been great for her that he's come out because it's given her back the father she never really had.

After Dad was let out for the first time, it became a regular thing. The first time he came to see me was at the Premier League. He was okay that time, but next time he appeared I realised that Dad being at a snooker tournament wasn't going to be the best thing for me. I had got so used to going on my own, having friends there supporting me, doing my own thing; suddenly having Dad there reminded me of when I was 10 or 11, and he kept telling people what to do.

'Go on, son, get the balls out,' he'd tell the fella getting the balls out, and it made me feel like a little kid again. It made me feel inadequate. I never said anything to him. I just thought, well, I don't want him to come to a major event. If I get to the final, then he can come down for the final – he comes down Sunday morning, and it's over by Sunday night. But having him there every day at a tournament was a no-no.

I had my routine, my own way of doing things. Anyone who

Running … my religion, my belief system, my way of keeping calm. (Mel Fordham)

Me and my personal trainer Tracey Alexandrou … she's a brilliant athlete and has been a constant in my life. Tracey gives it me straight. If I'm not fit, she won't pretend otherwise.

At the farm … I loved working there during my year away from snooker, but cleaning out the pigsties didn't half put me off my ham. (Tom Jenkins)

On my way to victory in the Lactic Rush assault course … it was bloody murder, but I was determined, especially after I heard one fella shout out to his mate, 'You can't let a snooker player beat you.' (Mel Fordham)

Running in Birmingham with the great Ethiopian Olympic 5,000m and 10,000m gold medallist Tirunesh Dibaba. She couldn't believe the miles I was putting in. (Alan Walter)

Me, Chris Davies, his family and friends. They promised me I'd do my PB in France and I did.

Me and Chris Davies and his wife Amanda in France. All the family are incredible runners, and I loved the fact that I became part of their extended family. Happy days.

At Woodford Green athletics club with Alan Rugg, Barry Elwell, Bernadine Pritchett and Terry McCarthy ... none of them cared that I played snooker, and most of them didn't even know. They just accepted me as a runner. (Tom Jenkins)

Me, Chris Davies's dad Terry and his mum Lyn in France ... we were staying in a hotel for £18 a night, running every day, eating pizzas, talking about running, and I thought I'd cracked life.

Love this pic … me, Lil and little Ronnie. Everything that makes life worthwhile. I took my year off the game to make sure I could get quality time with the kids.

Me, Damien and Irish Chris … vital men in my corner. Lovely fellas as well.

I'll tell Irish Chris how shit I think I really am at snooker and he just looks at me as if I'm mad. That's friendship! But here we are with a nice little world trophy.

(*over page*) In the first half of my career, it was drink and drugs that kept me on the straight and narrow – crazy though that sounds. This time round, it's been the running that's kept my head straight. Or at least as straight as mine will ever be. (Tom Jenkins)

interfered with that I'd get rid of anyway. It's non-negotiable. I've learnt over the years that I've got to look after myself first when it comes to the snooker. I don't care if that's my mum, my dad, my sister, my kids; if it doesn't feel right for them to be at the tournament then they're not going to be there. From the UK Championships onwards, I made the decision that it probably wasn't best for my career to have Dad around when I was at work, and I thought I'd rather nip it in the bud sooner than later.

We didn't really have a chat about it. We didn't need to because he came out with it first.

'I prefer watching it on the telly anyway,' he said.

'Result!' I thought.

Maybe he knew how I felt and was making it easy for me.

'Them snooker lot are not my cup of tea anyway. I don't like them,' he said.

It's true: they are a funny old bunch, but *I* like them. He's just used to a different world. My dad likes to have a laugh and a joke and push a few buttons, but in snooker they're not used to doing that. They're just there to do their job, and that's it. I learnt to fit in with that world, and it's not one Dad's used to. So it's probably the best decision he could have made for both of us not to come to tournaments with me.

He's happy enough with it.

'I can throw things at the telly,' he said. 'That's what I've been doing for the past twenty years, so why should I change now? When you miss, I just chuck something at the telly, and obviously I can't do that if I'm there at Sheffield or wherever.'

I think Dad actually misses prison a bit. When we used to have him at home at first, I'd take him back at the end of the day and he'd be back with his mates, and I'd be observing them, and thinking, he's got a good little set-up here; they think the world of him. That's not to say he wasn't desperate to come out, but he had made it home. He had to make it home to survive, and if there's one thing Dad is it's a survivor.

Then, after day release, he'd come out on weekend release. At the end of the weekend it was sad to see him. I remember crying one day when he had to go back because I'd got used to having him around. He was staying at my house, and I was in pieces when he had to go back.

'What's the matter?' he said.

'I'm just gutted that you're going. I don't want you to go back there now.'

He gave me a big hug and a cuddle. It was difficult. I'd got used to not having him around over the years. Then I got used to having him around and he'd be off again.

You hear of people who've done the kind of time Dad did who never make a life for themselves afterwards. They just don't know how to live on the outside. Some of them even get themselves back into nick for the security of it, or to see their old mates. So I think Dad has done amazingly. It doesn't surprise me because he is one of those fellas who will get on no matter what situation you put him in. It's a fantastic ability to have. I could do with some of that.

Sometimes I stay overnight at Dad's and there are periods when I'll see him every day. I've got a little bag there so I can stay over, brush my teeth, do my run from there. He makes me breakfast – boiled eggs on toast. That's why I eat boiled eggs on toast every day because he started making it for me and the kids. If I don't have boiled eggs on toast I'm done for; can't make head or tail of the day. What I like doing with Dad most these days is sitting in his flat, having a cup of tea, watch a bit of sport and get a takeaway – Indian or Chinese. Just chilling.

By the time Dad got out, Mum had got the old way of life

out of her system. She couldn't have been less interested in nightclubs. Me and Mum are pretty similar. Although she went out partying in the old days, she had Dad there and she was a young girl having fun. Now she looks back at it and thinks she was surrounded by so many vulgar people, and when he went away she saw all the people who'd come round and put drugs on the table and go: 'Here, Maria, this will get you through your grief.' She just went, 'Fuck off with your drugs.' Mum realised they weren't the type of people she should be around; they're rotten human scavengers who'd nick the eyeballs out of your head for a fiver, and she started to keep herself pretty much to herself.

Before Dad went to prison, there was no way they could have taken advantage of Mum, but when he went away they were like piranhas gathering in the water, just waiting and waiting. A few of them still occasionally come out of the woodwork, and Dad is a very forgiving person. It's a good trait to have, and I admire him for it, but I think he's too forgiving. Mum is a lot less forgiving these days. You fuck her over once, and that's it.

But I think it's much tougher being on the outside when your partner's in prison than being the one banged up. On the outside, you have to deal with the mess of life. Inside, you get your three meals a day; everything is provided for. Dad said: 'I stopped worrying about my kids, I stopped worrying about everything. I had to because in there they'll use it against you if they think you're attached to something.' So in the end he thought, well, I can't run the business from here, I can't look after the kids. Whereas my mum had to deal with everything – the lawyers, the problems, the family.

Managing relationships is never easy. Perhaps the first step is to understanding yourself better.

Working with Dr Steve Peters has made me more aware of

who I am and how my brain works, and however many sessions I have with him I'm never going to change my basic nature, and will probably always revert to type. It's about managing my weaknesses, and standing up for myself. Being with Steve has also made me more aware of other characters in my life. Thanks largely to Steve, I feel that I am getting better now at managing relationships. For example, I know if I speak to Dad in a certain way he can get agitated, so I'm focusing on talking to him in a way that won't worry him. The same is true with Mum.

Those people you're closest to tend to pounce on things when you make a point. Sometimes you're desperate to share stuff with people, but if it's going to provoke a reaction that's going to make you unhappy, you start to withdraw and keep important things to yourself. Sometimes people are just too close to you, and if you're upset with something and you tell them, they just take it too personally or it causes them too much hurt. So you offload, and then you realise you've made the situation worse because now you've got to worry about the fact that they're now worried about you. Bleedin' difficult life, at times. Whoever said it was a bowl of cherries had obviously got off lightly.

We never really get together as a family now. Mum and Dad don't talk much these days. He's been away for so long that he couldn't come out and expect everything to be the same as when he went in. But I say again: I think he has done unbelievably well since he was released.

So many people said to me: 'It ain't gonna be easy, he's going to find it hard, it could take him ten years. He won't be able to come out of the house.' And for a while he was like that; he couldn't come out of the house, he was scared of going down the shops. I thought, is he winding me up; is he really scared of going out for a bar of chocolate? But he said: 'I'm just not used to it; all this space and time, and people around me, I don't know what to do with it.' I was surprised that somebody as tough as him would say that. But now he's adjusted and he's here, there and everywhere. He's got a lot of new friends.

He's done a lot of reflecting in his time away, and has realised the lifestyle he was leading didn't do him any favours. 'Maybe I had low self-esteem myself,' he said to me, 'and I was trying to feed that by going out to clubs, and buying nice clothes and cars, but you can put a decent suit on and still feel like a bag of shite. Now I know that's low self-esteem, and I don't feel the need to dress up big or go clubbing.' He's calmed down a lot; people tend to come and see him at home, rather than them all going out together, and he's got a nice little network of people. He loves his sport, his telly, his films, and it's great that he's enjoying his freedom.

He's nearly 60 now, and he's finally given up on his dreams of being a footballer. To be fair, he gave up on that a few years ago. He was playing in prison a while ago and he said he got the ball, tripped over and went, ref!, and then realised no one was near him. His knees had gone, and he realised the game was up.

12

HEROES

'Bike at the gym, Fartlek session, a Swedish way of training – walking, running. No set distance, but I pushed myself hard enough so I felt it.'

I've always had my sporting heroes. When I was growing up, I played football, golf, tennis. But I was mad about snooker. I wasn't so much into team games, though I did like a game of football and had trials for Spurs at one point. But I felt I was an individual within a team. I never saw football as a team game – I didn't like to pass, was always greedy, always took on an extra man. I like to do something to excite myself, and that isn't the sign of a great team player. So I'd excel more in one-to-one sports. Rather than play football at dinnertime, I'd go and play table tennis for an hour, and I'd try to play with the best in the school. I was the best player in my year apart from one kid, Paul Hudson, who played for England Schools. He was unbelievable.

I found sport easy. Anything with a ball was easy for me. I think you've either got a feel for a ball or you haven't. So if I was going to kick a football or hit a tennis ball I'd instinctively know where to. Mum used to play tennis for fun with her mates, and Dad was a good semi-pro – he played for Leyton

Wingate and had trials for Arsenal and QPR when he was a youngster but never quite made it. Sport ran through the family. My granddad and his brothers were all boxers – the fighting O'Sullivans, they were called. I've never boxed, mind. I wouldn't mind having a go. I don't like fighting, but boxing is different – more of a science to it; science and ballet. I was never into fighting. That's probably why I became a decent runner – because I'd always run a mile from a fight. Not surprisingly, my heroes tend to be individuals rather than team players.

Snooker heroes:
Jimmy White, Steve Davis & Stephen Hendry

My first hero was Jimmy White, the most exciting snooker player of my childhood. Then the more I got into snooker, the more I wanted to be a winner and Steve 'the Nugget' Davis became my hero. I loved Jimmy – he was the people's favourite, the great entertainer, and hugely successful. But in the end he always fell just short – six world finals, all of them lost. I was so disappointed that I thought maybe I should make Steve Davis my role model instead because I wanted to be a winner. If I've got to become robotic and play like the Nugget to win, that's what I'll do, I told myself. He became known as Steve 'Interesting' Davis – that was a *Spitting Image* piss-take. He might have looked boring compared to Jimmy, but actually he was more aggressive than most of the other players of his time. Some of the players of his generation were so slow – Terry Griffiths and Cliff Thorburn were both great players, but I could get a quick 10-kilometre run in while they were considering a shot.

I was always a fast player because my brain worked quickly, but my style became robotic. I wouldn't move, kept everything still and just copied how the Nugget walked into shot, how his hips were, how his left leg was bent, how his right shoulder was over his right leg, how his left arm was bent, how far he was from the ball, how straight his arm was. I watched every bit, and mimicked it all. And I became more consistent, more machine-like, even though I was still fast. I still played the open game Jimmy White played, but I was more deliberate in my technique. As a junior I think my technique was as perfect as it could be. I've managed to get a few faults in my game since I was 16, and they've held me back a bit and stopped me being as consistent as I used to be.

So Davis was my first sporting hero. Then Stephen Hendry came along. I started to watch what he did and to mimic him. Where Davis was rigid, Hendry had that stillness but he was also a much more floaty player. Rather than punch balls in, he caressed them in, and he had more of a feel for break building. He was lighter in his approach, more delicate. He didn't have the greatest cue power, but around the black spot he could manufacture shots that nobody had ever seen, and as far as I'm concerned there's never been a better long-ball potter, especially under pressure. Under pressure, he's the best sportsman I've seen. So he was my biggest teacher. I played him lots of times and he taught me how to become a winner. Until then I was more likely to say: 'Well, I'll play that ball safe, just in case I make a mistake', but to do that against Hendry was the biggest mistake you could make. I'd try to put a red safe and leave the white on the cushion and two shots later he's got the red off the cushion, potted it and is on his way to clearing up. And he was the only one who played such audacious shots. I thought, if he's doing it and he keeps winning, he's obviously doing the right thing and the rest of us are doing it wrong.

In 2002 we had a ridiculous falling-out, and he didn't speak to me for three years. That hurt because he was my hero. But it was entirely my fault. Well, my fault and my mate the boxer Naseem Hamed's.

I was down watching Naz training and he said, when you play you've got to say I'm the best, I'm this, I'm that, and I was like, well, it's not me. Then I thought, well, maybe he's right and I'm wrong and I need to start being like Naz. The end result was I questioned Stephen's sportsmanship over a ball that had been called a miss ages ago (mad, because he's the best sportsman in the world), and announced in a press conference that I was going to send him back to his sad little life in Scotland. Jesus, I blush just remembering it. As soon as I said it I thought, what am I doing, I love Hendry, he's my hero. But I was listening too much to the advice of other people. It worked for Naz, who was brilliant at talking himself up, but it just wasn't me. Then when I told Naz what I'd said, he went: 'Oh no, what d'you go and say that for?' Even though Naz got me in shit, and not for the first time, I love him – his heart's in the right place, and he loves me and his family love me. Having said that, I'd never listen to him again, never go to a mosque with him again, never have a pep talk from him again. I'll have a bit of grub with him, but that's about it. He's huge these days – physically, that is. He looks like an Easter egg in boots.

I played Hendry in the semi-final of the World Championship in 2002, and it was a brilliant game, 12-12, and then I went 13-12 up and I had a red with the rest. I was shaking, and I missed the red, and he won five frames on the trot to beat me 17-13. I came off thinking he raised his game when I bottled it. The closer he got to the winning line, the more he went for his shots, the more aggressive he became.

That's what made Hendry unique. Even if you look at a great talent like Judd Trump, he sometimes plays more of a percentage game when he gets into a winning position, turning down shots that he would normally go for. He has a tendency to screw back to baulk just in case he misses when the pressure's on. Hendry was the opposite, and that was really intimidating. He was a train with no brakes, and at his peak matches were over almost before they'd started.

The difference between Hendry and Judd Trump, as he is now, is that Hendry went for it when it mattered. Hendry was 18 when he won his first world-ranking event and 21 when he won his first world title, and his record is unequalled. Judd is a good player, and he has won the UK, but he's got a long way to go before he starts even to glance at Hendry's record. Selby is a very good match player. Ding is a good player, but I think he's got a mental issue that stops him winning as many tournaments as he should do. I love Ding. In the Masters in 2008, he burst into tears when he was playing me in the final. I hated seeing him like that. He's a fantastic talent, but it's all about doing it in the final stages of the big matches, and that's where Hendry would have anybody. Tiger Woods, Roger Federer and darts player Phil Taylor are the only three sportsmen you could put in that bracket; when the pressure was really on, they went up a gear.

Tennis heroes:
Roger Federer & Serena Williams

Roger Federer is another of my heroes. It's the ease and grace with which he plays. Look at his rivals – Novak Djokovic, Rafa Nadal and Andy Murray are all amazingly good players, but they rely more on their athleticism so eventually their body will break down. Federer played so much within himself that he avoided injuries. He never spent much time on the court – it was always 6-0, 6-1, 6-2, and it was effortless. In all sport, it's a huge advantage if you can kill a game off early and conserve energy. He's light on his feet, incredibly graceful. He's the only non-grunting tennis champion I can remember. Even now, when he's past his peak, he still gets to semi-finals and finals of grand slams, which is an amazing achievement. To be ranked third or fourth in the world at 32 is another great achievement. And he has broken so many records throughout his career – more than 300 weeks at number one in the world, a gob-smacking 237 consecutive weeks at number one from 2004 to 2008, 17 grand slam victories and (hopefully) still counting, seven Wimbledon titles (along with Pete Sampras).

He never bottled it. Even when he got beaten, they'd nearly always be great matches with both players giving their best. When he lost to Rafa Nadal at Wimbledon in 2008 over five huge sets it was one of the greatest matches ever.

Tennis is my favourite sport to watch on telly – you get all the angles, the rallies. Golf is the worst to watch on the telly. They hit a ball and if you're lucky you see it land, and that's it. I like watching boxing, too. But really I watch for the players, not the sport. I'll watch Federer, Djokovic, Serena Williams, but not just anyone.

I love Serena Williams: she's the queen. What a record she's got, too. For me, it's not just about ability or style, it's about maintaining that standard over a career. That's what makes a player truly great. Serena has had so many problems with injury and illness, and personal tragedy in her life when her sister was killed, and then there were the critics who said that the Williams sisters were just part-timers and didn't really care about the game (like they'd said about me) and each time she would battle back and prove them wrong. Perhaps I shouldn't separate them – the Williams sisters are heroes of mine, Serena and Venus.

But if I had to choose it would obviously be Serena – so much power and passion, never knowing when she's beaten. Also she's like me in some ways. I think she's a lovely girl who doesn't like conflict, but sometimes finds herself in the middle of fights when she has been wronged. I always think of that time at the US Open final when she threatened to stuff the ball down the lines (wo)man's throat. Well, obviously that ain't a good thing to do, but think of the context – she had just wrongly called a foot fault, Serena was one set down, 6-5 down in the second set, 15-30. So the wrong call took her to 15-40, match point down. No wonder she went bonkers. Don't get me wrong – 'I swear to God I'm fucking going to take this ball and shove it down your fucking mouth' is not a measured response. Definitely worth a bit of a fine. But it just shows how much it matters to her. Serena is 32, and still miles ahead of any of her rivals in the world. In 2013, she regained her world number one spot, and in doing so became the oldest number one in the history of the sport. Perhaps this is even more incredible than Federer's achievement (though, having said that, he's had the greater competition throughout his career). In 2003, she won the Serena slam – holding all four grand slams simultaneously. Serena has won 16 singles grand slam titles at the time of writing (plus 13 doubles and 2 mixed doubles), and my bet is as you're reading this she's already won more. Phenomenal. *And* she scrubs up nicely.

Running heroes:
Haile Gebrselassie, Tirunesh Dibaba, Kennenisa Bekele &
Mo Farah

As for runners, I loved Haile Gebrselassie. What a story and what a man. Like so many of the great Ethiopians, he learnt his sport by running miles to and from school every day. He was one of 10 kids brought up by his parents in the hills of Asala, 160 miles south of Addis Ababa, and in the dry season he ran six miles to school and back every day. Things weren't so easy in the rainy season. Then he couldn't take a short cut across a river bed, and his round journey became 15 miles. Haile ran his first marathon when he was 15.

He's an amazing role model – for the people of Ethiopia and the rest of the world. He won successive Olympic gold medals at 10,000 metres in Atlanta in 1996 then in Sydney in 2000. Perhaps even more amazing, he just continued running into his thirties and in 2008, at the age of 35, he broke the world record for a marathon in Berlin, recording 2 hours 3 minutes and 57 seconds. He broke his own record by 27 seconds. Incredible. Gebrselassie then went on to become a role model as a business-man, running hotels, gyms and garages, and giving hope to so many Ethiopians.

He grew up in absolute poverty and is now worth tens of millions of pounds. He gets at least £250,000 for every city marathon he runs in. But running has never become work to him. He just loves it, and every morning he puts on his shorts and runs into work. Now there's a man who's got the buzz.

The fella's only 5' 5" and he's got superhuman strength and stamina. Apparently, he once ran 60 kilometres – he claimed it was just a nice little trot that took him four hours. Mad. Like my other heroes he dominated his sport for years. Decades in his case.

Kennenisa Bekele is also an incredible distance runner – which makes Mo Farah's achievement in beating him at the 2012 Olympics in London even greater. Bekele comes from this tiny village about 80 kilometres from Addis Ababa called

Bekoji where nearly all the young kids dream of escaping poverty by becoming runners.

They all go running at the crack of dawn, coached by this little fella called Sentayehu Eshatu, a retired teacher, who has trained half a dozen gold medallists, including Bekele, Tirunesh Dibaba, Deratu Tulu, Fatima Roba and Kennenisa's younger brother, Tariku Bekele. Kennenisa won silver and gold respectively at 5,000 and 10,000 metres in Athens in 2004, then followed up with double gold in Beijing. Ridiculous.

What I love about Kennenisa is the ease with which he raced. If they wanted to go fast, he'd go fast, if they wanted fast laps then slow laps, he was happy with that. It didn't matter how the others wanted to run the race, he was always aware of what was going on, and knew where the threat was and knew when it was his time to go; and at his peak when he did go nobody was going with him. He didn't even bother looking back. He knew nobody was going to get past him. That's what separated him from the other runners. I watched him once in the world cross-country championships and his shoe came undone. He was in the lead, and had to stop and put his shoe on; it took him about 20 to 30 seconds, the others overtook him, then he just made his way back through the pack with such calm determination and won the race. I thought, he's given everybody a 30-second start and still won the race so how much more has he got left in the tank? That was when I thought, this fella's special. You just knew he'd be able to pull them back and maintain his pace to outsprint them at the end. And to think Mo Farah beat him at the 2012 London Olympics . . .

Mo Farah's feat in taking double gold at 5,000 and 10,000 metres off him in London is impossible to overstate. What an achievement. He was only the fifth man ever to pull off the double. To be honest, I didn't think he had a chance beforehand, but the work he put in, training at altitude in Kenya, leaving his family back home, giving everything, really paid off. He transformed himself as a runner through sheer discipline and hard work to become the first British man ever to win double Olympic gold in these events.

Mo tells amazing stories about how he walked away from his honeymoon when an ash cloud interrupted their flight back from Zanzibar and he told his wife that she and their daughter would have to make their own way home while he went back and trained in Kenya. But that's what it takes to be a great world champion. He's incredibly cool under pressure – and not just on the track. He became the first contestant, celebrity or member of the public to win the jackpot and beat the Cube in the TV game show *The Cube*, and won £250,000 for charity. *The Cube* is all about pressure – contestants have to stand in a 4 × 4 × 4-metre Perspex cube and complete challenges. It's claustrophobic just looking at it, never mind being inside it.

In 2009 I met Tirunesh Dibaba and was star-struck. She's one of the greatest distance women runners ever, and also comes from Bekoji in Ethiopia. In 2008, at the Beijing Olympics, she won double gold at 5,000 and 10,000 metres, and in London 2012 she held on to her 10,000-metres title – that made her the first woman to win back-to-back Olympic gold at 10,000 metres – and this was after she had been out for 16 months with injury in 2010–11.

I met her in a hotel in Birmingham where she had had to pull out of the Aviva Grand Prix because of injury. We had a lovely little chat and I showed her my weekly running schedule to see what she thought. She said she couldn't believe the miles I was putting in. I had so many questions for her – what pace she trains at, how many track sessions she does, how many laps, how she psyches out her rivals. I wrote down all my questions before meeting her because I was worried I'd be so nervous in front of her that I'd forget everything I wanted to ask.

She's a lovely girl and suggested I go and train with her in Ethiopia. I'd love to give it a go.

Golf hero:
Tiger Woods

Tiger Woods is relentless. He's such a competitor. People say he was the first billionaire sportsman. He became a business, a brand, yet he retained that focus to be the best he can be. He's not won a Masters for five years, but for me he's still up there. The exposés about his private life coincided with his loss of form. Before that he'd won the US Open on one leg when he was injured. That's how good he was. He had that air of invincibility. Then there was the time away from sport; he had the horrors in his personal life and other players caught up with him. You read the comments about him and realise there are a lot of Tiger haters out there, but that always surprises me. Even when he smashes his club and spits on the floor I still love him; that's part of his desire to win. He's just psyching himself up, and when you're out there you just become a different animal. I don't think people realise that you're not always conscious of what you're doing out there. Tiger the golfer is different from Tiger the person. It's the same with all the world's great sportsmen. They give off that air that they're the boss, and Tiger's no different.

Darts hero:
Phil Taylor

Phil Taylor is the greatest sportsman in any sport. Sixteen world titles: who gets near that? He did me the honour of coming to watch the final at Sheffield in 2013. The geeza's awesome. He never looks as if he's going to lose. Does he ever not hit a treble? He's unbelievable. Snooker and darts have one thing in common – sums. But that's the only thing. I would say snooker is closer to golf. Both are still-ball sports. If the ball goes off line, you've got nobody to blame but yourself, whereas with all other ball sports it's more reactive – you have to react to what the opponent or team-mate is doing to the ball and you're on the move with the ball. With golf and snooker, everything points back to you.

Coaching hero

Ray Reardon was a great coach for me. He was a funny mix – so relaxed in some ways, so demanding in others. He was, like: 'Go into the club, have a little practice, get out your cue and if you don't feel like it put it away, have a cup of tea, chill out, relax, come back to the table when you're feeling better, yessssss.' Ray is very funny. 'Go and play some golf, you've got all the time in the world, come back later.'

That was a pep talk from Ray. Fantastic. The funniest man I've ever met. Ray is my hero, the king, I love him. Perhaps he should be a snooker hero – after all, he won the World Championship six times – but he's more of a coaching hero and all-round-person hero to me. He is a father figure, granddad figure to me. I felt that man loved me, and that was so important to me.

I worked with him in 2004, the second time I won the World Championship. Ray taught me things that only a mathematics genius could know. I adopted his philosophy, and for a time I played every shot Ray Reardon would have played. The games became long, drawn-out matches. I became like Mark Selby, the Torturer. Pre-Ray, whenever I played a match I'd come off at the interval (after four frames) and look at my screen at the other matches and see 1-1, 1-0, and think, Christ, they're going to be there all night. But when I started working with Ray I'd come in at the interval, and I'd look at my screen and they'd already be back out there playing, 4-2, 4-3. And I'd think, what's going on here? I was torturing my opponents. I became a nightmare to play against.

It was a new way of playing, and I understood why that game was getting me results and why I was now being classed as the complete player, but it felt weird. I wasn't blowing players away, I was outtacticing them, outthinking them. Ray would think so many shots ahead it was incredible. He once told me that if you get a respotted black, it would go like this: he plays this shot, you play that, he plays this, you play this, he plays that, and on it went. Anyway, one day I thought I'd try this against John Parrott and it was an eight- or nine-shot sequence and Ray was absolutely right. That's how clever that geeza is. He played snooker like chess. Ray knew what shot he'd be playing in four shots time, whereas I'd just go bang red, split 'em open, make a mistake, game over. Ray taught me how to play snooker like chess.

Did I like playing like that? Well, I won the world title and learnt a huge amount along the way. But after a year and a half with Ray I felt I needed to get aggressive again and do it my way. I knew I had his game to fall back on, and it gave me confidence. I could go back to playing aggressively, and then I had the more defensive game to resort to when things weren't going well.

In the end, though, Ray got a bit too much for me. I couldn't cope with the play-this-shot, play-that-shot, and if I didn't play a shot the way he wanted he'd get the hump. It put a lot of pressure on me and I felt I couldn't please him. Every time I made a mistake he'd be going: 'Ohhhhh!' That's how I felt anyway. He was a harsh taskmaster. I'd be telling him my hips aren't right, my stance isn't right, my head's not right and he'd just say: 'Oh no, don't worry about that, put the ball here, put the ball there, don't worry about that.' And I'd say: 'Well, I am worried about my stance and my head because if I can get those right potting the balls is easy, but you're asking me to do something I can't do at the moment because my cue action is so shit.'

He couldn't get his head round that. He just said I was unplayable. 'You're unbeatable, Ron. You pot better than anybody and you've got the defensive game.' It might have been true theoretically, but if your head's not screwed on right it doesn't count for anything. He used to say: 'Once I make you impregnable you'll be unplayable.' He was right to an extent, but I suppose the bottom line is I like to play it my way.

A friend who was sitting next to Ray in a match said to me afterwards: 'If he could have got out there and played the shot for you he would have.' And that put pressure on me. In the end I was playing terribly in the UK Championships against Mark King, and I started going for everything, thinking this will give Ray the hump. I knew he'd go mad. I came in at the interval and I was going to say: 'Ray, drop me out, I ain't having it', and as I came in I said to my mate: 'Where's Ray?'

'He's gone home,' he said. 'He got up and walked out of the crowd and went home.'

That was the last time we worked together, and we haven't talked about it since.

I was shocked when I discovered Ray had gone. But he knew what had happened. He knew he'd done my head in, and just went. But we still love each other. I don't speak to him much, but I know I'm welcome to go down to his house in Torquay any time and he'll put me up. The time I spent with him was one of the best 18 months I've had with anyone.

His one-liners, his little laughs, his manner, were so funny. He'd slaughter people in the nicest way. You'd listen to him and think, he's ruined that person but he's done it with a smile on his face, and you'd think, I wish I had that skill! And it is a skill, make no mistake. Just before a match, when people came up to us, he'd say: 'Right, shop's open. No more talking! See you later! Bye bye!' He'd say it to everyone. He took no prisoners, and I was the opposite. I'd think, how can you say that to people, but he'd be like: 'No. Shop's open, time for business, shop closes later, then it's time for fun.' Basically, fuck off, get out of the way, we're here to do business, ta-ta, but always with a smile on his face. And he was right to say that.

I saw Ray after I won the World Championship in 2012. He was sitting just behind me in the crowd, and I was winning 17-11, one frame short of victory, when I caught him. He just gave me a little look, and I thought, blimey, he's watching me. Pressure! But he was so happy when I won.

Ray couldn't stand Scouse John, who's one of my best mates. I think he misread John. Every time Scouse John has been at Sheffield I've won because he makes me laugh. Ray didn't realise that, and he got the hump with him. John used to call him Raj, not Ray. It drove him mad.

One day we were in Brighton, having breakfast. Ray's a class dude: smoked salmon, poached eggs, he's chatting to the girls who love him, he's immaculate. Every day we're sitting there, overlooking the sea for breakfast, and it's all well classy. Then one day we get there and there's a camper van in front of us – Scouse John's camper van. And Ray's going: 'What's this? What's this? Where's the view gone?' I can't say it's Scouse

John's van because he'd just go: 'Move it. What's he doing here?' So he goes to the woman in charge and says: 'Can you find out whose van this is, and get rid of it?' She comes back and says: 'It's Mr O'Sullivan's.' Typical Scouse John that is.

Even though he ended up walking out on me, I like to remember the good times with Ray. He's a gentleman. Snooker brainwise, he's the best coach I've worked with. There have been a few other decent ones. Frank Adamson, an old boy from Bristol, was good. He's around 80 and has supported me massively over the years. Frank looks at light and lines, and I couldn't be more different. So in the end, to spin his head out I said, here, look at this, Frank, stood on one leg, played it left-handed and started rifling balls in. I have to prove to people sometimes that what they're saying is not the only way.

In a way the best coach I've ever had has been myself. I've always learnt from people when I've watched them. I can watch a player and know why the ball's doing this or that, and I'll take that in and say, okay, I'll use that. I did it with Steve Davis and now I do it with all the youngsters on the circuit today.

Rock friend hero:
Antony Genn

Antony used to be with Pulp as a kid then went on to form The Hours. He has been like a brother, top mate, heart of gold, one of the funniest geezas you'll meet in your life, and he can eat chocolate for Britain. I love him to bits. He's a bit of a sensitive soul, like me – we take things to heart. He's a northerner. I love northerners.

It was 2008 when I first met him. I won the World Championship, but was in a terrible state personally – splitting up with Jo and caning it. I was incredibly fit – but I was also abusing my body like there was no tomorrow. I met Antony at Sheffield, but we didn't really get chance to chat. He was with Damien Hirst, and they both seemed like nice fellas – not that I knew anything about them. We swapped numbers, and a couple of weeks later met for a bit to eat at the Ivy. We had some dinner, and I was looking at these two blokes sipping their Perrier water and Antony was telling me all the addiction horrors he had been through – that I was going through. Maybe he was on a mission, and could tell I was in pieces. To be honest, he looked so fit and together I didn't really believe him.

A few weeks later I was in a terrible state at my mum's house – couldn't move, fever, sick, pissing blood. The doctors initially thought it might be my kidneys, and put me in a hospital ward full of old men wearing colostomy bags. They did tests, and my kidneys were fine. None of the doctors could work out what was wrong with me, but I knew – it was payback time for not looking after myself.

When I started to feel better, the first thing I did was call up Antony and ask him how he got clean. We started going back to NA meetings, but I couldn't really cope with them. So Antony said, no worries, why not just hang out with me. And that's how we got close. We'd meet for lunch or dinner, just chat, there was no temptation because he didn't drink or take drugs. He and Damien showed me a different way of living, and since then I have been clean. I'll stay clean for them because I don't want to lose my friends, and I don't want to be around them if I'm wrecked, so they have become my motivation. Whatever state I'm in I can pour my heart out to Antony. If I'm in a state I know I can ring him and he'll always some say come round, there's a bed for you at mine.

Artist hero:
Damien Hirst

Only one candidate here, and that's my mate Damien Hirst. On the outside people see this mega-rich artist with an attitude to match. But his outward persona is so different from who he is. He is perhaps the most generous and kind-hearted person I've ever met. He's been my wingman during three championships, of which I won two. He's made me laugh when the shit has truly hit the fan.

He's one of the few people I want around when I'm playing. He's invested so much time and energy in helping me through those difficult times and I don't want to let him down when I'm playing.

Damien comes to lots of tournaments with me – Sheffield, Wales, Gloucester, Germany, Premier League. I've hardly ever lost when he's been there. He plays a lot; he's had a break of 40-odd, and he loves snooker. He can come in at the interval and I know the player is trying to fuck me about, and he'll say: 'What's his game? Why's he doing that? Don't let him freak you out. But if you do get beat, fuck it, we'll go to London and have a good time. Who gives a shit?'

Damien came to watch me in the 2008 World final. I didn't have a clue who he was at the time. He came down with Antony Genn. Gradually I got to know Damien, and we just got on great.

He came to about five or six tournaments a couple of seasons ago. He stayed for all 17 days at Sheffield – he went back home for his kid's birthday, then came straight back. He said, I've got to go and do the birthday with the boy, but I'll be back – bang! Sylvia, his PA, is a big snooker fan so it was just like the three of us. And when I took my year out of snooker, I said to Sylvia, it feels like I'm never going to see you again, because snooker was our way of meeting up. She said: 'No, no, no, it won't be like that' but I was right – I didn't see Damien for about nine months. The snooker was a great excuse for Damien to say, I'm not working for a week.

Damien did me a massive favour with Rolling Stones guitarist Ronnie Wood. Ronnie and I go back a long way now – years ago, when he was still with his wife Jo, me and Jimmy White used to go round to theirs and play snooker epics while getting slaughtered with him and Keith Richards. One night we were off our heads and me and Jimmy just hit century after century. It was probably the best we've ever played, and nobody was there to see it except a couple of blitzed Rolling Stones. Keith said I was the Mozart of snooker – I may not be up on classical music, but even I know that's a compliment.

Anyway, every so often one of Ronnie's family would ring me and say: 'Can you help get Ronnie straight? He's got to go on tour – he's in a state and Mick wants him straight.' I think they called on me because they knew all about my past, and that I was an addict who really was trying to keep straight despite my relapses. Ronnie could never get it, and so his family had come to see me as the best person to come down and take him to the Priory. I think for Ronnie it became a bit like, oh, here we go again, ring me up, go down the Priory, show willing, but he knew he wasn't going to get clean, he was just doing it to keep the family off his back. I'd taken him to the Priory a couple of times after being summoned to the house.

By now, though, Ronnie seemed to be in a worse state than ever. He'd gone off with the Russian girl I was indirectly responsible for introducing him to. It was the premier of the Rolling

Stones film in 2008 and we were on a mission. It was just after the World Championship and I was like a lunatic, hanging out with the Stones' kids, just an unbelievable night, and it ended up with me, Jimmy and Ronnie stuck in a hotel room at about five in the morning, and I've gone, come on, let's go to a club, so we end up going to some London bar, so we get a couple of girls, and Ronnie only goes and falls in love with a Russian girl. This was the year of my binges.

Ronnie's going: 'Thanks, thanks, for the night', and I'm like: 'What are you talking about, you need to get a flight soon.' And he's still thanking me.

The next day I get the phone calls: 'Where's Dad? Where's Dad?', and I said: 'I left him in his hotel room at seven this morning and he looked all right. He was in bed, and I had to go.' And Ronnie's son Jamie was saying: 'But he ain't turned up!' Anyway, he did manage to get the flight to Kenya to join the family. When he came back from there I put him in the Priory. He didn't intend to get clean, not because he didn't want to but because he didn't know how to.

He then came out and was holed up with the Russian girl in Ireland and his family were in pieces.

This time when Jamie rang me I was at a loss as to what to do. So I thought about it and said: 'I think I've met somebody that Ronnie might listen to; that he might respect.' I think Ronnie respected me as a person and as a player, but we'd done too many drugs and too much drink, too many nights out for him to take me seriously as the rehab man. I thought, Damien is a hugely successful artist, so Ronnie, who is a very good artist himself, will look up to him, and I thought maybe I could persuade him to do it for Damien.

I hardly knew Damien when I asked him if he could do me a favour. He said: 'Yes, what is it?'

'Ronnie Wood is in a bad way,' I said. 'His family are worried sick, and he needs to get away, can you help? I can't do any more – he's not listening to me, he's not listening to Mick Jagger.' Addiction's such a powerful thing that not even Mick knew what to do with him, but I just had an instinct that Damien would be able to help. I'm not the most clued-up person, but sometimes I can put things together and can see things working out. And boom! It all happened so quickly.

Damien said, leave it to me and he and Antony hired a private jet, and Damien phoned him up, and said, where are you? He said, I'm in Ireland, and Damien said, right we've got to come and get you. So he went over to Ireland to get Ronnie with Antony, who has been clean for well over a decade and has been there and done it. Antony had done all his research – he said, I'm not just banging Ronnie up in the Priory, we're going to do this properly. Damien and Antony didn't know Ronnie at the time.

He couldn't get out of his house in Ireland because it was surrounded by photographers waiting for him to emerge with the Russian girl. But they managed to smuggle him out of the back of the house under a blanket, into a car and on to a plane. If it had been me I'd have said: 'Just get in the fucking car, Ron, you're life's fucked, who cares?' But they did it the right way. He said: 'We're sending him to this place in England, make sure he's got no mobiles, no this, no that, there's no fucking about here, it's one month intense.' It was classic Ronnie as he went in – 'I've got to have a drink before I go into rehab.' So they stopped off to let him have a pint and they got there. I phoned Antony and said: 'How did it go?' and he went: 'Fuck me, it was a long and emotional day!' But Ronnie went there and got well.

When Ronnie came out he moved into Antony's for a week or so, and Antony looked after him. Then Damien rented a house for him, and the day he moved in a big lorry pulled up outside; it was full of art equipment – stencils, pencils, paints, brushes, boards, you name it. Damien did that all off his own back. They've all stayed mates, and Ronnie has stayed clean, which is brilliant. Ronnie obviously takes the credit for that, but Damien and Antony played a massive part.

Along with Irish Chris, Damien is my man in the corner these days. I met Chris through AA, and he's another motivation to stay clean as he's one of my best mates and I want him in my life. The great thing about Chris and Damien is that I can be myself with them. I'll tell them how shit I think I really am at snooker and they just look at me as if I'm mad. That's friendship!

Although Damien and I had great fun, and he's been a brilliant support, we've never been on a bender together. He's been straight ever since I knew him. Damien has been an amazing friend to me. He thinks I've got autism. He says: 'The way you play snooker, it's like a form of autism.' I think it's a compliment! He means that the way I play is beyond teaching and he might have a point.

Before I met Damien I didn't have a clue about his pickled sharks and horses and butterflies and what not. I didn't know he was the most successful artist in Britain. But now I know a bit more about art I know just how talented he is. I was with him the night he did his auction at Sotheby's in 2008 and made a fortune. The funny thing is we weren't actually at the auction. We were in a dingy snooker hall in London's King's Cross.

Damien decided to flog an entire show called 'Beautiful Inside My Head', and nobody had ever done that before.

Well, nobody had ever done that before and made so much money.

Damien gave me a ring before the auction and told me about it and then said he wasn't going to be there for it.

'What's going on, Damien?' I said. 'Why are you not gonna be there?'

'Well, normally when an auction's going on I just go down the Groucho Club and hit a few balls,' he said. 'It's too much for me to be around it, and I just get someone to ring up to tell me what's going on. And I just love playing snooker.'

'Right!' I said. 'I'll bring the balls and the cues and meet you there.' And he was like: 'Yeah, lovely, come down.'

So we got there for around 6 p.m., hit a few balls and the auction was kicking off at 7 p.m. No one knew what to expect because the banks had just gone bust and nobody knew whether anybody was going to spend money. Then the first lot came up and Sylvia said: 'D'you want me to tell you how much it goes for?'

Damien went: 'Well, course I do.'

Sylvia was taking the phone calls. 'Five million,' she said. It was meant to go for about £3 million.

'Five million for the first lot?' I said. I couldn't believe it. My head was rushing – £8 million, £9 million, £13 million, £14 million, £850 grand for an ashtray.

I went: 'That ashtray just got eight hundred and fifty grand and there are another two of them!'

As the auction went on, I thought, I've just got to start potting balls to take his mind off it. So I started making a few breaks, doing the shots, entertaining him, and we had a good night.

'Why are they paying so much for an ashtray? I don't get it,' I said to him.

He started laughing. I couldn't get my head around it. And after an hour and a half he finished with £111 million. My head was gone. To be fair, so was his. We just got back to the hotel, and me and Ronnie and my little mate T and a few others were sitting in Damien's room, but he had just disappeared. I thought, where's Damien gone? Antony texted me to say: 'We've had to get out and get another room just to lie down!'

The thing that's surprised me most about Damien is his ability to cook. He really is a genius in the kitchen. When I stay at Damien's for four or five days, I'm on a mission to eat as much as possible because I don't know when I'll be there next. Pizza, lasagne, roasts, curries, he can turn his hand to anything. If you ask me he's an even better cook than artist.

Damien made a painting for me of the 147 I made in record time in the 1997 World Championship (5 minutes 20 seconds, seeing as you're asking). I can't keep it at home because I've not got a wall big enough for it. It's the same size as a snooker table – 12 by 6. I don't know what it's worth, but it must be a fortune. He kept saying to me, have you got a wall 12 by 6 in size? And I'm like, what are you talking about?

I'd heard he made paintings for people, but I just thought, I don't want him to do anything for me, I just like his friendship. I've always been like that with people – I'm not good at accepting gifts. I don't want to be a sponger. Bollocks to that. So whenever he asked about my wall I just ignored him. Then one day I got a call saying: 'Damien would like you to come down to the studio' and I thought, oh no, he's done something for me, but I didn't have a clue what.

I was just walking through the studio when he said: 'What d'you think of that?' and I looked at this painting, and just went: 'Wow! That's my 147! I can see what you've done. I can see where the balls are.' It was the most beautiful thing. He said: 'If it isn't right, tell me, and I'll do it again.' I was like: 'No, it's perfect.'

13

DODGY DEALINGS

'Sunday morning, Epping Forest, easy eight and a half miles. Did not enjoy my run, lost my love for it at the moment, it feels like an effort.'

When you're involved in a sport you hear all sorts of rumours about what's going on. I think there are elements of corruption in any sport. In snooker, there must be players who think they could make more out of this match than they could probably make out of my whole career if they just take a bit of a fall. We're all doing maths with our careers. And there will be players who say, I could give everything to my next five years and if I'm lucky I'll make £50,000–£100,000, or I can throw this match or frame and make £100,000, maybe get away with it, and continue playing as if nothing happened.

That's how I reckon some snooker players must think. They like their money, they like their gambling, they like a certain standard of living. If they can get away with it, they will. I could think of seven or eight who have done it. I reckon 80–90 per cent of it is at a lower level, then there are a couple at the top level who would do it.

I was shocked when I saw the story in the *News of the World* about John Higgins apparently agreeing to chuck frames. It was a sting operation, undercover in a hotel room in Kiev, and the paper alleged that he had agreed to lose four frames in four different matches for €300,000. John issued a statement the day the story came out saying he'd only agreed to it because he was shitting himself and wanted to get out of the room alive. He reckoned he was talking to the Russian mafia and didn't want to end up swimming with the Kiev fishes. In the end, he received a six-month ban for giving the impression he would breach the rules and for failing to report the approach made to him and was fined £75,000 but was cleared of corruption charges. 'If I am guilty of anything, it is naivety and trusting those who I believed were working in the best interests of snooker and myself,' he said when he was banned.

In a way John had a bit of a result. He could easily have been thrown out of the game for longer, perhaps even banned for life. His manager, Pat Mooney, looked like the guy who was instigating it, but obviously John was there in the room and they've got him on camera saying: 'Oh yeah. Frame three I'm going to lose, yes, yes', and that was never going to look good, whatever his excuses.

To be fair to John, I don't believe he would ever throw a big tournament.

I wasn't only shocked when the news about John came out, I was also upset. John and I have always been close – as friends and rivals – and he's a hero to me. Only Hendry has ever played the game like him and an even bigger desire to win. In the post-Hendry generation, I suppose it's often been me and John fighting it out for the major tournaments. Our families have also got on well. I'll never forget how generous he was the first time I won the World Championship, and how the first thing he did was pass on his congratulations to my dad. So I'm glad he's managed to put the *News of the World* sting behind him. I'm sure it taught him a lesson.

In October 2012, Stephen Lee was suspended by the World Professional Billiards and Snooker Association after allegations of irregular betting patterns. It wasn't the first time there had been allegations made against Stephen. In February 2013 the WPBSA dropped charges against him in relation to matches played in 2008 and 2009. The charges all related to betting and entering into an agreement to influence the result of the match.

It's a shame that he's got himself suspended because he'd got his form back, he got back up to number eight in the world, won £200,000–£300,000 last year, was doing well for himself. His form was as good as it had been for years. Stephen has denied any allegations of wrongdoing through his lawyer, Tony Miles. 'He does not accept that he has been involved in any breaches of the rules and regulations and is gravely disappointed that a decision has been taken to bring proceedings against him.'

While I sincerely hope Stephen is found innocent, if he is not he obviously wouldn't be the first player to succumb to temptation. I'm not sure what goes through their minds, but throwing matches is never going to end up well.

There had always been rumours that this kind of thing went on. I remember the South African snooker player Silvino Francisco being arrested in 1989 after he'd lost 5-1 to Terry Griffiths and it was discovered there'd been heavy betting on that score, but he was released without charge (though he was later jailed for three years for smuggling cannabis). But all the gambling stuff was hearsay till the John Higgins sting. Then, when Barry Hearn came in to run snooker, he said, we're not going to tolerate this; we're going to police the game properly. Barry actually put a superintendent on the investigating panel looking into betting scandals. It was a deterrent as much as anything – he was saying that if anybody was tempted to break the law, they would be caught out.

I was once offered money to throw matches, but I said no chance. Someone rang me and said he'd like to meet me over in the forest and have a walk through the woods. I knew the fella, and it was someone you don't want to mess around with. I thought, fuck me, what have I done wrong here, I'm in trouble. When people say that to you, you think, hold on, am I going to come back alive?

Typical that it was Epping bloody Forest, too. The same place I went to run to get my peace of mind.

I met up with the fella because I didn't know what it was about. I was nervous. There was just the one fella. 'Alright, Ronnie, how you doing?' he said.

'Yeah, I'm sweet,' I said, though I felt anything but sweet.

'We'll just go for a little walk up here,' he said. Jesus. I thought, okay we'll just go for a walk. You don't want to get on the wrong side of these people. They're nice enough as people, but you still don't want to piss them off. I try to have nothing to do with them so they don't have any reason to dislike me.

'You're playing in the Premier League,' he said.

'Yes.'

'And we've got people who can put big bets on.'

Oh, great, I thought. Just what I need.

'If you lose this frame and this frame we can get enough on it to make some money. We'll give you this out of it.'

What they were offering me, 20 grand, I could get for a couple of nights' work. Not that the amount would have made any difference. I just didn't want to be there, let alone talking about throwing a match. So I told him straight I couldn't do it. They were perfectly nice about it.

'No problem, Ron, fair enough, we respect your wishes.'

The whole thing lasted about 15 minutes. He was good as gold. I think he respected me for being straight and upfront. That all happened about 10 years ago. It was the only time I've been approached, and I came away thinking, blimey that was a bit weird.

If anyone could get away with it, I could. I could just play one-handed, or left-handed, or just put a towel over my head and pretend I was going nuts. But it's not something I would or could do. I couldn't live with myself; I'd feel that I was robbing somebody.

I think my honesty goes back to when I was a kid and I was a bit of a liar. I'd get in trouble at school, lie about nicking money out of Dad's wages – those little packets that came through the door, I'd take a fiver out of them. And I got to the point where Dad slippered the lies out of me. In the end, I just couldn't lie, and that has followed me all the way through. In some ways I wish I could lie. Everybody else seems to be saying one thing but meaning another. Dad is basically honest, but whereas I say everything I'm thinking, he'll be like, no you shouldn't say this, you shouldn't say that. I suppose I'm a compulsive truth teller. I find it difficult to be any other way because then I just feel as if I'm spewing out words.

14

BACK ON TRACK

'Tuesday, gym, Terry. Fifty minutes. Weights, top half, chest, thighs and shoulders, sit-ups, worked hard and felt strong.'

I trained hard yesterday, it was tough for me, but I felt okay this morning. It's April 2013 and I'm just beginning to get back to fitness. Last year, after winning the World Championship, the running fell by the wayside. I was just getting back into it when I broke a bone in my foot on a run – the metatarsal, a common bone for footballers to break. When I broke the metatarsal I was gutted. I was getting fit at the time and I was running with my mate Alan. We'd had a lot of rain, it had been First World War trenches, but this was a nice sunny day. We were running through the forest, putting a few nice little efforts in, and there was a woman walking with three of her dogs – big dogs, Staffies. And I thought, fucking hell, here we go; I've been chased by a few dogs when I've been running so I slowed down and as I did I went boom! and twisted my ankle. I tried to run through it, but this time I couldn't because it was so painful, and I knew I'd done something bad. I hobbled back to the car, went to hospital the next day and they said, you've broken a bone across the middle of your foot.

For three months I was on crutches, then for the next three I wasn't in the mood for training. So I put on a bit of weight, got fat, no snooker, and cranked myself up to 13½ stone – two stone heavier than when I was at my fittest. I'd put my clothes on, they didn't fit, and it made me feel shit.

There's six weeks to go to the World Championship and I want to be at my best for my comeback. This means a lot to me. Now I've said I'm coming back I don't want to make a show of myself.

Today I did some one-to-one training with Tracey. She's been a big part of my life. I've known her since I was 15, and I really admire her because she's one of those who walks the walk. She's 50, looks brilliant, comes third and fourth in loads of the local races, always number one veteran. She's a fantastic athlete, and has always been there for me. Tracey Alexandrou has been a constant in my life. For 20 years on and off she's been training me, though only seriously for the past 10 years.

Rather than just running, I decided to train with Tracey because she does lots of core strength work. Typically we'll meet in Hainault Forest down the road, do maybe a mile warm-up, then she'll put four cones down and a bench, and I'll do 20 dips, run round, 20 dips, run round, 20 dips, run round. Then it will be 20 press-ups, run round, 20 press-ups, run round. Murder. Each circuit was like a boxing round – three minutes. At the end we'd run back, but I had to walk back because my legs were burning.

'Trace, I'm done, man, I've hit the wall.'

'What d'you mean, you've hit the wall?' she said.

'I'm done, I'm slaughtered, we've got to stop.'

'Don't worry, darling,' she said. 'You've worked really hard, you're really fit, you've done great today.'

She's lovely, so supportive. If I'm not fit she won't say it for the sake of it. She gives me straight talk, and that's what I like and need.

I suppose there are a lot of people in my world who don't talk straight to me. Mum, Dad, my mate Irish Chris, Kimo, Damien, Antony, Tracey, my Scottish mate Chip, whose son is an unbelievable snooker talent (four foot nothing, 12 years old and already under-14 champion in Scotland), they all talk straight to me. But I've learnt over time that a lot of people have an ulterior motive. Although most of them care about me and like me, I know they are also saying things to me because it will benefit them.

That's not people in general, just some people in the snooker world. Basically, they don't care if I'm depressed, in pieces, so long as I'm out there playing, potting a few balls, and making them look good. It's not nice to find that out about people. I've always been a bit naive, but as I head towards 40 I'm beginning to see the world for what it is.

Even people who are rooting for me, such as my manager Django, if the relationship is professional there has to be a mercenary element to it. Django has come from a tough background, a bit like my dad, where he had nothing and with him every penny and every shilling counts. Django's done brilliant things for me and he'll always be my mate, but when it comes to work we have different mentalities. I wish I had his ruthlessness. I love him, and he is the best cook in the world. I'll always owe him for showing me how to cook a decent Chinese!

Django thinks I'm a soft touch. He calls me the ATM – the automated cash machine. 'You've got so many people poncing off you, right left, and centre,' he says.

'But I don't care, Django,' I say.

'You've got to stop it.'

'But I can't help it if there are vultures out there,' I tell him.

While Django's always had my best interest at heart, plenty are interested in nothing but the money. When I quit snooker as I've said I want to do a bit of media, radio, television, commentary, interviewing. But I don't want to be controlled by some corporation, at their beck and call. What I do want – and need – is something to get me out of bed in the morning; something to occupy me. A bit of media, a few personal appearances, motivational talks and I'll be happy. If I can do something, a social event, and somebody comes away saying they really enjoyed it, well, that will do me nicely.

The least vultury people I've ever met have been through running. And I've met lots of them. There was a period when I was picking up strangers by the day. I became a proper running tart. It was Dad's idea really. 'Why don't you just treat tournaments like a training camp?' he said.

So when I went to tournaments I'd get my friend Terry McCarthy from Woodford Green Athletics Club to get in touch with the local running club and hook me up with a runner.

Terry the fix-it-man would give me a ring. 'Alright, Ron, I've got Eddie for you in the morning and Trevor at night.'

Lovely. So he'd leave me the number, I'd give them a bell and say: 'Eddie, I'll be up Saturday so if we can meet Sunday. That would be great.'

Boom. Job done. I come downstairs in my shorts at 8 a.m., look for another fella in shorts. 'You must be Eddie?'

'Yeah, you must be Ronnie?'

'How far d'you want to go?'

'Five or six,' I'd say. And we'd be off. We wouldn't have a clue what each other was like. Sometimes you'd think, God, this geeza's quick; occasionally you'd think, cor, he's a bit slow. But nine times out of ten you'd think, he's run 34 minutes for

10 kilometres, he's quality. I picked up a lot of my close friends this way.

I was lucky to belong to such a good club – Woodford Green has produced loads of brilliant athletes, including Sally Gunnell, who won a gold medal in the 400 metres hurdles at the 1992 Barcelona Olympics. There are so many great coaches and runners there, and they have contacts with runners all over the country. They put me in touch with a bunch of lovely fellas. I was just about to go up to Telford for the UK Championship, so I asked Terry if he could help me out.

'I've got Chris Davies in Telford,' Terry said. 'He's done 10 kilometres in 28.37.'

'You're havin' a laugh, aren'tcha, Tel?' I said.

'No, you'll be alright with Chris. He's a lovely fella.'

Chris was Terry's hero. Terry said: 'Oh, there's a good club in Telford, and Chris Davies will meet you for a run with a group of people. He's the bollocks.'

So I got up there, and a woman called Claire met me. Then we walked round to the house and I met this fella – massive legs but a tiny body. I thought, he can't be a runner. Most of them have skinny little legs. As he was talking I thought, blimey, he must be Chris Davies, but he can't be, he looks wrong. Then we started to run, and I realised it must be him.

We ran through a forest and then a thing called the Wrekin, which is a legendary hill that can pass as a mountain. Apparently, from the top you can see 15 counties, and it inspired Tolkien's Middle Earth in *The Lord of the Rings*. Awesome. And that's where they did their Sunday morning long run.

'Look, I can do about nine miles,' I said, 'but I'm playing today so I don't want to go mad.' I got up the hill quite comfortably and then found Chris Davies running alongside me. So I thought, I'll up the pace a bit, not run as fast as I can, but just put it in. So I gave it a go, and I thought, this geeza ain't even out of breath by the end. I was blowing out of my arse, and he was just casually chatting away. He was on another level.

Chris ran in the Commonwealth Games, and he was a postman. They've moved from Telford to Stoke where his in-laws live, and he trains up there now. The whole family runs – his brother-in-law does 2 hours 20 for the marathon, his girlfriend runs 35 minutes for 10 kilometres, his other brother-in-law, David Webb, runs 2 hours 15 for the marathon and competed in the last World Championship. And his other sister, Sian, runs 34 minutes for 10 kilometres. Imagine that little family set-up. Mad. But lovely people. They'd come and watch me play – Chris, his dad, Claire, and another runner – but they weren't really interested. They were just there as support, which was great. Then we'd go out for dinner, have a Chinese and talk about running. We were all running bores.

There seemed to be an inverse correlation between how well I was doing in my running and how well I was getting on with Jo. The more time I gave to running, the more our relationship suffered. She thought it was self-indulgent, and she probably had a point. But I'd made such great friends through running – normal, decent people who weren't into all the celebrity crap – and I wanted her to realise how special they were. But it just didn't happen. It didn't help that I was no good for anything after exhausting myself while I'd been away.

Jo was the nicest person on the planet when I felt shit. I'd ring her up, tell her I was depressed and she'd be so supportive. But if I'd just won the World Championship, we couldn't seem to be happy together.

I was often at my happiest when I was running, but running became a running sore between me and Jo, if you'll excuse the pun. She thought when I was running I should be with the kids, or that I spent too much time with my running mates. When we rowed it was often running-related.

After a while I had a runner in every port. There's Jason Ward in Sheffield who is an absolute legend. I was going to the World Championship and I was in the best shape of my life. I'd won the five-kilometre race in Epping, and this was when I got it into my head that I wanted to run for Essex, and that I'd happily give up snooker if only I could achieve that – even though there would be absolutely no money in it for me. It was a mad pipe dream.

I'd just come 180th in the southern cross-country league on Parliament Hill. There were 1,200 people competing, pretty much all of them decent runners. There were a few plodders, of course, but 1,000–1,100 of them would have been serious 35-miles-a-week people, and then you had the top boys who were running 27–28 minutes for 10 kilometres. They were flying machines – the best of the best. Well, I was never going to challenge them, but I'd just done 35 minutes for 10 kilometres and I was in good shape. I'd come 27th in the Essex cross country. So I'd got sharp, super-fit without really realising it.

It was 2008, and I said to Terry, get someone for Sheffield because, if all goes well, I'm up there for 17 days. Terry's on a website called Eightlane, which is for all the people who are into running, and he knows all the decent runners in the country. Terry was a good runner in his day, but now he just takes the class at the club on Tuesday nights. So it was Terry who got me in touch with Jason.

'I've got you a really good guy up there,' he said. 'He's called Jason Ward and he runs five kilometres in fourteen minutes.'

'Fucking hell, Tel, you winding me up?'

'No, class athlete,' he said. 'But you should be alright with him. You were alright with Chris, weren't you?'

'Really?' I wasn't so sure. With Chris, there'd been a few of us running. I was daunted, intimidated by him. So I phoned him before.

'Alright, mate, it's Ronnie here.'

'Yeah, I'm alreet,' Jason replied. 'I've just done five kilometres in fourteen minutes.'

'Fucking hell, you're on fire,' I said.

'Aye, not bad, not bad. Good race, decent pace.'

I was terrified.

So I got up there and texted him, and he took me on this route. We drove just out of Sheffield where he does a lot of his runs, and we ended up doing about nine miles. I was so fucked. When you've got a good runner you worry that you might be slowing him down; you don't want to ruin his run. I went as fast as I could so he'd want to run with me next time because I liked the fella. If I was blowing out of my arse, I'd tell him: 'Look, Jase man, I've got to slow down', but at the time I was fit. I could have gone out with anyone in the world at that time and given them a good, steady run. Anyone in the world is happy to run at six-minute miling. Mo Farah? He'll say, six to seven miles at six minutes will suit me down to the ground. At the end, I got in the car and thought, Jesus, that was a run.

The only problem was I had to play in the World Championship in a couple of days and I was already knackered. I got back to my hotel room, had a shower and just lay on my bed for an hour and a half. I was gone. I thought, I've got to go to do some practice now, but I couldn't.

Running had taken over my life. I knew straightaway that Jason was a nice guy. We chatted loads about running. I'd ask him where he ran, who he knew, what courses he'd done, what mileage, what sessions. I was a running junkie and a running information junkie. I could talk all day about running. I was your ultimate running bore.

When Jason isn't running he's one of the area managers for Iceland. He's got a good job, and it suits him down to the ground because he can run to work, run home. He said he could have devoted himself to becoming a full-time athlete, but he had a good job, and you wouldn't earn much as a top athlete unless you're Mo Farah. Jason is a pacemaker for the London Marathon – so you'll get the top guys going for 2 hours and 16 minutes, and Jason would have set the pace for about 20 miles for this lot.

I told Jase that I loved the first run but it had killed me. 'It was just too far,' I said. 'I've got my snooker and I'm happy to do that pace for five miles, but another nine miles would just see me off.'

'Alreet, mate, we'll just do a fiver next time,' he said.

He became a great friend. We just ran and ran. He's started coming to the snooker, and we hang out. It's nice to know he's in the crowd, supporting, even if he doesn't really care about snooker. I always say to him, look, there's a ticket, if you're bored you don't need to bother, but he normally turns up.

Jason was a typical runner. He wasn't a snooker fan and hadn't heard of me before. They are a different breed of people. They're not into money or status or what you do for a living; they're just into their running. Now every time I get to Sheffield Jason is the first person I call. If I'm in reasonable shape I'll run with him, if not I won't bother. I don't want to waste his time.

When I was away in Sheffield or Telford with Jason and Chris I was at my happiest. I'd get depressed about the thought of going home. I felt sad when I left. I had such a bond with these people, and they didn't want anything off me. We just ran and ran.

Occasionally, I'd hook up with someone abroad. One time I was in Malta, talking to the gym manager, Nick.

'Yeah, I'll come out running with you,' Nick said.

'I just want to find a couple of routes round here.'

'Yeah, we'll run there and back, it's about five miles,' he said.

'All right, lovely. Sweet.'

So we went out and he set a good pace, and he said, right we'll turn round now. I thought, well I know the way back, so I'm off now. Boom! And I lost him. I got back to the gym, and they said, where's Nick, and I said, well I turned and went and when I looked back I couldn't see him. I was really fit then; on the way back I was probably 5' 30" miling, which is good going. Next day when he came back he said: 'Fuck me, you can run!' He was a fit guy, but he wasn't a proper runner.

Some of the best running I ever did as with Eamonn Martin, the last Englishman to win the London Marathon. I was training with the six best runners in Essex and we were doing anything from 800 metres to six miles. One kid could run the 1,500 metres in 3 minutes 50 seconds, and we had one fella who could run 10 kilometres in 29 minutes. They were animals, so I wanted to train with them. I did about three months and got so fit. When I took my top off I was ripped to fuck. I was working hard with my personal trainer, Tracey, at the time, too. Some days when I went to train with Tracey I'd be so knackered we could only do strength stuff because I was too exhausted to run around. This was 2009, the year I beat Mark Selby in the Masters. I remember looking at my face at the end, and I was gaunt as hell.

I'd get up in the morning after a training session with Eamonn and I couldn't walk for about 15 minutes. A typical hill training session with Eamonn was Monday night. We'd meet up and start with a two-mile jog to the hill, with a stretch for 20 minutes, so that would take you about 45 minutes. Then we'd do the training session which was six x one minute up the hill – you'd run up the hill for a minute as fast as you could. I'd be at the back but I'd be hanging on for dear life. Then you'd jog back down and do it again. Six times all in all. Then we'd do 6 x 30 seconds up the same hill, jog back down, then 6 x 45 seconds and jog back down. Then we'd have a breather, change our clothes, put some warm stuff on and jog back for two miles. All in all the session would take two hours. It was a beast but I loved it.

Then on a Wednesday we'd do longer reps – anywhere between three and five minutes. So we'd split up into two groups, and I'd be in the slower group, and we'd do three minutes, then five minutes, then three minutes, totalling about 30 minutes of quality running. It would be the equivalent of six x five minutes, plus the two-mile warm-up, the stretching. Again, the whole session would last two hours.

On the Saturday we either raced or we met over in Basildon at Langdon Hills and we had this little route. They'd give me a head start and I'd run with the record-breaking half-marathon champion Nick Weatheridge. He was carrying a bit of a belly, but he could still go out and do nine miles at five and a half minutes, no problem. He's a class athlete. He's like me with snooker. I might not play for a year, then can still come out and hit a century.

Nick would give me a head start of about 30 seconds and our rep would be about three minutes, but Eamonn would be waiting at the finish point, so when I got to two and a half he'd say, come on, and he'd push me all the way. Nick would get past me after about two and a half minutes, and as soon as he came past I thought, I've just got to hold on. We'd do about six x three minutes on a Saturday. The faster boys would do the longer loop. We were going as fast as we could.

Eamonn has got a dodgy hip and has just had a replacement; he's in his mid-fifties and I've learnt so much from him.

It took me an hour to drive there, an hour back and two hours for the session. So twice a week I was taking four hours out of my evening. I didn't mind, but Jo wasn't happy about that. I became super-fit, but because it caused hassle at home I thought I better back off. When I went back down the gym, they couldn't believe how fit I was. But I'd been training with proper athletes. I could do any machine, I could train for two hours, I never got out of breath.

2008, when I was at my fittest, was the year of my running triumphs. I've won three races, all of them in that year. My first win was probably the greatest. It was a fun run in Epping to raise money for Rhys Daniels, a girl who died of a rare degenerative disease called Batten's.

I'd just won the world championship. All my wins came around that time when I was at my fittest.

My second victory was a handicapped race at Orion running club. Everybody was handicapped so the slowest runners went off first and the fastest last. So, say, somebody runs five miles in 45 minutes and I run it in 27 minutes, she would start off 18 minutes before me. The idea is that everyone comes in roughly together. I was one of the last to go off, and I thought I'd never catch the two in front of me. I ended up winning that race, which was a great feeling, and I won a cream cake or bacon sarnie, something like that!

The third race wasn't a pure run – it was an assault course

called Lactic Rush, devised by my personal trainer Tracey, and about eighty people took part. It was a criss-cross course with loads of obstacles, so you could see the others as you were running. One of the fellas shouted out to his mate, 'You can't let a snooker player beat you.' And I thought, right, I'll have you for that! He was just winding me up, and it worked. It made me more determined. He was an army bloke and was good over the assault course – up mud hills, through streams, over tyres, so I just watched how he got over it and copied him. I stayed behind him, conserved a bit of energy, and watched how he went through the assaults. Then over the last mile his shoe came off and I went boom! As soon as I got in front, he died. I won it by more than a minute in the end, which was a lot considering we ran the first six miles together and it was a seven-mile assault course. That made the *Brentwood Gazette*, which gave me a buzz. I won £100 of vouchers. Result.

Soon after that I went on a running holiday to France with the Telford mob – Chris who runs 10 kilometres in 28 minutes, his brother-in-law Mark who runs the marathon in two hours twenty, his wife and Mark's sister Amanda who runs 10 kilometres in 35 minutes. There were a few others with us from Telford – slower than Chris and his family, but decent nevertheless.

The trip didn't start off well. We got to the ferry at Portsmouth and I realised I'd forgotten my passport. I had to get a courier to bring it, and that delayed the trip by ten hours. The others went off except for Chris and his dad Terry, which worked out great because I could just talk about running to them. I had them all to myself, but I felt really guilty because I thought these people are going to have the right hump with me now and think I'm a nightmare. But actually they were lovely about it.

We got to France, and I was a bit nervous because the guys are obviously proper athletes. It was probably how an amateur would feel playing me at snooker – fuck me, I'm in trouble here. But they didn't make me feel like that at all; they were so encouraging.

Terry told us the idea behind the holiday. 'We're gonna get PBs,' he said. 'You're gonna get a PB,' he said looking at me. 'She's going to get a PB, Chris won't get a PB but he's going to win the race, and Mark's going to do a good time in the half marathon.'

Mark, who is a top man, said he wasn't going to do the half marathon because he wasn't fit enough, but he was going to pace me round the 10 kilometres. 'You will be getting a PB tomorrow,' he said, like he was stating a fact.

We got to Caen in the north-west of France, booked into our little hotel for £18 a night. Next day, me, Mark and Chris went for a jog, just to keep our legs turning over. I thought fuck me this is going to be fast, but it wasn't. It was a leisurely jog, and this is when I discovered that top athletes were happy going out running 7-8 minute miles, and not going flat out all the time. I studied the way they trained and raced, the same way I studied snooker players.

We had breakfast together, enjoyed each other's company. Amanda beat 3,000 people to win the 5 kilometres for women in 15 minutes on the Thursday night. Then we had the 10 kilometres, half marathon and marathon to come.

So Mark paced me round and said just stick in with me. At 5 kilometres I was gone. 'I can't do this,' I said to Mark, 'it's killing me.'

'Up on your toes,' he said. 'Chest up, chest up, up on your toes, and keep on the balls of your feet.'

'I can't, Mark, I'm fucked.'

'You're doing well,' he said. 'Chest up.'

Every time I slowed down he went 'tuck in behind me, tuck in behind me'. So I just tried to hang on.

When we got to four miles I started to overtake some runners. I thought fucking hell, we're picking a few off here. It gave me confidence. He said, 'You're doing well, you've got another mile and a half to go.'

'I'm fucked, Mark, I can't keep going.'

'No you can. You can.'

I had a mile to go and I was thinking I must be running a good time.

'You're on for your PB,' Mark kept saying. 'You're on for your PB.'

My PB was 35 minutes 50, so anything under that was great.

'You've got half a mile,' Mark said. 'Keep going, keep going.' I knew I wasn't going to stop by then. I thought I've come this far. I'd learnt that you can run in a lot of discomfort. We got to the last 400 metres and Mark went, 'Right, go! If you've got anything left, go!' And I sprinted like a lunatic and got over the line in 34.50. I couldn't believe it.

Chris had come in at 30 minutes. I sat on the side, and said, 'How d'you do, Chris?'

'Yeah,' he said, 'I won it. And you beat your PB.'

Then Terry, Chris's dad, came over and said, 'See, I told you, you got your PB. *You got your PB!*' He was ecstatic. I caned my PB; beat it by a minute – five forty miling, good running.

I was made up. My family life was a mess, but I was so happy just then with my running friends in France. We had pizzas, watched the World Cup and I thought I'm around beautiful people, I've just got my PB, I'm a running bore, I've won the World Championship, I'm staying in an £18-a-night hotel, no one's drinking, no one's taking drugs, I ain't got to worry what

I'm eating because it's just burning off, I thought I've cracked it, I've got the recipe for life.

The next day we got up and they said we're going to the beach. It sounded great, but you knew there'd always be a run involved along the way. So we got there and Chris said, 'Right, I'm just going for a little jog with Amanda, d'you want come?' and Mark said, 'Yeah, great,' and I joined them. Mark and I ended up doing a five-mile run at a lovely pace along the beach, just shorts, no top, no trainers, and we were flying. We must have been six-minute miling along the beach, and I didn't even feel tired. I felt as if I could do this for ever. I'd worked hard to get to this level of fitness, but it was worth all the effort – life doesn't get any better than this. It was the happiest I've ever been.

15

RONNIE'S HANDY RUNNING HINTS

'24 minutes, 3 and a half miles, easy felt good, nice rhythm, trying to kick my legs back at my bum and stand tall.'

Break those distances down

I've been fortunate enough to work with some good trainers over the years and people who give you good advice. The easy thing to think is you've got to run loads and loads and loads to get faster and fitter. In fact, to run fast you simply have to run fast, and to do that you have to break it down into mini-segments and interval work. The idea with interval work is that you run a lot faster than you normally would, but not to the point where your technique is suffering. But you can run 400 metres faster than you can run a mile so you break that mile down into four reps of 400 metres, so you do 4 x 400 metres off a two-minute recovery. In other words, you have a two-minute gap between every 400 metres. The advantage of the recovery is that you can run each 400 metres faster than if you ran one continuous mile flat out.

Listen to your body

You also need to listen to your body. A cliché, but true. I would often go out and get injured because I was overtraining, pushing myself too much, trying to get too fit too fast. If you've got that mentality, you'll end up knackered and unable to train so it becomes a vicious circle. The best advice I ever got was from Chris Davies's dad, Terry, in Telford. He trained a lot of the good runners up there. I'd train the first day, then a second, and the third day I'd go running and I'd have to stop. I went to have a massage and my calves were so tight, but I didn't realise it was my calves till I had the massage. So after I broke my foot I phoned Terry up and said: 'Look, I'm really out of shape because I haven't trained for seven months. I'm struggling, carrying a lot of weight.' He said: 'Look, just do twenty minutes every other day for the first five or six weeks.' So I did that: I was able to run with no injuries and after four weeks I found myself getting faster and faster, not having to stop as much. In short, I was listening to my body; not overdoing it. I was enjoying each run I went on because my muscles weren't killing me. It's hard to listen to your body when you're obsessive! But if you get too enthusiastic, you're just going to end up on the runners' scrapheap. As I write, I'm being sensible. Not as fit as I have been, but doing nicely enough. Getting there slowly. Every other day I do my nice little four-mile loop because that's all my body can take at the moment. To push it further would be silly. Once I get three or four months' training under my belt I'll push it a bit further.

Run tall

There's lots of advice you can give on posture etc., but then again there are so many exceptions to the rule I'm not sure how worthwhile that advice is. For example, I watched Paula Radcliffe run and her head bobbed like a crazed chicken's – hardly classic – but she was winning all her races. So I thought, I'm going to try that, and it worked for me because it stopped me thinking about having sore legs. I was just focusing on bobbing my head about. But you tell any coach that and he'll laugh you off the track.

Coaches will tell you that to run well you've got to feel that you're running tall. When you're not fit you slouch and sit on your hips and your stride gets shorter. A lot of the time I used to sit on my hips and shuffle along because a lot of the runners I ran with were long-distance runners and they shuffled along on a shorter stride. To increase your stride you've got to do a lot of drills – get your knees up high. It's hard to change your natural stride pattern, though. People tend to have a naturally long or short one, and sometimes you just have to go with what you've got. But the fitter you get, the stronger you get; the less you sit on your hips, the better the rhythm you'll have. When I wasn't fit and I was tired, I had a tendency to run out of energy; then my shoulders would slacken and I'd sit on my hips and shuffle along. But when I was fit I always felt I was pushing the top half of my body through, and that makes you feel you're having a good run. And if you feel you're having a good run that tends to become a self-fulfilling prophecy.

Run on the balls of your feet

The best runners run on the balls of their feet because it's quicker, whereas if you go heel-toe, heel-toe you're doing more work for the same distance. If you go toe-toe, toe-toe, you're going to have energy and be quicker, but it's hard to run on your toes. When I'm running well I feel my feet are hitting the ground quicker, but I'm still not running on the balls of my feet.

Give those fry-ups a miss

My ideal diet would be a slice of toast before I run, then porridge for breakfast when I get back. Then I'd have tuna salad at lunch and fish with boiled or jacket potatoes for dinner and natural or Greek yoghurt with a banana and a bit of honey. When I'm not training I fall back into the bad roasties and fry-ups habit, but when I'm training I just can't do it. I used to run a food diary as well as the running diary. As I say, I'm obsessive. If I was tempted to eat something bad, the diary would stop me because I knew I'd have to write it down at the end of the night.

16

MAD MOMENTS

'Felt sluggish, don't enjoy easy run, weekend mileage 25 miles.'

I have my moments. My mad moments. Unplanned and, until now, unexplained. I'm probably as famous for doing daft things as I am for my snooker. But my mad moments haven't come unprompted. Yes, there was a reason why I walked out in the middle of the Stephen Hendry match in the UK Championship; there was a reason why I put a cloth over my face when I played Mark King. There was even a reason why I gave myself the world's worst skinhead in the middle of a match. It's time to fess up.

Walking out on Stephen Hendry

It could have happened in any of the previous half-dozen matches. It was 2006 and I was playing in the Premier League, against Steve Davis in the semis and Jimmy White in the final. Jo and I were going through a terrible time, and my head was completely up my arse. I didn't want to be at the tournaments. My brain wasn't right. I wasn't happy.

I played Davis, was 3-1 up, and missed a ball and went to

shake his hand because I just wanted to walk out. And as I did, I said to myself: 'What are you doing? You can't do that!' I was 3-1 up! It was the Premier League, the tournament before the UK Championship, which was in York. So I just about stopped short of shaking his hand and sat back down again. My mind, though, was, shake his hand, get out of here, you've had enough. But I held back and went back to my chair.

I pulled myself together, won the match and got through to the final against Jimmy White. I was 4-0 up, had barely missed a ball, I was potting really well and then, boom! I missed a ball, he cleared up, and it went 4-1. In the next frame I missed another ball and I did the same thing – I went up to shake his hand.

I thought, Jesus, that's twice on the trot. I didn't do it, but the thought that I'd wanted to do it was worrying enough. I was in such a mess because of the state of my home life that I couldn't face being there. I felt like the loneliest man in the world. I didn't really know what I wanted. I didn't want to be at the tournaments, but nor did I want to be at home because I was so miserable there. I suppose the bottom line was that I wanted a happy home life.

Lily was just a few months old at the time. She was absolutely gorgeous, adorable, but even her presence couldn't help improve things between me and Jo. Before Lily was born we argued like most couples do, but we always got through it. Then, as soon as Lily was born, things took a dive. If we hadn't had Lily I would have just left at that point. But I felt this overwhelming guilt and sadness. I was determined not to mess up as a dad as I had done with Taylor, my first daughter.

So as I went to shake Jimmy's hand, again I thought: 'What the fuck are you doing? You can't do that. You're 4-1 up, then 4-2 up, you're going to win the tournament, what are you doing, you nutter?' So I got through the match, won the tournament, but I had a feeling that wouldn't be the last of it. And it wasn't.

A pattern was developing. I'd almost walked out twice, and then I was at York for the UK Championship and I'd won two rounds before playing Stephen Hendry. But in both matches I'd felt the same – I wanted to walk out. I managed to hold back, though. Then I was up against Hendry. I was playing terribly, couldn't pot a ball, played a bad shot, went into the reds, 4-1 down in the quarter-finals, he was playing well, and I thought, fuck this, I'm out of here – I'm going straight out and I'm going to have a night of it.

It was about 4 p.m., and I was thinking, I've got a couple of my jockey mates up here, they like a good booze-up. I'm going to get smashed tonight, absolutely wasted. Even though I was still running well, I didn't feel good in myself. It's funny: to the outside world I looked in great nick – healthy, trim, fit. Everybody was saying, you're looking well, but I was in pieces. I wasn't eating my way out of depression, but I was running my way out of my depression. But even the running didn't always do the trick. And now I just wanted out.

It was the first to nine, so Hendry still needed another five frames to win. We weren't even at the halfway mark, but I simply didn't want to be there. I turned round, shook the ref's hand, shook Hendry's hand, said: 'Good luck, Steve', and walked out. Since then I've seen Stephen Hendry's reaction on YouTube, and he just didn't know what to do with himself – did he stay there or walk out? – and he was saying: 'Well, what do we do now, Jan?' to the referee, Jan Verhaas. And Jan was: 'Well, I suppose it's game over because he's conceded.'

A few people in the crowd shouted: 'Come on, Ronnie! You can't do that!' and I thought, well, I can do what I like really.

Why can't I do that? Not surprisingly, everybody started talking about my mental issues and unstable mind.

Nobody could believe what I'd done. Least of all Stephen. He was quite gracious about it at the time. He must have realised there was something really screwy with my head for me to do that. 'I didn't have an inkling anything was wrong,' he said after I'd walked. 'He seemed in good form beforehand and we were chatting backstage. Ronnie's obviously got his reasons and I'm not going to criticise him. He just said he had had enough and wished me good luck for the rest of the tournament. Only he knows what he feels inside. I can't criticise someone else for that, but I've never seen anything like it. It's just bizarre.'

I issued a statement apologising for my behaviour. 'I wish I could have played a better game today, but I had a bad day at the office,' I said. 'Anyone who knows me, knows that I am a perfectionist when it comes to my game, and today I got so annoyed with myself that I lost my patience and walked away from a game that, with hindsight, I should have continued. I'm sorry I didn't stick around to sharpen him up for his semi-final. I'm also really sorry to let down the fans who came to see me play – it wasn't my intention to disappoint them, and for that I am truly apologetic. At this present moment in time I am feeling disappointed with myself and am hurt and numb, but I am a fighter and I will be back on my feet fighting stronger and harder than ever very soon.'

But that wasn't enough for most people. Most of the pundits thought I was a disgrace to the game and had brought shame on snooker.

I think it was inevitable that I would walk out of a tournament. There was something in me that wouldn't be satisfied until I'd done it. It was just a matter of time before I got into flight mode. It did cross my mind to get to the final and just not turn up. I thought that would be the ultimate thing to piss the authorities off. Part of me just wanted to have a go at World Snooker. I'm not saying this is the action of a man who was thinking at his most logical. But I also had people revving me up in the background. Friends were telling me they couldn't get in the players' lounge and they couldn't get into matches, and they were encouraging me to have a pop at World Snooker. My mates the Scouse twins Bobby and Les were revving me up – nice guys, love 'em to pieces, but they are wind-up merchants. And they kept saying that the authorities were this and they were that, and they had a point; some of the people in the World Snooker hierarchy might be jobsworths who just want to make your life difficult but that's my working environment and I have to get on with these people.

It's important for me to keep it sweet with the authorities, but the Scouse boys didn't want to keep it sweet – nor did they want me to keep it sweet. I was a bit of an idiot for listening to them, really; for letting them wind me up. For a while it became like a war between me and the authorities because I felt my mates had been wronged. And that was just daft.

When I walked out there was a fair old hooha. The fallout was worse than I imagined it would be. I couldn't understand why they made such a big fuss. I wasn't feeling well, I was depressed, Stephen Hendry's had a bye: happy days. Then they fined me £25,000 and I thought, what the fuck! What's happened here? They came down hard on me and I thought, I can't do this again. When they fined me I was fuming. It made me feel even more alone.

That night I just got absolutely smashed. I phoned my mate, one of the jockeys, and said: 'Dino, we're out, mate!' He came over to the house and just assumed that the match was over.

The Scouse twins, Bob and Les, were with me as well.

When I got home I told Jo what had happened. Because I was so down, she became supportive again. That's how it always worked. She said: 'Don't worry, it's the best thing you've ever done. That's your truth.' I went: 'My truth? That's not good. I've just been fined twenty-five grand. That ain't good.'

I thought the fine was too heavy, but they were right to fine me. After all, I was a liability if they thought I could walk out in the middle of any match. And if the fans thought I might do that, maybe they'd do the same thing – or just not turn up in the first place.

I sat down with Rodney Walker, who was then chairman of World Snooker, and told him I was depressed and had family issues but said I didn't want to go into them. 'I'm having a hard time, not finding it easy, and I cracked,' I said. 'As you know, I'm quite highly strung and when I get it in my head that I'm going to do something I do it, but it was really because of personal stuff going on at home.' It was the truth – but not the entire truth. I didn't tell him the bit about being so pissed off with World Snooker.

'Okay,' he said. 'No problem, glad you told me.' But they still shoved it up me with the fine.

Perhaps they also worried that I'd set a trend and other players would start walking out of matches, but I don't reckon they had much to fear on that front. Other players aren't mad enough to do it.

The fans turned against me a bit. I got a couple of boos when I played a match in Preston, then when I played in the Masters at Wembley, which was the very next tournament. John Parrott was slating me, saying, if he isn't stable then he should get his problems sorted out and come back to play snooker when he's ready. I thought that was wrong – kicking a man when he's down rather than showing a bit of empathy. Hendry was good about it. He said that for me to have done that I must have had a lot on my mind. But the others just said I had no excuse – if you're a pro you just go out there and play.

At the Masters the pressure was really on me. I'd just walked out, and everybody was asking what I'd be like; whether I'd play well, whether I'd even stay long enough to know if I was playing well. That was the tournament in which I beat Ding in the final and he started crying. The reason I won that tournament was because I was sitting at home on the Sunday when Ding was playing and he was really flying, and John Virgo said: 'This is the new guard, this is the guy who's going to take over the mantle from Ronnie O'Sullivan.'

I went, cheeky bastard! I love John, but I thought, Christ, you're writing my obit a bit premature, Virgo. It gave me a reason to go and win the tournament. Perfect motivation. I never said anything to John about it, but I remembered it and every time I was on that practice table I thought about what he had said, and how I had to shut my critics up.

Ironically, then, it was Ding who I met in the final and he was playing really well. He went 2-0 up, and I thought, I've got a right battle on here. But I knew my form was okay – coming and going – but when it came it did so in spades. So I thought, wait till I've got a bit of form and just see how he responds with what I hit him with. I didn't panic when he went 2-0 up, then it went 2-2, then 5-3 at the interval – I'd outplayed him, out-fought him, by then, and he knew he was in for a hard match because I was playing some nice shots.

Then it got to 9-3 and he wanted to walk out. Funny because Ding is the last person you'd expect to do something like that. Maybe he was taking a leaf out of my book. Ding started crying, and then it was the interval with me only needing one more frame, and he went to shake my hand. I thought about my own problems, and said to him: 'No, mate. You can't do that. They are going to ruin me, and they'll ruin you if you do it. You cannot do it.'

Well, when I say that's what I said to him, it's what I got Django to translate for me, and I put my arm round him and said: 'Come and have a cup of tea.' Maybe he was so gone that he didn't know the score or he thought he'd already lost. So we went and had a cuppa and I said: 'Your mum's watching, your dad's watching, this is bollocks, one more frame and it's over.' He was sobbing. I took him into my dressing room and Django was with us. I said to Django: 'Tell him he's got to go back and play, everything's sweet', and I asked him if he liked racing cars, Ferraris, and said we could go down to Brand's Hatch for a day.

He started to chill out. His manager, Gary Baldry, was there, and I said: 'He's got to go out and play.'

'Yeah, I know,' Gary said.

'Come on, let's go out and do one more frame, get it over and done with, and that's it, otherwise World Snooker and the press will slaughter him just like they slaughtered me and that's no good for him.'

So we went out, played the last frame and one person in the crowd slagged me off. He shouted out: 'You're just as bad, walking out.'

'Shut up,' I said. 'If you've got nothing nice to say, go home.' That was while I was clearing up in the last frame. I thought, I'm not having this idiot saying that.

So even though the walking-out experience was bad for me, in a way it made me aware of things, and enabled me to help Ding in the end, when he was in the same situation.

I've never spoken to Ding about what happened. There's

no need to. He learnt from it, just as I learnt from my proper walkout.

The wet towel over the head

I was playing Mark King. Some players you can watch and enjoy and think: 'You know what, I'm getting a pasting here, but I've got the best seat in the house' – Stephen Hendry, John Higgins, and you're going you know that this geeza's class, but then I'm playing Mark King and there's nothing good about watching him play.

He probably knows he's a hacker. He's not one of those who thinks he's brilliant. He's honest and open. He knows he's done unbelievably well for the talent he's got. He's a bit of a banger. He's got no touch. But he's got more fight and spirit in him than anyone in the game. Having said that, sitting there and watching him play isn't a dream day out.

Everything he does is wrong; the way he stands, the way he holds his bridge hand, the way he flicks it in, there's nothing smooth about the way he plays. So, no disrespect to Mark – okay, a bit of disrespect to Mark – I had to put the wet towel over my head so that I didn't see it. And I was afraid I'd be able to see him through the towel. So as I put it over my head I thought, Christ, can I still see him? But I couldn't, thankfully.

I could just hear balls going in, and by the time the referee had called out the ball and he'd got round to potting his next ball I thought he must have walked round the table twice. A good player around this area when he's in the balls just goes bish bish bish bish, done. Mark probably does four times more walking round the table than I do.

I just found it very difficult to watch – it was a long match, best of 17 frames, the UK Championships, and I thought, I can't watch him. But he isn't the only one. There are loads I can't bear watching. In some ways that's why I wish I was shit because then I wouldn't notice all the faults. Sometimes I wish I wasn't so aware of what makes certain players good and certain players bad. When you play a bad player you can pick up on their bad habits, just as when you play someone good you think: 'Oh, I'll try that', and you can learn from them. With Mark King there was nothing I could feed off. I don't think he ever knew why I had the towel over my head. He will do now, mind.

He beat me 9-8. That was the match Ray Reardon walked out of because I was smacking the balls all over the show. They brought in a rule after that saying you weren't allowed to put a towel over your head because it was ungentlemanly conduct.

It was similar to when I played Selby and I started counting the dots on the spoon. I knew I wasn't allowed to put the towel over my head, but he's the same type of player. He's got so many things wrong with his cue action that when you watch him you think, how is he potting balls, he's going to break down eventually, he's mistimed this one, miscued that, and I'd find myself watching and criticising in my mind. And it's not something I wanted to do. I couldn't help it. It's like a compulsion. So my idea of counting the dots was so that I didn't have to look at him or watch him play because he's not good on the eye.

I think I could be a good coach, but I'd be a bit like Ray Reardon – baffled and frustrated when players didn't play the way I wanted them to play. People call me instinctive but I don't think that's right. I think it's more the other way round. You have to be technically good before you can be truly instinctive. If you're technically good you can play the shots with ease and precision, which then allows you to not worry about potting the ball and where the white goes; you're just worried about getting from one shot to the next. You're thinking, where do I want to be, rather than, I don't like this shot; I'm jabby with this one, or I'm here but I don't fancy getting there.

Being technically good frees you up and enables you to concentrate on the game itself rather than struggling with shots. That's why I've often said I thought Selby would struggle with the tournaments that were over longer frames because, like me, he's had his technical problems. Interestingly, he's never won the World Championship, and only won the UK this year when they shortened the matches to first to 11 frames instead of first to 19. In the longer matches, technique tends to come to the fore because you're more likely to struggle at some point if the match is over a few sessions, and if you lose a session 6-2 or 7-1 you've really got to battle to get back in. I used to think I would never win the World Championship because I felt I was struggling with my game technically. Thankfully, I was wrong.

The famous nosh in China

I'm not sure if this counts as a moment of madness. I thought I was just having a laugh, though not everyone saw it that way. The problem was I didn't realise the cameras were rolling and the mics were all set up. If I had, there is no way I would have said what I did.

I was sitting next to Ivan Hirschowitz, head of media for World Snooker. Ivan's one of my mates and he's got a good sense of humour. They asked me the first question then translated it into English, and I thought, blimey that sounded a long question in Chinese then really short in English.

'Fuck me,' I said to Ivan. 'That was the world's longest question.' And he started laughing.

The journalist said: 'D'you think you gave 100 per cent today?'

'I thought I performed well, but Marco just performed better,' I said. I had the microphone in my hand and then put it down. I whispered to Ivan: 'Look at that, it's the size of my prick and the same shape.'

'Well, that's a funny shape,' Ivan said.

'Well, what shape's yours then, Ivan,' I said.

I didn't realise I was all mic'd up, and we were just having a giggle. Then I looked round and said: 'Anybody want to give me a nosh? Anyone want to suck my dick?' And I was looking at the lady in the front row, saying: 'You want to come and have a suck on this?' She was looking at me, smiling, and Ivan was pissing himself laughing, tears rolling down his face. I only said it because she didn't understand. It was stupid, but I'm not rude and offensive normally. We were just having a laugh.

I only realised that the mic was on when I got home and Dad phoned me up and said: 'You've been done for lewd comments; it's all over the radio.'

'What?' I said.

I didn't know what he was on about. I was staying at my mate's house in Ongar, and had no internet connection so I just had to take Dad's word for it. The first I saw of it was when I bought the *Sun* the next day. I'd got home on the Monday and the transcript of it appeared in the *Sun* on the Wednesday. When I read it I just started laughing. That's fantastic, I thought, really funny. But at the same time I was worried because I knew World Snooker was looking for an excuse to come down on me and I think they assumed the Chinese would find it offensive and say that I was a rotten lot. I was convinced World Snooker were looking for the first opportunity to ban me, and thought this would be the perfect chance – Ronnie goes out to the new superpower, asks them to suck on his cock and upsets the Chinese. I thought they'd say, we need to come down on him; he's not bigger than the sport, and I started to shit myself.

I had a few friends in China and asked them if they could do some digging to find out what the vibe was over there; to see whether they were really appalled by what I'd done. They got back to me and said: 'No, no, no, they don't get it, they think you're great, and they're just gutted that you've gone home.' My friend said: 'They love you here, and they don't understand what all the fuss is about.'

So I thought, thank God for that. We put an apology out on their sports channel, I apologised, said, I love the Chinese snooker fans, I'm really looking forward to coming back. This was done without World Snooker, off my own back. By then the Chinese Snooker Association and Chinese press were on my side, so I had nothing to worry about from them. I just needed World Snooker to know that I had made up with the Chinese and apologised, and I knew that no damage had been done.

Sometimes it feels as if I'm in an abusive relationship with World Snooker. They love me, and know that I'm good for the game. But at the same time they resent me – they think I think I'm above the sport. To an extent they have been dependent on me over the past few years, and they hate that. And I know I've never been one of their sheep; never just done what I'm told and fallen into line. If I did that I'd quickly lose my own sense of who I am.

I thought, what's the worst thing World Snooker can do to me? Ban me. And if they did, and I convinced myself I wasn't enjoying playing, was depressed, they would have been doing me a favour. So every time I felt World Snooker had me by the short and curlies, I'd try to turn it into a positive – I told myself that being banned would be good for me, and put myself out of my misery. No more snooker depression: great. I decided not to compromise. They could ban me if they wanted, but they'd look as if they were cutting off their nose to spite their face – 'Good luck to you when you go and talk to sponsors because you would have been the ones who made the decision to ban me in the first place. I don't have to worry about that now. Happy days!' That's what I told myself – and more or less what I told them.

It is weird that they are so dependent on me after all these years; that no one has come along with the personality and talent to kick me into touch. I think it's the personality thing that's the biggest factor. Snooker players are all boring bastards basically. Even those who are hugely gifted technically don't have that thing that makes the public really care about them like they did about me or Jimmy White or Alex Higgins. I suppose our instability has always added to our appeal. We're all pretty vulnerable types one way or another, and you never knew what was going to happen next when we were around.

The public adored Jimmy and Alex. Jimmy was such an amazing entertainer – and also the fact that he lost all six of his world finals turned him into even more of a people's champion. We were all desperate for him to take the crown. Perhaps it's the Hurricane that I'm most similar to, both in touch and in our demons. But I think the public see an important difference – 'Yes, he's like Higgins, but there's the other side where he's relentless in how he wants to be a champion, and he's got these demons, he's fucked up, we don't know what he's going to do next, but he's healthy, he's fit, he's an athlete.'

World Snooker know the public feel like that about me, and it's a problem for them. Sometimes I think there's nothing more they'd like to do than get rid of me once and for all. With Higgins they could do it – he wasn't potting any more, wasn't winning, so it was easy to give him lengthy bans when he misbehaved. Of course, when he was winning, they tolerated much of the bad behaviour.

With me, they are suffering it while I am doing okay, but I know the minute I'm not doing well, or the minute they think snooker fans have given up on me, they'll get rid of me. It's just a matter of time. But I've always thought I'm going to walk before they push me. I've always planned to leave on my terms rather than be pushed. I don't want to do an Alex Higgins and be forced out. That's why last year, world champion, best player on the planet, I went, you know what? Ta-ta. It was on my terms. And in the end they moved every goalpost to have me back. And that was me winning the battle.

In a way they must be looking forward to me retiring. Sure, they'd miss the stories and the will-he, won't-hes, but at least they'd feel they had more control over their sport and be able to keep everyone in line easier. They would be like, Ronnie's history, let's move on.

People have talked up Judd Trump as the new me. But, again, I think there's a difference. There's a lot going on with me, for good and bad. Underneath it all, though, there is a burning desire to win and an intelligence in my game. I don't just go out and hit balls and hope for the best, smash them round the table. I've walked out of a match, come back next tournament and won it. I've always managed to come back, and I think that makes people respect me – that I've come back when I'm down. People like that. It's like Rocky or Muhammad Ali – get knocked down, get back up, win again. Ali was banned from boxing for being a conscientious objector and refusing to go into the army. In 1966, he famously said: 'I ain't got no quarrel with them Viet Cong.' He came back three years later and won the world title.

With all my demons, and my mum away, and dad away, and the drink and drugs, the kids, the maintenance, the keeping fit, the obsessions, the depressions, in between all that I've managed to win four world titles, four UKs and four Masters. I don't know how. I've won 24 ranking events, 10 Premier Leagues, more than 50 tournaments altogether. It's not bad going for such a fuck-up!

The Hurricane won two world titles, which is a fantastic achievement. He had the bottle to produce his best when it mattered. But he wasn't relentless like I've been. He'd be out on the piss, I'd be out running eight miles (and sometimes doing both). Sometimes I would win in spite of myself. I think people have always expected me to crumble; blow up. Look at me, and you can understand why. But I've been going as a professional, winning events, for more than 20 years, and still feel I've got a few more victories left in me. But those who did think that, or who say that I'm weak mentally, don't really know me. I'll eat commentators like John Parrott for breakfast. All right, I have blowouts, my moments when I crack up, but over 20 years I reckon I've been far stronger mentally than most of my critics.

I'm not saying I'm mentally strong in the way, say, Peter Ebdon is, where he can grind through frame after frame at tortuous pace. I wear my heart on my sleeve, love my game, and ultimately as a player I do hold it together.

I might be inconsistent, contrary even, but so many real people are. Who can't relate to that?

One day you love the game, next day you hate it. I bet loads of people feel that about their work (if they're lucky). One day you love being around the kids, next day they're driving you mad. That's just life. For me, it's how I manage my emotions that's important in how I go forward. In the past, my emotions dominated me. I'd have to go so low that there was nowhere else to go but up. Hopefully, I won't spiral out of control now. I can nip it in the bud when I see things going downhill – breathe, think, ask myself what I want, try to enjoy the game.

I think most players, most people, have extreme highs and lows, but they just don't talk about it. I'm very vocal. If I'm guilty of anything it's being vocal about what goes on in the mind.

Shaving my head at Sheffield

It was 2005 and I was in the World Championships, playing pretty shit. I'd had a great season, winning four of the eight available titles. But at Sheffield I wasn't dealing with the pressure very well. I felt ugly, low, sluggish. Nothing felt right. There was a clip on the telly of me, with the scoreline, and I looked at it and thought, ugh, look at the state of you. My hair was long at the time. I said to my friend Mickey the Mullet, get the razor out and give me a number one. The Mullet said: 'No don't be daft.' But he did it anyway.

I went to the venue next day and thought, they're going to think I'm mental. I looked like I'd just been given a lobotomy. Ken Doherty walked in, took a second glance and thought, who's that lunatic playing over there? It was like they'd let some serial killer into Sheffield.

It was bad.

That was the year I played Ebdon in the quarters and he tortured me into submission. He drove me to the torture chamber. For large parts of the match I sat in my chair slumped against the wall with my hands over my head. At other times I just chewed my fingers and grinned and grimaced at Ray Reardon. I was in bits. Ebdon made me scratch my forehead until I drew blood. He ruined me. I was relieved when he beat me. He had a 12 break in 5 minutes and 12 seconds. I was sitting there and asked this geeza in the audience the time. He said about 11 a.m. and I thought, Jesus, there's still two or three more hours of this to go. I now know what it's like to be waterboarded. It was like sleep deprivation. There's not a sympathetic bone in Ebdon's body. To him that was the art of winning, the art of sport. We call him Psycho because he looks like Anthony Perkins. I like Ebo; he's a nice guy, but he is a torturer of the worst kind. Everybody thought I was distraught when I lost, but I was relieved. It was over! It was holiday time.

I'd had the haircut halfway through a previous match. Lucky I didn't kill myself rather than just shave my head. That's how bad I was feeling. I got off lightly. I was playing so badly – 8-2 up at one point, but proper pony, all over the gaffe. But Ebdon did me like a kipper. I didn't blame him – he had a wife and four kids to feed, and if that was the only way he could win, so be it. But I had to go and get smashed after that.

From Alcoholics Anonymous to Sex Anonymous

I keep moving things from here to there to there. On my kitchen table I've got my pad and my phones and my bowl, and if it looks messy I try to tidy it up. When Damien's cooking it's like a bomb's hit the place. So I tidy up. It doesn't annoy me. It makes me feel better because it gives me something to tidy up after. I always have to do things. My mate said, you're a human doer, not a human being. I suppose that's an obsessive thing.

I never realised I had an addictive personality till I went to the Priory. Until then I just thought I had a bit of a problem with drugs, and that I needed to stop using them, or at least learn how to control it. I certainly didn't consider myself an addict. Then it probably took another 10 years after first going into the Priory to accept that I was an addict.

I supposed I rationalised things to myself. I'd say, well, if I've worked hard, or had a good run I deserve a little night out. So I'd tell myself I wasn't as bad as the others; I was different. I'd say, if I can have a month or six weeks clean then have a little blowout that's better than doing it every day. I was trying to manage my binges, and I told myself if I could do that I didn't have a problem.

A typical day on the binge would start with a bit of drink. Always vodka and orange. I don't actually know much about drink, don't know my beers and spirits; all I know is vodka and orange will do me. Ronnie Wood is a pro. I realised I wasn't a drinker when I started drinking with Ronnie. He had a drink for every different type of situation, so he'd start off on the Guinness, then he'd go on to the vodka, then he brought out this lovely drink early afternoon. I can't remember what it was, but it was his early afternoon drink. He drank by the clock, and I thought, this geeza is an expert. Me, I'm just an amateur, I'll drink anything without knowing much about it. But Ronnie was educating me.

I don't actually like alcohol, I just like the effect. It obliterates everything nicely for me. So a good day I'd be on the vodka and orange, about 10 of them, then get home at 3 a.m. and the wine would come out. Any old drink: it didn't really matter by then. Throw in a few spliffs. Then at 7 a.m. the sun would come up and I'd think, oh, Jesus, I've done it again. The birds would start tweeting and I'd think I'm bang in trouble. Then it gets to 11 a.m.–12 noon and I'm sunbathing on the floor, just thinking, what have I done? Then it takes three or four days before I feel normal again.

When I was on a bender, I'd talk shit all night, drive everyone mad, bore them to death.

When I went into the Priory I thought, how am I going to survive without anything to numb me? And it was hard for a while. I didn't think it was possible to give up drink and drugs just like that. If I was clean, I'd lock myself in the house and not come out. I'd do the same at snooker tournaments – I wasn't good at mixing with people and felt paranoid.

Spliff gave me the confidence to have a laugh and a joke. I got so used to puff I could function on it. I could play golf, snooker, anything: it just levelled me out. By the end of it I was so immune to it that it never got me stoned, it just levelled me out.

I was frequently tested, but if I was fucked or over the limit I'd just pull out of the tournament. But after I'd been done once I thought, they're not going to forgive me a second time, so I knew I was better off missing a tournament rather than risk getting banned. I was always running the risk of a ban, but when you feel miserable and in bits and you know a little spliff is going to lift you out of that depression, you think you've got to have it. When I stopped taking drugs I got really depressed. I was struggling with life. It's a bit chicken and egg. I was depressed because I'd stopped drinking and taking drugs, but I only drank and took drugs in the first place because I was depressed. Ultimately I'd rather be clean and depressed than on drugs and depressed. At least there's a way out, and you're reliant on your natural feelings – if you're down you really are down; if you're up, you are genuinely up.

After the Priory I spent a long time going to AA meetings. They provided a lot of relief at the time. They helped the depression. I'd go there, share, say I was depressed 'cos I missed the drink and drugs, and everybody would be sympathetic, tell me to keep coming back and pray to God! So it took me out of it for a bit. I would go back to AA if I had to. AA is Alcoholics Anonymous, but I did all the As. I did NA (Narcotics Anonymous), FA (Food Anonymous), all of them. I thought, if I've got addictions, food is one of them so let's see what they have to say about food because I love my grub. They'd say, don't eat this bread, don't eat those potatoes, but I was reasonably fit at the time and thought I didn't really belong there; I thought, I've got that one under manners.

At one point I tried SA – Sex Anonymous – for sex addicts. I'd been single for two years and thought I'd see some sick, dirty, rotten sex addict who wanted to give me a really good time, but they were all off their heads in there. I thought I'd see what's around; there might be a few nice birds there. Some of them wouldn't even hold hands because their addiction was so bad – or they thought it was. I thought, no, I can't handle this.

Sex Anonymous sent me back to drugs. It was so mad in there I thought, fuck, I've got to get out of here. I don't want to end up like that mob. It's funny: you see the same things in there as you do in NA. It's like they've had problems with drugs, they get well and outgrow NA, and they start looking for other addictions they can 'cure'. So some of the people I saw in NA, who were really sound people, I found them in Sex Anonymous, and I began to think this recovery lark is just continuous; it goes on for ever. And I don't want that. I want to be able to live my life and be in control of it. I'll take my chances.

You don't have to talk at Sex Anonymous, which was good because I thought, I've not really got anything to say to them anyway. I never actually felt I was a sex addict. The opposite. I'm not a sex addict at all. If I'm with a girl and I'm attracted to her, great. But I'm not craving it. I can go without. So I knew at heart I wasn't a sex addict, but I just wanted to try them all out.

Running is the best addiction, though. It's not that dissimilar to AA and NA and all the As. RA – Runners Anonymous! We meet once a week, a group of friends, talk to each other, help each other stay fit, push each other on, there's always someone ahead of you and always someone behind, so there's always someone to help and always someone to get inspired by. Runners are addicted, and some of them start to look unhealthy with it. But I'd much rather look like that than Steve Lee, just feeding off pork pies, eating my way out of it. I've been there, and I know what that's like and it ain't nice. I just wanted to run. Run, run, run; that was my cure for everything. Perhaps it's better to confront things, but I've never been good at that.

When I'm running I'm just thinking of the strides; of keeping a nice rhythm and tempo, just staying within myself. When I do a proper workout, 12 x 200 metres or whatever, I'm thinking, why am I doing this, what's the point? I just want to stop. You can't make any sense of it at the time, but when it's done you're on holiday, and you're glad you've done it. It's never enjoyable, but the fitter you get the more pain your body can tolerate.

As well as running I found walking therapeutic. I learnt that when I lost my licence a couple of years ago when I got done for speeding. I really began to enjoy a good walk down the Manor Road to the Tube station.

The reluctant 147

In 2010, Barry Hearn decided there wasn't going to be a prize for a 147. It used to be £25,000 at the World Open, and then they just decided to get rid of it – so the only prize was £4,000 for the biggest break in the tournament. To me, that's crazy, an insult – after all, the 147 is the ultimate, the greatest thing you can do in the game; snooker perfection.

So, rather than complaining about it, I thought, what's the best way to get this out in the open? And I thought, well, if I get in the position where I'm on for a maxi I could just stop short, ask the ref what the prize money was, he'd tell me that there wasn't any, then I could sabotage it at some point in protest. So, sure enough, I was on the 147 and I had a word with the referee, Jan Verhaas.

'What's the prize money for a maxi,' I said.

'Four thousand,' he said.

'I'm not making the 147 for that.'

I was only on about 40 or 50 at the time; it was early days. He didn't say anything, but I reckon he thought I was joking. Every time I potted another black I told him, I'm not making it. You can just about hear it on the telly. So I got to the yellow.

'I'm still not making it,' I said.

I was quite excited by now. I thought it was a good protest and would be better remembered than a 147; that it would be more exciting for the punters to be able to say: 'I was at the match when Ronnie refused to make a 147' than at the match where he did make one – after all, I've made plenty in my time. That might have been as remembered as the fastest 147 – though, obviously, for very different reasons. No snooker player had ever made 140, then decided not to pot the black. It would make history.

Dennis Taylor said: 'He's smiling and joking with Jan Verhaas, the referee.' But they didn't know what I was saying then.

'What can you say?' said John Virgo. 'Last frame it looked as if he wasn't bothered, and this has just been sensational. *Sensational.*' I was on 134. 'Come on, Ronnie,' he said.

One hundred and forty, and a huge roar from the crowd.

I then just shook Mark King's hand. I'd won 3-0. The black was simple. You could have potted it with your knob. Mark looked as if he was in shock. The whole arena seemed too stunned to take it all in. Jan wasn't having any of it, though.

'Come on, Ron, do it for your fans,' he said.

I thought, you bastard, guilt-tripping me in my moment of glory. So, sure enough, I ended up smashing the black in.

'Have you ever seen anything like that in your life?' said Virgo at the end. Well, if I'd not potted the black they certainly wouldn't have.

Barry Hearn came up to me straight afterwards. 'Thank God you potted that black because you would have been in big trouble. We've got the superintendent here who's clamping down on the betting scandals and we're trying to clean the game up. For you to do that in front of him would not have looked good.'

There were only a few seconds between shaking Mark's hand and actually potting it.

The reaction was mixed. To me, it was obvious I was having a laugh and making a point – ruffling a few feathers. But the authorities thought it was shocking. Mark Williams was critical too. 'Ronnie's break should stand at 140 because he'd shaken hands before he potted the last black. He should have potted the black without messing around or played safe [if he wanted to make a point]. But that's why people come to watch him, to see what he's going to do,' he said.

Some players were supportive, though – after all, they were pissed off about the prize money, too. Neil Robertson said he thought it was great. 'To pot one red and black and then ask the referee if there's a 147 prize is pure genius. No other player would have done that. He knew there wasn't a prize, he was just setting it up. No one is bigger than the sport but he does make it more attractive when he does something like that.'

17

MY GREATEST WINS

'Ran hard, pace felt fast, slowed down at halfway
for a bit then worked hard up the hills.'

My first World Championship in 2001 was so important because it had taken me longer than everybody had thought it
would. The pressure was mounting, the longer I went without
winning it. I was 25 years old, and beginning to think I'd never
do it. So in a way this was the most important and toughest one
to win.

Even at 16, when I went on that mad winning run, I still
didn't think I was destined to win the World, despite what
everyone was saying – I didn't know how good the top players
were, but I assumed they were a lot better than me.

I just thought I'd play, enjoy the game, see where it took me.
It was only much later in life when I'd played all the best players
and seen my form dip that I realised how well I was playing in
Blackpool as a 16-year-old. I realise now that at 15 or 16 I was
playing as good a game as anybody had ever played. But I didn't
know it at the time because I'd not mixed it with the top boys,
and I assumed they just didn't miss.

Before the first World Championship victory, I wasn't in a
good place. Far from it. I was in about as bad a place as it's

possible to be. I was free of addiction so I couldn't blame it on that. I was winning virtually every tournament I was playing, so I couldn't blame it on my snooker. But I just felt dark.

I had nothing to say to anybody, low in myself, no confidence. Classic depression. I was just putting on a front all the time. And it got to a point where I just got fed up doing that. I was being interviewed on the radio, and I think they were expecting a nice, bouncy pre-World Championship interview, and I just said: 'I'm not feeling too good, I'm really struggling, I don't want to be here.' They didn't know how to respond.

The previous night I'd called up the Samaritans, and told them I was desperate. I didn't give them my name, but I had told them I was a snooker player, was having panic attacks and didn't want to play any more. There was a lovely girl on the other end of the phone.

'Do you have to play snooker?' she asked.

'Well, it's my life. It's what I do for my job. I want to be able to play.'

'Isn't it more important for you to be healthy?' she said. 'Haven't you ever thought of giving up snooker?'

'Yeah,' I said. 'I've thought of giving it up for the last eight years!' I'd only been professional eight years.

It didn't sort anything out, but I felt better after calling the Samaritans. I decided there was no point in hiding how I felt, and then it all came out on the radio. After that, I got straight on to the doctor and said I better try the anti-depressants he'd offered me earlier because I had nowhere else to go. I thought I had nothing to lose, so I got the prescription and started taking them at the beginning of the tournament.

It's a risky thing to do – often people feel shit when they start on anti-depressants for the first couple of weeks, but I couldn't see any alternative. I stayed on them for a couple of years, and they really worked for me. But I suppose I didn't want a life's dependency on anti-depressants – you read stories in the papers about people becoming addicted and it fucking their lives up, so I thought, it's better getting off them if I can. I always felt I could go back on them if I needed to – a bit like AA and NA. I'd much rather have the natural remedy: that's why I go and do my runs and get my serotonin boost. I love that feeling of sweating, working hard. Your body's a machine, and you've got to respect it – even if I do occasionally go and blast it. I reckon I blast it for about 10 days a year. That's about 3 per cent of the year. Not bad. I reckon 20 per cent is just being a lazy bastard sitting on the settee, recuperating, and the rest of the time is keeping fit.

I felt relief more than anything else when I beat John Higgins 18-14 in the final. He'd already won one world title so the pressure was on me to win it. John is a different player from me, but in some ways he's got the more complete all-round game – he's more tactical, great break-builder, great potter. He's a 9 out of 10 in all departments, just a class act.

I think I've always been more of an instinctive player, and somehow I stop people playing their natural game. I don't think I'm a better player than him, but perhaps my style ruffled other players more than his did. John Higgins was always machine-like, and I don't think opponents felt intimidated by the way he played, which they did – and I hope still do – by me. He was snooker's equivalent of the Germans at football – they destroy you with efficiency. It might not always look great, but they take you apart, and they're always tough to play against. With me, it's much more bang bang bang bang, and it might be over before it started. Maybe I'm more Brazil than Germany.

In 2001, the pills started working really quickly. I became

less self-conscious and just got on with the game. I tend not to speak to many people during tournaments, but I was on the phone to Dad loads during the two weeks.

He could hear the difference in my voice. 'You sound so much better, Ron. They're obviously working for you. I can hear it in your voice.' He could also tell that my game was more natural.

'You're going for all them long shots,' he said. 'Crunching 'em in. I can't believe some of the shots you're going for.' Speaking to him made me feel better too. He didn't really understand depression, but he could certainly tell I was in better nick.

The final against John was a toughie. I started well, went 6-2 up even though I wasn't playing great. Then the gremlins crept in. I went 7-2 up, but it was embarrassing, the worst frame of snooker you've ever seen from both of us. Then John won the next three frames. 7-5. Jesus. I went in at the interval and said to Del Hill, who was then my manager: 'What is going on here? I'm having a nightmare. I can't pot a fucking ball.'

'Look, just stick in there,' he said. 'You're not playing badly. You've missed a few, he's missed a few and he'll miss a few more.' I came out and had a good final session, and on Sunday night I went to bed 10-6 up. Good day's work. Monday afternoon, I turned it on with breaks of 138, 90 and a couple of half-centuries. 14-7. But then he came back at me. 14-10. The World Championship is like the marathon – it just goes on for ever. Seventeen days of snooker and by the end you're half dead. You can see it on the players' faces – those who get through to the last four are normally white by that stage – all that time in the dark, all that pressure, standing up, playing, sitting down, watching, watching, watching. Murder. There's no sport in which players are so exposed – the cameras zooming in on your face as you're sitting in your chair, picking your nose, scratching your ears, pawing your face. There's no escape.

As it happened, the doctor who had prescribed my anti-depressants was watching on the telly, and he phoned up Del.

'He was watching the match on the telly,' Del told me. 'He saw your concentration level was falling. You were fading away.'

'What d'you mean, fading away,' I said.

'Just talk to him, please,' said Del.

'I ain't phoning no one,' I said.

Del begged me, and finally I agreed.

I wasn't in the best of moods, mind. 'Look, what's the matter?' I said.

He was lovely, patient, caring. 'Just take an extra pill. It will help you stay alert. Take one now, and in an hour or two you'll come alive again.'

He was right. I went 15-10 up, had a mini-wobble in which John got back to 17-14. Just one more frame to go. By then I could already see the headlines about how I'd chucked it all away and couldn't get over the finishing line. But I did – in the end.

It was a brilliant feeling. John was a gent, and he said the best thing he could have said. 'Tell your dad, well done. Well done, I'm so pleased for you and your family.' He knew just how much it meant to me and Dad, and all of us. Mum was in tears.

'I'm so proud of you,' she said. 'I'm so happy. You've done brilliant.' We went back to the tiny changing room. There was me, Mum, Danielle, Jimmy White, Ronnie Wood, his then wife Jo, and everyone was going mad, shouting and wearing the trophy on their head. I was the only calm one in the room.

Three years later, in 2004, I won it for the second time. I was feeling good then, doing my running. That was the year of the long hair and the Alice band. I started off playing well, then got worse as the tournament went on. I cut myself off from people at Sheffield, but there's always someone who has access to all areas, who can get the teas and coffees in, get the balls out, be there for me if I need to chat.

Although Damien Hirst is the man in the corner these days, along with his PA Sylvia, if they're not around it will be one of my running mates. It's just nice to have a friendly face there, someone to play for. At that stage I don't want anyone there who's trying to make me a better player or planning for me to conquer the world. I need someone to lighten the mood. Of course, I want to achieve more, but I'd rather do it by having a bit of fun instead of having someone try to find the missing piece in the jigsaw. In the end I've got to be the master of my own destiny.

There are so many talkers out there and not many people who walk the walk. When I come across those people who tell me it's easy and are full of advice I'll just tell them: 'Here's my cue, here's my hotel room, there's my suit, catch you later for dinner, good luck, you've got John Higgins today, not a bad player.' They don't know what to say when you say that to them.

People often ask me which are my most important victories. It's a tough one because there have been so many and they all mean a lot to me one way or another. But if I was on a desert island and could only take three trophies it would be this lot: the 2012 World Championship – my fourth victory after my horrible run of form for two years – the Champions Cup, when I came out of the Priory in 2000, and the European Open in 2003.

The Champions Cup was the first trophy I won when I was clean in 2000. It's not a huge tournament, but it was just great playing, feeling well, with a fresh frame of mind and perspective. My third one, the European Open, wasn't even televised. It was 2003 – again, not a massive tournament, but I played really well and had a great final against Stephen Hendry. I won

9-6, and both of us were on our game – high-scoring, good potting, attacking. It was a flick of a coin in the end.

People often don't believe me when I say it's how I play that's so much more important than whether or not I win and what I win. But it is 100 per cent true. Sure, you want to win the World Junior when you're a kid, then the World Amateur, then the UK and the World Championship. But for me I've got clearer memories of playing Jimmy White at Ronnie Wood's house than some of the World Championship finals I've played in. I've had some of my worst times at Sheffield even when I won the World Championship.

In 2004, I beat Graham Dott in the final. I didn't feel I'd played well, but it was great for the CV. Two-time world champion: that meant a lot to me because just the once can seem like a fluke. I celebrated that one by sticking my Dracula teeth in my mouth. My friend Scouse John said in 2001: 'If you win it again, will you put these in?'

'Yeah, yeah, yeah, no worries,' I said at the time, then I forgot about it.

At the beginning of the tournament, he reminded me. Perhaps he had a feeling.

'No, no, no, I can't do it,' I said.

'Go on, it will be really funny. It'll be in the papers,' he said. 'And you promised.'

Anyway, I thought it was never going to happen, and I had made the promise three years earlier, so I told him okay.

Everybody thought it was a tribute to Ray Reardon, but it wasn't. It was just Scouse John's crazy teeth. I didn't even realise I looked like Ray, I was just doing it for John.

It was another four years before I won the Worlds again. I remember that for one reason. I thought the authorities were going to come down heavy on me after the noshing incident in

China. I thought: 'Shit, they're going to ban me, I'd better do something here.'

I made a maxi, and if you watch it on YouTube you can see I had a really clenched fist; that was my way of saying: 'Right, now try to ban me.' I thought, I've given you a problem now. I've done a 147, I've set the tournament alight and now you're going to have to ban me. That was my incentive. It was the tournament just after China, and I was desperate to do well. Winning it was the icing on the cake. After the final, I said: 'I think I'm probably going to take some time out now.' I just wanted World Snooker to know that I could take time out if I wanted. But I didn't in the end.

It's not as if I'm trying to provoke the snooker authorities. Often I just do silly things because I can't help myself. And that's when World Snooker tries to clamp down on me, and I sense a ban coming my way. But it tends to bring the best out of me. In 2004, I got a bit of stick for my attitude and they said I'd been banging the tables and I thought: 'You know what, you're trying to pot me off here, you're trying to dig me out.' So that was a bit of an incentive to win the Worlds, which I did. So when I won the Worlds in 2008 after China, and when I won the Masters after walking out against Hendry in the UK Championships, it was my way of saying: 'Fuck you.' Some of my greatest wins have come after I've got myself into trouble.

18

THE WHORE'S DRAWERS

'Six x 1 minutes by police station Manor Rd. Got faster with each rep. Felt good, legs felt like they could fly and they did.'

It was May 2013, and I'd been away from the game for 11 months – in court, on the farm, being a dad, running, living – and now I was due to make my comeback at Sheffield. I was excited, and bloody nervous. For weeks in advance, every time the BBC trailed the World Championship they did so by hyping up 'the return of Rocket Ronnie'. They made it sound as if there was no one else in the competition. It was embarrassing. And after all that I didn't fancy returning and going out in the first round with a whimper.

Towards the end of March I started practising. I gave myself six weeks to get match fit.

The first couple of weeks' practice I felt great, as if I'd never been away. Initially, I was just playing my friends Chick and T, and that was fun for me. After a couple of weeks I went to the Academy in Romford, Django's place, and he's got three or four top Chinese players, so it's one of the best training places in the country. I was on fire. I was playing 25 frames and making five or six centuries. We'd often play best of 25 to replicate Sheffield.

But as it got closer and closer to the start of the finals, it began to feel more like hard work.

Everybody was welcoming when I got to Sheffield. Funnily enough, the first person I saw was Barry Hawkins. I remember meeting Barry when he was 14 and I was 17. He was playing in a junior championship and I'd just turned pro and had won the UK Championship. I got invited to hand the prize out and play the winner. I remember thinking all those years ago, blimey, he hits the ball well. When I saw him at Sheffield he was as good as gold, asked me how I was, said it was great to see me back. Nobody really knew why I'd been away.

Hazel Irvine, the BBC presenter, was great. I love her; she's the best. The BBC were definitely pleased to see me back. It wouldn't have looked good to not have the defending world champion playing in the World Championship, and I suppose they must have worried what it would have done to viewing figures. The BBC has always been good to snooker, and we're like a family together, so I'd missed them and was glad not to let them down.

What made me nervous was not so much the thought of playing again, but all the media interest.

Nearly all the snooker headlines involved me in some way – lots of speculation about why I'd been away and what my head would be like on my return. There was a fair bit of suggestion that it had all been staged to increase interest in the finals. That was nonsense.

Some people were saying the Ronnie O'Sullivan circus was in town, and that I just turned up when I fancied. I think some of the players felt that as well – that I could just turn up and play, that everything comes easy to me. When I hear that I find it hard to believe – it's anything but.

I was talking to John Higgins the other day – John and

Stephen Hendry are the two greatest players I've played. I played John the other day; he was brilliant and beat me, and when we came off the table I said to him, when you're in that form I don't know how you can ever lose. And he looked at me as if I was taking the piss. 'Apart from Hendry,' I said, 'there's nobody who's ever played the game like you.' I meant every word of it, but he wasn't having any of it. My mate Jason Francis was with us, and he said later that John might have thought I was patronising him.

'That's the last thing I'm doing, Jase,' I said. 'When he plays like that he's unbelievable.'

'But they all think that about you,' Jason said.

I suppose I do play with instinct and I do flow when I'm on it, whereas most players have to think more and set themselves up for every shot. So in that respect I probably see things quicker than most players. But other players are more deliberate than me, more consistent, more reliable, whereas I tend to be either really good or really bad.

Maybe I'm being too tough on myself. I used to be really good or really bad, but I think Steve Peters has helped me play decently even when I'm not on top of my game. I am definitely more disciplined than I was, thanks to Steve. He's taught me that giving up is just my emotional chimp sabotaging me, which it will do in certain situations. So I don't listen to the chimp's voice in the match. I will do afterwards but not when I'm playing, so I'm giving it 100 per cent in the game. So many times I've lost matches because in my mind I've given up.

My work with Steve had made me less emotional about the game, in a good way – more, this is your job, now do it. You don't need to enjoy it, I told myself – after all, who always enjoys their job? Whereas before I was: 'I need to be buzzing, I need to find that perfection.' I told myself I had nothing to prove – I'd won four titles, so I was content in that way, and nobody had retained the World Championship title since Stephen Hendry in 1996 (incredibly, the fifth of five consecutive wins), so there wasn't pressure on me to do that. My head was in a good place. I thought, I'm just one of 32 players here, I've got as good a chance as anybody here, I just need to win five matches. In my practice sessions before the tournament I was playing well, getting the better of good players and I thought, well, it's no different from going out and doing it at the Crucible. In fact, with the adrenaline and the crowds, I can play better in Sheffield than I had in practice. As with all sport, so much of snooker is psychological. Probably even more than most.

The crowd were really supportive. I got standing ovations whenever I went out. They've always been brilliant to me at Sheffield, but this felt different. It was really touching. I thought, well, I've been around a while, and maybe they gave it to me because they now regard me as an elder statesman. A lot of these people have been watching me for 20 years and they think, he's one of us, he's an old boy.

My first match was against Marcus Campbell, a tough, tough Scottish opponent. Marcus is a good, solid match player. The previous year I'd played him in China and just scraped home. But I always think Sheffield is different from anywhere else. Experience counts for so much at the Crucible – experience of the atmosphere, the intensity, and experience of having done well in the past. You can go there with bad form and do well if you've got the belief.

I was 7-2 up after the first session, playing decently, potting the balls. My long potting wasn't great, but it's never been brilliant so I wasn't that concerned. In the evening session I went 9-2. Almost home. Then I started missing balls. I began to panic, and thinking my game's gone; it's only day one and I've got another 16 days of this shit, if I survive that long – and that was a huge if.

I won 10-4, and was so down when I came off the table. Damien Hirst said to me: 'You'd think we'd lost.' He was making a joke of it, telling me how shit I'd made everybody feel. What he was basically saying is that I'm nuts. 'You've been out for eleven months, you've won ten-four, you've played some lovely shots, yes you've missed a few, but that's the game.' He's like another Steve Peters – he gives me perspective all the time.

In the evenings, when I wasn't playing, I went to the casino with friends. We played blackjack, roulette, had some dinner, watched the snooker on the telly. A great way to spend an evening. I went in there with £500 and told myself that it had to last me 10 days because I don't like gambling, don't want to get sucked in to it. When I played, I bet anything between £3 and £50. We had a little team – me, Damien, Sylvia, Chick, Irish Chris, Taz and Scouse John. I ended up about a grand up after the first night. Sweet. My luck couldn't hold out, though.

In the second round I played Ali Carter. Even though Marcus is a good player, he's not got Ali's experience at the Crucible – I've played him in two World Championship finals. The match started brilliantly for me, and I was 5-1 up in the first session, cruising. Then he won two good frames and came back to 5-3. We came out for the second session, and my game just wasn't there. I couldn't score, was coming off second best at the table. It got to 7-7, and I wasn't feeling good.

At 7-7, Ali put me in a snooker and I smashed my way out of it and potted the white. I thought it was unlucky, but actually it was a touch because I got away with it. He had to take on a long ball after the white went in it, and he missed it by miles. Lovely, I thought, and I knocked in a 70. In the last frame of the evening I made an 80. So I'd gone from 5-3 to 7-7 to 9-7.

I'd struggled, Ali had played really well, and I'd come out in front, which was brilliant for me. The most telling sessions at Sheffield are when you're struggling rather than flying. If you can win or draw a session when you're off your game, that's the stuff that wins you the World Championship.

It gave me confidence overnight, thinking, I'm two up, I've had my bad session, that's out of the way. I came out the next day, played well. Long one, boom, 70. Long one, boom, 80. I played good safety, too. It helps when your long shots are working – it gets you in earlier, and puts pressure on the opponent. In the end, I beat Ali 13-8, and thought, that's more Championship form.

I was in the quarter-finals, and a lot of the big names had already gone out: John Higgins, Mark Williams, Mark Selby, Mark Allen, Neil Robertson They'd all fallen by the wayside, but it didn't make me feel that this was my big chance because I've always said that if you're going to win the world title you're going to have to play someone who's on top of their game. There's not a lot in it among the world's top 16, and anyone who's in their best form can beat you. So I wasn't really worried about who'd won and lost; it was always more about my game.

The one big negative was that I couldn't run at Sheffield. I tore my calf muscle when running just before the World Championship. I was in the gym doing stuff on the bike, but that was about it. It's ironic really that once I stopped playing and thought I'd be able really to focus on the running I kept getting injured, so I got fat and lazy. Then, when I did start playing snooker again, I thought I'd better get fit, probably did too much running too quick, and tore my calf muscle. When I was in Sheffield I saw my running mates Jason and Lee. We couldn't run together because of the injury but I went out for a couple of meals with Jason, and saw Lee down the gym. Between matches I'd speak to Steve Peters, who lives between Sheffield and Manchester, in Chapel-en-le-Frith. I'd pop over there whenever I could, stay overnight, have a chat.

In the quarters I got Stuart Bingham, and went 7-0 up in the first session. His nickname is Ball-Run Bingham because people say he gets the run of the ball. But I don't think he's lucky. In my book he's unlucky – he's a good player; if he was lucky he would have won more tournaments.

Even though I wasn't really confident with my game I was able to put the bad shots behind me. And there were quite a few of them. But my break-building was good – 79, 111, 87, 133 and 78. The commentators were saying it was snooker from the gods, but it didn't feel like that at all; not like when I'm potting balls for fun. I felt I had really to work hard for it. I got to 7-0, then took my foot off the gas.

In the last three frames of the session against Stuart I couldn't pot a ball. My concentration had gone. I got down on myself, thinking, I've got to concentrate so hard on every ball in every session to win this tournament and I can't do that. I felt I was just taming the monster, caging the chimp, but it could have broken loose at any time. What made it difficult was having all these thoughts going through my head, and thinking, I'm not playing very well, then hearing Steve Davis and Stephen Hendry in the studio saying it's the best snooker ever. It didn't make any sense to me. I thought, are they winding me up? I think the truth was somewhere in the middle. It wasn't coming to me as easily as it had in 2012; that year I had to graft for it, but was generally consistent.

I ended up beating Stuart Bingham 13-4, despite the fact that I was beating myself up so much. After the match, it has to be said I wasn't at my most positive. I said I hadn't missed snooker, that this was possibly my last major tournament, and I'd only come back to pay the school fees. It didn't go down well. But I've always had a love-hate relationship with snooker: when I hate it I really hate it and when I love it I really love it. Sometimes I love it and hate it at the same time.

As for the school fees, some people found it funny, and some thought it in poor taste and made me come across badly. Others simply didn't believe me. Some thought it made me sound snobbish in that I needed to send the kids to private school, but that couldn't be further from the truth. I have no choice but to take them out of their schools unless I go to court, and I don't want to do that. I do want to pay for their schools out of my income, but, actually, I'm not really a believer in private education. I think state school is good enough for all of us; it's just a matter of whether you want to apply yourself. I went to state school and didn't apply myself. But there were loads of highly intelligent kids there who did, and who went on to university and good careers. I don't think many people believed that I was short of money, but it's true. Yes, I've got my home, and the home for the kids, and a couple of properties with my mum, but the bottom line was that if I didn't go back to work I'd have to sell my home.

The commentators kept saying how relaxed I looked this year, and I think I did on the table. But there were times when I felt so paranoid, especially after I'd just finished a session. It's hard to explain, but it's the classic symptom of paranoid depression – you can't talk to people, can't look them in the eye, you think people are laughing at you, you think you're going to be exposed but you're not sure why or about what. It's a horrible, destructive waste of energy and life. Then I'd get out there and be alright. Playing was escapism – I felt okay playing; playing was a distraction. What I couldn't handle was the thoughts and anticipation when I wasn't playing. And that's what I wore my friends out with.

Everybody became exhausted. All my closest mates, Scouse John and Damien, I'd tell them, I can't do this no more, I'm getting a new job, I'm going to work in the media. And the next day I'd get on the practice table, I'd be hitting the ball really well and I'd be going: 'Yessssss. I'm going to play this game for the next ten years!'

Whatever I was like, Damien remained a great support. He just said: 'If it makes you feel like that, just don't do it. If it's making you feel like this, fuck it off. You've just got to be happy. You're the king, the best snooker player ever, but I just don't want to see you down.' I don't think I am the best ever, but it's nice of him to say it. Damien never seems to get down.

Sheffield is exhausting at the best of times, but I was so gone early on. After each session, up until the semis, I was so tired that I'd just sleep all the time. I think that was because I wasn't used to the adrenaline pumping through my body and playing match after match. My recovery powers were not good. Even my mates, who'd seen me down plenty of times, thought I looked in a bad way when I'd come off at the end of a session. I'd think to myself, what am I putting myself through this for? I was happier when I was working on a farm and had no money. As soon as I was done I'd strip down to my pants and an old T-shirt, but I couldn't sleep. Yet everyone told me how confident I looked when I was out playing. I thought, I've got to look after myself. I've been down this road before, with glandular fever, and my health is more important than the snooker. I felt I was living the life of the fella out of *Breaking Bad*. I thought, I just don't give a fuck any more. But at the same time I was desperate to win.

Your view of yourself is at such odds with that of others when you're paranoid that you start to question your own sanity. You think, are they just saying things because you're a top player and they feel they have to say nice things about you, or am I just getting this completely wrong?

Paranoia is a form of depression. Other people probably don't even notice it. You feel that everybody else is enjoying themselves, having a good time, and inside I'm feeling so uncomfortable. I just want to be in my room, on my own. I want to duvet dive, I want to watch the telly, get loads of room service sent to me, I want to start smoking, go on my mate's barge and sit there and moan my bollocks off because he doesn't care. Little Mickey has a barge on the canal. He was in the army for years, then split up with his missus, and he bought himself a barge to live on. I can just go there, let my shoulders drop, moan, tell him I don't want to play any more, and he just goes: 'Alreet, mate', and he's got his little dog there who hates my guts because every time I turn up there I go: 'Come on, Mick, let's go out for a cup of tea', and the dog hates me because he has to lock it up and they're like husband and wife. I told Mick, the fucking dog hates me, and he goes: 'No he don't, mate, see, he's wagging his tail', and I'm like: 'Look, I'm a threat to that dog. All that dog thinks is, whenever I come you disappear with me. I ain't good news for that dog.'

On the surface, I looked composed. Probably was pretty composed for me. But I certainly had my moments. At times I couldn't bear being in the Crucible, couldn't bear seeing people; every little thing was getting to me.

I got better towards the end. I remember saying, three more days of brushing my teeth, two more days of brushing my teeth and it's done; one more day. All my friends in the dressing room kept me sane – Irish Chris, Scouse John, Damien and Sylvia, and two close friends from Sheffield, Iyaz and Taz.

252

Despite my doubts, I was through to the semi-finals and drew Judd Trump – a huge match and potentially a real crowd-pleaser. Both Judd and I play an attacking game. We were still going down the casino in the evenings. By now I was back down to £500 worth of chips left and I thought, fuck it, it's time to win big or lose it all. I lost, of course. But it didn't matter by then. I was happy with what I'd achieved at Sheffield.

I was 4-1 up in the first session, but it ended up 4-4. I came out and I thought, I've outplayed him by a mile and we're drawing. It didn't give me much confidence for the second session because I thought I should have been 6-2 up, maybe 5-3, but at least I should have had a lead. A pattern emerged in Judd's game, and one that I've noticed before – he always played well when he was three frames down, but when he got level he went negative. I picked up on that and it gave me confidence.

At 7-6 to me he missed a red, and I thought, right, now's the time, I've got to clear up and pull away, and that's what I did. At 11-8, I felt that mentally he gave up, and that made my job easier. I thought, all I have to do is stay disciplined, and if he gets close kick on again and just be professional. In other words, it was mine to lose rather than Judd's to win.

There was a mini-controversy in the semi with the score 13-9 in the middle of a long, boring frame. I made a 'motion' with the snooker cue – some people might call it a wanking-off-the-cue gesture, but not me! I had the cue between my legs and just gave it a little rub. To be honest, I've often done it when I'm pissed off with myself. The referee, Michaela Tabb, gave me a quick but stern talking to: 'Don't make obscene gestures again, okay?' I said I was just wiping something off my cue, and: 'I want to go home.' It probably put me off for a bit, and I ended up losing that frame.

It was a tense match, and I enjoyed the first session. But I didn't feel I was flowing in the other sessions or that I had momentum. It was just bits and pieces, but tactically I had my wits about me, my safety game was good and I did enough.

To get to the semis and the one table was a nice feeling (until the semis there are always two matches going on at any one time), but to get to the final was great. I felt a real sense of achievement. I'd made it from 32 players, the first one into the final, defending champion, and I hadn't played for a year. I didn't think it was possible at the start.

When the bookies had me down as one of the favourites at the start I thought they were mad. When the players said I was the favourite it annoyed me. I thought, you've been playing all year; when is someone going to stand up and say, I'm the governor of this sport, I'm number one, I'm going to win the World Championship? But I never heard one player come out and talk with that confidence. I really want to see that because it will be great for the game and it would probably spur me on again. But no one's really grasping the nettle. In a way it's good for me because it means my competition isn't that confident, they don't believe in themselves enough, but it isn't good for snooker.

Perhaps Judd should be that man, but sometimes I think he lacks the killer instinct. He seems as if he's just happy to be there – he's got a bit of money, enjoys the lifestyle, wins a few matches and the odd tournament, but what he really should be doing is trying to write his way into the history books. There isn't a Hendry or a Davis out there who wants to devote his life to it, someone who says: 'You're going to have to scrape me off the table if you're going to beat me. I want this so bad I'm going to make it happen.'

When I got through to the final my first thought was, I don't fancy Barry Hawkins, he's flying, he's going to smash me. Daft, because, as I said, you're always going to meet someone in form in the final. I went through everything Steve Peters had taught me, and told myself to get a grip – every day's different, every player's different, forget the catastrophic thinking, let's get the facts, let's get the truth. With Steve I was trying to reverse the belief system that I had grown up with, one that was based on fear and negatives – you've got to win, don't make me look bad, don't show yourself up.

So I gave myself a good positive talking to – whatever happens, nobody's going to smash you; the worst that could happen is that it might get close, then I'll get my chance to win. So it was about staying patient. I never felt I was going to be blown away. I'd been here before, won four finals out of four, am reasonably good under pressure, not going to bottle it, and I just kept thinking, if the opportunity comes to win the match I fancy my chances.

Just when I'd talked myself into enjoying it, I discovered they'd changed the cloth on the table for the final. They told me they'd changed it but I expected it to be the same as before – fast and slick. But this was really slow. A faster cloth suits me better, and I think a slower cloth suits Barry better because he hits firmer with the ball; he's a bit more punchy whereas I prefer to float balls in. You can't float them in on a slow table, you've got to bang them in. I can do that, but it's a different technique – it's like going from clay to grass in tennis. So I thought, who did that, and why? The conspiracy theorist in me believes it was done to try to stop me winning the World Championship. But every little thing that could have set me back I've tried to turn into a positive, so I told myself, right, if there are people out there who don't want me to win, I really need to do it now. It made it more of a challenge, more of a buzz.

Maybe I was being paranoid, but even a couple of knowledgeable ex-players said to me: 'I know why that was done!'

'Why?' I said.

'They didn't want you winning the World Championship. That was to try to stop you.' This was after the final, so they weren't trying to wind me up.

I loved the final. It was the only match in the World Championship in which I thought I played really well. It wasn't until the semi-finals that I got my energy back, and I thought, I've got a chance here. The first session in the final was good – I took a 2-0 lead, then he came back to 2-2 and I thought, we've got a game on here. Then he went 3-2 up, and it was the first time in the whole tournament I'd gone behind. I then had three really good breaks, two centuries, and I went 5-3 up, and I thought, lovely, we're involved now! This is a proper ruck. I've set my stall out, let him know I'm here. I know that he's there as well, so it was a good first sparring session.

I've never played really well in the second session in a final at Sheffield. The first session you're all excited, it's the final, you play really well, then the second session, on Sunday evening, always seems a bit of a come-down – you can't win the tournament, but you can have a poor session and put yourself in a bad position for the next day. Sure enough, it did get a bit tense that Sunday night.

Last frame on the Saturday night I played a great snooker against Barry when I tucked him up behind the black. If I won the frame I'd be 10-7 up overnight; if I lost it the score would be 9-8. I would have been so disappointed if I'd lost it because I'd played well in the frame, but somehow it had come down to the colours. That would have hurt. Thankfully, I won it, and to go in 10-7 up was a massive boost.

Then, come Monday, I played great. In the afternoon I was dominant, cueing well and scoring from nowhere. In one frame I was 54 behind, 59 left on the table, and I cleared up with 56.

The final red was really difficult – a long pot in the bottom corner, then I had to screw back for the blue. But that still left me with another long yellow. That went in really sweet. Boom. Which left me with a tricky green – against the bottom cushion – and I had to come back with side for the brown. The white landed perfectly, and that was that. Lovely. The frame was to go 12-8, and it was one of the best clearances I've ever made.

I was pleased with my patience – potting, making a few good breaks, then playing a few snookers. Rather than having to make it happen straightaway I thought, no, I'll bide my time, and that gave me confidence. I played well on the Monday afternoon, and I just thought, okay, we'll have more of that on the Monday evening. This was the test of my work with Steve Peters – I'd done it the year before so I knew I could do it; but would I be able to do it again? Barry came out, long red, and made 130. Then he won the next frame with a good break, and all of a sudden the score's 15-12 and I'm getting a bit twitchy.

Next frame he was on 20-odd; he took on a tricky red, and I thought the way he'd been playing he obviously fancied it, so I didn't expect him to miss it. But he did. I heard the roar from the crowd – disappointment from Barry's fans, anticipation from mine – and I thought, right, I've got to win the frame in this visit. I made a 70-80, went 16-12, and won the next frame with another good break.

At 17-11 I went in for the interval needing only one frame to win, but my head wasn't quite all there. After the final, Scouse John reminded me what I'd said to him.

'What's the score?' I'd said.

'Seventeen-twelve,' he said.

'So that means he's got to win six frames on the trot to beat me.'

What Scouse John didn't get was that I was being serious

– for the whole 17 days I didn't think I was good enough to win it. John thought I was taking the piss, but I wasn't one bit. I thought there was every chance Barry could pull off six frames. As it happens, I came out and finished the match in style with a break of 77.

I picked the trophy up – very nice, thank you very much, five times world champion, first person to retain it since Stephen Hendry, proud moment. I was really happy. I'd achieved what for me was the impossible. To win it five times sunk in straight-away. When I wrote my first book 12 years ago, I'd just won the World Championship for the first time. Two years ago I'd won it three times. Not bad, but there's a world of difference between winning it three times and winning it five times. Now I'm only one behind one of my all-time heroes, Steve Davis, and two behind Hendry.

My lasting memory is having little Ronnie on the table, jumping up in my arms and we're smiling into the cameras. It doesn't compare to the year before because in 2012 I'd had such a bad time personally and professionally I never thought I'd win it again, but it was still wonderful. There's a lovely picture of me with one hand on the trophy, and little Ronnie standing on the table with one arm round my shoulders and another on the trophy. Beautiful.

In the after-match interview I caused another bit of contro-versy. Hazel Irvine said I'd made it look easy, but what had it actually been like behind the scenes and to whom did I owe a debt of gratitude? I said I didn't think I'd have won back-to-back titles without the help of Steve Peters because; 'Everyone knows me. I'm up and down like a whore's drawers.' Hazel didn't know what to say. I'm not even sure she knew what I'd said – she just sensed it wasn't something for prime-time telly. The audience burst out laughing. 'I think we'll forgive the industrial language,' she said. 'D'you want to rephrase that or just plough on?'

'It's a bit late, it's live, Hazel!' I said.

I thought it was funny because I knew Hazel would be thinking ahead to the next question and I thought I'd just throw it in there to see how she reacted. She came up to me the other day and said: 'It did take me by shock because I was thinking of the next question and all of a sudden I heard the crowd and I thought, what's he just said? And I had to deal with it.'

I also said I was planning to play in more of the little PTC events, and again there were lots of sceptics saying why would I want to do that when the prize money isn't that great for winning them. But I love the small-time atmosphere of them, and also that they don't last long, which is perfect for me. Whereas lots of the tournaments are 10 days to two weeks, and the World Championship is 17 gruelling days, these events start on Friday and you're back home on Monday. So you keep your eye in, there's not loads of pressure on, and you're not away from home for ages. And if you love the game you love the game. It doesn't have to be a World Championship for it to matter to you. You get around 20 grand for winning most of the events, so it's decent money, but not like winning the World Championship, where you get 250 big ones. I can understand why people think I'm mad to want to play in these events, but my situation means I can't be on the road 12 months a year. I want to see little Ronnie and Lily and still play regularly so I thought the best way to manage that balancing act was to play in a few of the smaller events and have a bit of fun. If you play just for the money you're going to be screwed anyway. Sometimes, all money brings is misery.

A month on from winning the World Championship and I'm feeling good. I know I'm not the most positive fella in the world, and I'll probably always struggle one way or another, but I also know I'm blessed. Blessed with great family and friends, beautiful children, good health, a strange gift for snooker, and blessed with a fan base that sometimes I've probably not deserved. I've also got a great girlfriend who's brought stability to my life. Laila is an actress, probably best known for playing Amber Gates in *Footballers' Wives* and Sahira Shah in *Holby City*. She also got to the semi-final of *Strictly Come Dancing* in 2009. She's been a fantastic addition to my life. She's been a good support, a calming influence on me. And I think we make for a good team. Her heart's in the right place, she's a good girl. She has enhanced my life. She's got some great friends and she takes me out to places that I've never been before. She comes from a Moroccan Muslim background, and a lot of her friends are Moroccan. Most are not drinkers. They just talk rather than drink, and there's a lovely openness to them – that's the Moroccan mentality. Most of my friends are: 'Yeah, go here, go there, do this, do that', and that's not for me. Laila's brought a new world to my life. Like me, she doesn't like the celebrity world. That's one of the things we've got in common. She's a clever, shrewd girl, but she's not into all the celebrity rubbish.

I'm also beginning to get into some media work; preparing for the end of my career whenever that comes, and I might even have a go at writing a novel. As I reach the end of this book, I'm planning my next year, have paid the school fees, have won the World Championship, got a bit of money in the bank, and have got my self-esteem back. And as for the running, I'm getting fit and beginning to look nicely gaunt again. In just over two years' time, when I'm 40, I'll be able to enter Masters races as a veteran, and then I can really make my mark. So, all in all, the whore's drawers are back up, and with any luck they'll stay that way.

INDEX